Characterising Local Southeastern Spanish Populations of 3000 – 1500 B.C.

M. J. Walker

BAR International Series 263
1985

B.A.R.

122 Banbury Rd, Oxford, OX2 7BP, UK

BAR -S263, 1985: 'Characterising Local Southeastern Spanish Populations of 3000 - 1500 B.C.'

ISBN 9780860543350 paperback
ISBN 9781407342443 e-book
DOI https://doi.org/10.30861/9780860543350
A catalogue record for this book is available from the British Library

This book is available at www.barpublishing.com

CONTENTS

****

Please note that additional material is available to download from www.barpublishing.com/additional-downloads.html. The original foldout has been reduced in size to match the A4 format of this book, the image is therefore not as clear as the original foldout. Please refer to the original foldout via the download for the original content.

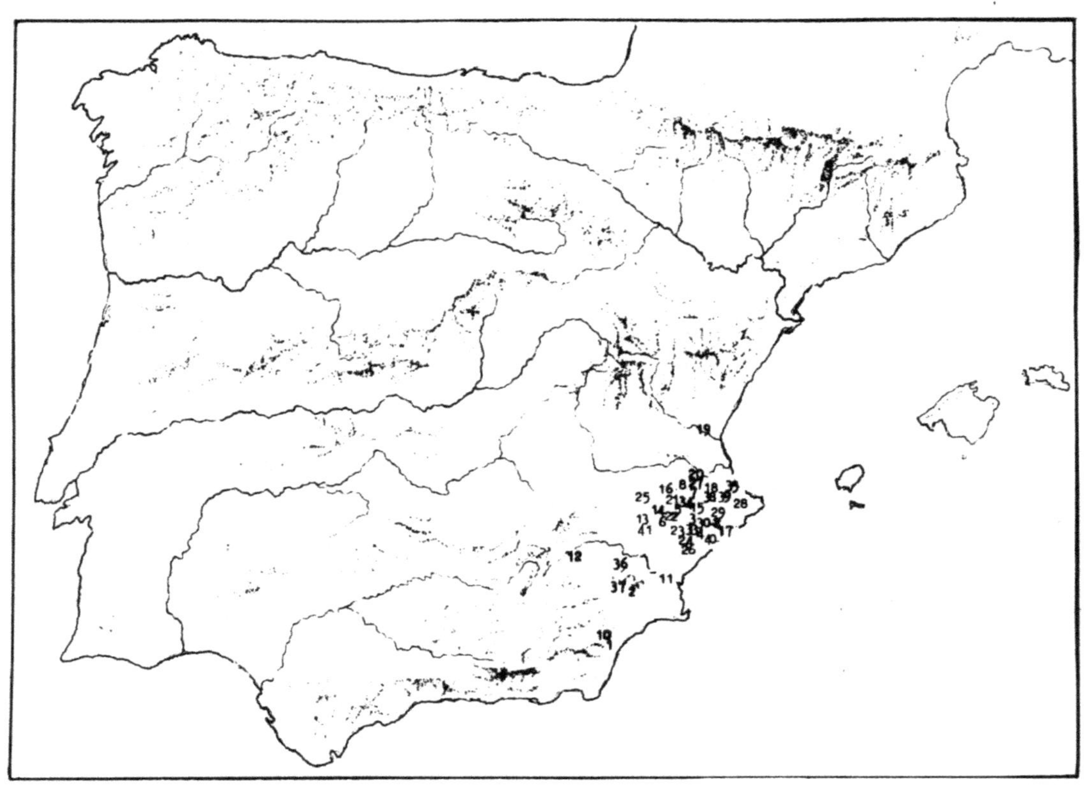

Distribution of Sites Investivated

(Utilisation of site probably falls within ranges in brackets)

1	El Argar	(3750-3000 b.p)
2	La Bastida	(3750-3000 b.p)
3	Cova de la Pastora	(5000-3500 b.p)
4	Cova del Morro de la Barsella	(4500-3500 b.p)
5	Cova de Les Llometes	(4500-3500 b.p)
6	Cueva de las Lechuzas	(5000-3500 b.p)
7	Cova de Beni Sid	(5000-3500 b.p)
8	Cova del Camí Real d'Alacant	(5000-3500 b.p)
9	Cova del Palanqués	(5000-3500 b.p)
10	Cerro El Serrón	(5000-3000 b.p?)
11	Puntarrón del Chico	(3750-3000 b.p)
12	Cerro de las Víboras	(4000-3000 b.p)
13	Cerro del Cuchillo	(4000-3000 b.p)
14	Cabezo Redondo	(3750-3000 b.p)
15	El Puig	(3750-2500 b.p)
16	Cabeço dels Alforins	(4000-3000 b.p)
17	Isleta de Campello	(3750-2500 b.p)
18	Rambleta	(4000-3000 b.p)
19	Torreta del Mal Paso	(4000-2750 b.p)
20	Rocafort	(5000-3000 b.p)
21	Cova dels Anells	(5000-3500 b.p)
22	Covacha del Alto	(4000-3500 b.p)
23	Peñón del Trinitario	(4500-3000 b.p)
24	Cueva del Hacha	(4500-3500 b.p)
25	Cueva Santa	(4500-3500 b.p)
26	Serreta la Vella	(4500-3500 b.p)
27	Ereta del Pedregal	(4500-3500 b.p)
28	Cova de Montgó	(5000-3500 b.p)
29	Cova d'En Pardó	(5000-3500 b.p)
30	Cova del Barranc del Sinc	(4500-3500 b.p)
31	Cova del Rebolcat	(4500-3500 b.p)
32	Cova Bolumini	(6000-3500 b.p)
33	Cova del Mas d'En Felip	(4000-3000 b.p)
34	Cova del Moro	(5000-4500 b.p)
35	Cova Frontó	(5000-3500 b.p)
36	Cueva Amador	(5000-3500 b.p)
37	Cueva de los Blanquizares	(4500-3750 b.p)
38	Cova de l'Or	(7000-5000 b.p)
39	Cova de El Parpalló	(30,000-10,000 b.p)
40	Barranco de las Ovejas	(?125,000-75,000 b.p)
41	Cueva de los Tiestos	(4500-3600 b.p)

Characterising Local Southeastern Spanish Populations of 3,500-1,500 B.C.

M. J. Walker

1.

INTRODUCTION

While the original purpose of these enquiries was to press palaeoanthropology into the service of southeastern Spanish prehistoric archaeology, their development highlighted some fundamental questions of craniometrical statistical methodology and of the biological significance of the results for interpreting variations between human groups, questions which are brought to the fore in this study.

For 100 years southeastern Spanish prehistoric burials have provided a singular abundance of human skeletal remains of the 2nd and 3rd millennia and, notwithstanding the loss and dispersal of some major collections, there still exist large numbers of skulls and postcranial bones in the museums of the 350 x 100 km coastal belt between Valencia and Almería. In broad terms they can be divided into remains from collective burial vaults antedating the appearance, about 3750 bp*, of the Argar Culture, and single (or at most double) inhumations at settlement sites thereafter.

Radiocarbon dates for cave burials range from 4780±80 b.p. (SUA-2070) for calcite enveloping bones from the Cova del Moro at Agres (Alicante) to 3790±115 b.p. (HAR-160) for burnt barley spilled over burials and 3600±80 b.p. (HAR-358) on bone at Cueva de los Tiestos near Jumilla (Murcia). These last-mentioned dates overlap with the onset of the Argar Culture: 3735±55 b.p. (GrN-5594) at Cerro de la Virgen (Vogel and Waterbolk, 1972), 3670±70 b.p. at Herrerías (Almagro Gorbea, 1976), 3625±40 b.p. (GrN-6634)

* b.p. = radiocarbon date (uncalibrated) "before present", i.e. before 1950 A.D., and it is therefore identical to B.P. in the journal **Radiocarbon**. Following modern practice in the U.K. B.P. is reserved for dates before 1950 A.D. calibrated to sidereal years (thermoluminescence dates; historical dates; calibrated radiocarbon dates) and represents the sum "years B.C. + 1950 years". 3750 b.p. may be roughly calibrated to 2230 B.C.. For the convenience of the general reader in interpreting b.p. dates given in this study, the following may serve as a rough and ready guide: 4000 b.p. = 2600 B.C., 4250 b.p. = 3000 B.C., 4750 b.p. = 3600 B.C..

at Cerro de la Encina (Arribas, 1976) and 3620±35 b.p. (GrN-7286) at Cuesta del Negro (ibidem).

A complication is that sporadic single inhumations outside settlements may occur at any period, particularly when in caves or rocky fissures because such natural vaults are often the location of third millennium collective burials; indeed the dispersal of nineteenth-century skeletal collections from the Los Millares passage graves means that cave series represent the bulk of the collective burials available for this study.

It is often archaeologically difficult to date isolated burials, and one subsidiary aim of this enquiry was to see whether cluster analysis of skulls might link particular isolated cases to one or another major chronological group. Even here however one must tread warily,because a burial vault may receive cadavers and skeletons over many generations (some caves continued to be visited as late as 3750 b.p., see above).

It has from time to time been suggested that demographical dislocations were associated with the onset of the Argar Culture, especially in the southern (Almería-Murcia-Granada) part of the region - variously involving possibly nomadic groups with decorated Bell Beaker pottery and sea-borne groups with shiny, angular El Argar pottery. Many prehistorians are sceptical about these however. Others hold that, even if they were to have taken place, they may not so much have swept away as merely modified the local indigenous and well-entrenched culture, at least in some areas. Nevertheless there remains a doubt in the minds of palaeoanthropologists as to whether the skeletal remains under consideration might not perhaps derive from as many as three human communities with separate genetic histories and which moreover are not necessarily separable into neat chronological compartments where regional demographical uniformity can be presumed.

A parsimonious approach assumes a population homogeneous in time and space and looks for departures from the assumption. If anomalies in time and/or space are detected for series likely to represent biological communities, then isolated burials similar to one series or another may throw light of interest to prehistorians on inter-group relations in time and/or space. To seek anomalies by reference to the Null Hypothesis, it is of fundamental importance to abide by strict statistical criteria. Once series for comparison have been chosen, intra-series anomalies should be sought by inspection of univariate distribution of variables. Differences between series can be identified by employing Student's t at a probability level of ±2.5% or by using the Behrens-Fischer statistic should the probability value for the variance ratio contraindicate proceeding to Student's t. Comparing raw measurements does not allow us to assess the relative significance of different measurements in determining the differences between series measured. We cannot do this until intercorrelattions among the measurements we have taken are eliminated. A convenient procedure for this elimination is principal components analysis of a correlation matrix or a covariance matrix.

It is a procedure which allows series to be compared and contrasted in terms of independent, orthogonal components. In carrying out the analysis, it is unsafe to use statistics such as "indices", which combine measurements as ratios, because in some of our series there are correlations between measurements used as the numerator and denominator of some common "indices"; while correlations between the numerators or denominators of different "indices" can also be seen when some other series are considered. In other words, if composite statistics are taken as a reflection of degrees of relationship between series it can become a distorting mirror because of differently varying intercorrelations of different variables - and this applies not only to "indices" but also to Penrose coefficients and to discriminant functions when used for that end.

The "common yardstick" attitude (to using statistical measures in osteometrical comparative characterisation) may not always be appropriate, and by eschewing it our goal of determining which descriptive aspects of particular series are unlikely to be due to chance variation, and hence may draw our attention to intelligible models for their explanation, far from being thwarted is more readily achieved. Reinforcement may be added by augmenting metrical results with non-metrical epigenetical observations and they will be used in this study to highlight similarities and differences between major series, sometimes detecting dissimilarity even where rigorous metrical comparisons cannot.

Once major series are characterised in the foregoing way, cluster analysis is used, less to confirm them, than to draw attention to the possible relationship of isolated individuals which previously had been regarded as members of one or another series. The reason cluster analysis cannot itself be relied on to define the major series is that it is predicated on the presumption of a "common yardstick" to which are referred all of the constituent series it finds.

There is a fundamental problem here concerning the possibility of representing accurate relationships between series, when the characteristics responsible for defining independent series may be different, and when, even if common to two or more series, they may covary differently (in ways perhaps hardly amenable to interpretation in terms of discrete functions defining shapes but perhaps analogous to the assortment of varyingly associated genetic factors determined more by likelihood of mating than by probility of approximation to predetermined morphological types).

The investigative strategy proposed stands or falls on the initial choice of series for comparison. It is likely that burial vaults in the northern Alicante-southern Valencia highlands were severally reserved for use by discrete human communities between which minor morphological skeletal differences due to intra-group positive assortative mating should be anticipated although out-mating might also be expected to give rise to sporadic interments of individuals standing out in a burial group.Some groups however might also exchange sexual partners so often as to give rise to very similar human remains in two or more vaults (cf. segmentary societies) so that these should not be unexpected either. The 2nd millennium village burials of the Murcia-Almería lowlands might be anticipated to present fewer extremes and to represent a homogenisation of earlier communities, although it is probable that any mass immigration which were to have occurred from far afield could be reflected in a different Argar Culture morphology readily detectable by the sensitive procedures proposed.

2.

SELECTION OF DATA

1. Skulls, Assemblages

Only crania and mandibles were used because of the impossibility of assigning postcranial bones to particular individuals in vault assemblages. All measurements and observations used were made by us, except for those of El Argar which are taken from Jacques (1887). Several assemblages had also been published by Fusté (1957), and our measurements are in close correspondence. Cranial measurements used for statistical analysis are listed in Table 2. Some assemblages comprised skulls too fragmentary for any values for a given measurement to be available and for El Argar only 33 measurements taken by Jacques could be compared*.

In fact, the study reveals that there is no need for an exhaustive list of measurements for each and every skull series because principal components analysis shows extensive inter-correlations between particular groups of measurements. There seems to be some redundancy in the craniometrical variables chosen. Only when the number of variables falls below about twenty does there seem to a risk of conflating independent aspects of skull composition. Nevertheless, certain variables may be uniquely indepedent - bizygomatic breadth, for instance (see below).

In addition, epigenetical traits listed by Berry (1968) were sought as well as intrasutural and accessory ossicles, presence and extent of metopism, degree and site of sutural obliteration, pathological features, and tooth numbers, wear and *in vivo* and *post mortem* loss. Upto 216 characters per skull were recorded.

This study deals with skulls from 39 stations in addition to Jacques' El Argar skulls, namely** :-

* There are problems of definition when using Jacques' data. For instance his "maxillo-alveolar breadth" values are far too low for Martin's measurement 61 but appropriate to 62, internal palatal breadth, which we presume it to be. Jacques' work predates the Monaco coventions (enshrined in Martin, 1906).

** Numbers given here for some sites are slightly higher than the ones used for craniometrical computation as they include fragmentary skulls on which only non-metrical traits were studied.

Table 1

SITE	TOTAL CRANIA	LOOSE CRANIA	CRANIA +MANDIBLES	LOOSE MANDIBLES	TOTAL MANDIBLES	TOTAL CASES
MAJOR SERIES						
El Argar (Antas, Almería)	75	47	29	14	43	89
La Bastida (Totana, Murcia)	15	11	4	13	17	28
Cova de la Pastora (Alcoy, Alicante)	47	36	11	10	21	57
Cova del Morro de la Barsella (Torremanzanas, Alicante)	15	14	1	8	9	23
Cova de Les Llometes (Alcoy, Alicante)	27	22	5	5	10	32
Cueva de las Lechuzas (Villena, Alicante)	14	11	3		3	14
Cova de Beni Sid (Vall d'Ebo, Alicante)	23	16	7	17	24	40
Cova del Camí Real d'Alacant (Albaida, Valencia)	25	23	2	14	16	39
Cova del Palanqués (Navarrés, Valencia)	8	8		27	27	35
OTHER ASSEMBLAGES						
Cerro El Serrón (Antas, Almería)	2	2				2
Puntarrón del Chico (Beniaján, Murcia)	1	1				1
Carro de las Víboras (Bagil, Moratalla, Murcia)	1		1		1	1
Cerro del Cuchillo (Yecla, Murcia)	2	2				2
Cabezo Redondo (Villena, Alicante)	4	2	2	1	3	5
El Puig (Alcoy, Alicante)	1		1	1	1	1
Cabeço dels Alforins (Onteniente, Valencia)	2		2	1	3	3
Isleta de Campello (Campello, Alicante)	3	1	2		2	3
Rambleta (Rótova, Valencia)	1	1				1
Torreta del Mal Paso (Castell-novo, Segorbe, Castellón)	2	1	1	1	2	3
Rocafort (Valencia)	1	1				1
Cova dels Anells, Bañeres (Alicante)	2	1	1		1	2
Covacha del Alto (Villena, Alicante)	4	3	1	3	4	7
Peñón del Trinitario (Elda, Alicante)	1		1		1	1
Cueva del Hacha (Elda, Alicante)	3	2	1		1	3
Cueva Santa (Caudete,Albacete)	1		1	8	9	9

Serreta la Vella (Monóvar, Alicante)	4	4				4
Ereta del Pedregal (Navarrés, Valencia)	1	1				1
Cova de Montgó (Javea, Alicante)	3	3		8	8	11
Cova d'En Pardo (Vall de Gallinera, Alicante)	6	5	1	9	10	15
Cova del Barranc del Sinc (Alcoy, Alicante)	1		1		1	1
Cova del Rebolcat (Alcoy, Alicante)	2	2				2
Cova Bolumini (Alfafara, Alicante)	1	1				1
Cova del Mas d'En Felip (Ibi, Alicante)	3	2	1		1	1
Cova del Moro (Agres,Alicante)	1	1				1
Cova Frontó (Castellón de Rugat, Valencia)	11	7	4	2	11	18
Cueva Amador (Cehegín,Murcia)	1	1				1
Cueva de los Blanquizares (Totana, Murcia)	1	1				1
Cova de l'Or (Beniarrés, Alicante)	2	2				2
Cova de El Parpalló (Gandía, Valencia)	1		1		1	1
Barranco de las Ovejas Alicante, Alicante)	1	1				1

(The "Total Cases" exceeds the likely number of people represented. Because some unassignable mandibles no doubt belong to some crania entered as lacking mandibles, and also because some unassignable maxillary fragments may belong with calvarial fragments, the total number of crania slightly exceeds, in all likelihood, the total number of individuals. The last two crania in the list are Upper Pleistocene and were included to see if cluster analysis would separate from the rest; it did not.)

2. Sex

Vault assemblages rarely admit the sexing of skulls in terms of masculine or feminine apparel or jewellery, and anatomical criteria must be used. It is unfortunate that the pelvis, which is the best guide to the sex of an individual skeleton, cannot usually be invoked in collective burials. The sexing of crania on anatomical grounds rests on impressions about the development of muscle markings, supraciliary arches. and temporal and nuchal lines, together with general impressions about robusticity or gracility and about overall size, especially of zygomatic arches, mandibles and teeth. Argar Culture inhumations in graves more readily permit accoutremnts to be also considered, but their reappraisal in terms of masculinity or feminity by Lull (1983 and n.d.*) cautions us against clutching too eagerly at straws. Sexual identifications of El Argar skeletons were offered by Jacques and of skulls from some Alicante-Valencia caves by Fusté (1957).

Using both impressionistic assessment and also some of the sexing discriminant functions of Giles and Elliot (1963)**; which require only cranial measurements, attempts were made to sex the skulls. Impressionistic assessment is in fair agreement with the conclusions of Fusté for assemblages in common where particular skulls were identifiable craniometrically. This however does not mean the criteria necessarily are either objective or reliable. A hint that they may be comes from the discriminant functions. The approximately 375 "cases" included 82 crania sexed impressionistically as 50 "males" and 32 "females". Of 26 crania assessable by discriminant functions, 12 came from those 82. The 26 were broken down into 6 unequivocal males and 12 females, but no fewer that 8 defied assignation; of 12 singularly complete skulls, where both approaches were possible, half showed agreement, 2 disagreement, and the rest equivocal results (evenly divided, however, between doubtful agreement and doubtful disagreement***). If these findings are taken as reinforcing impressionistic judgements, then the indeterminacy of the latter for upto one-third of skulls, regardless of the approach chosen, must also be admitted, and if separation of skulls into sexual groups, for comparing metrical

* Data presented at the Coloquio de Pre- y Protohistoria, Homenaje a Luis Siret, Cuevas de Almanzora, 1984, the Actas of which are being edited for publication by Dr. O. Arteaga at the Deutsches Archaeologisches Institut, Madrid.

** Unfortunately only 6 of their 20 functions could be used owing to failure to take mastoid process measurements, on which many of them depend, due to ignorance of the existence of the functions at the time our measurements were made (1969-72).

*** At Cova del Morro de la Barsella, out of 8 intact skulls, 5 were sexed impressionistically, of which 2 were suitable for discriminant function sexing, with agreement on one and disagreement on the other. At Cova de la Pastora, out of 7 intact skulls, 7 were sexed impressionistically,of which 2 were suitable for discriminant function sexing, with disagreement on one and possibly on another. At Cova de Beni Sid, out of 10 intact skulls, 9 were sexed impressionistically, of which 2 were suitable for discriminant function sexing, with agreement in both instances. At Cova del Palanqués, out of 4 intact skulls, 3 were sexed impressionistically, of which one was suitable for discriminant function sexing, with agreement found. It was also found for one of 2 intact skulls from Cova de Montgó which was amenable to sexing techniques. At Cova de Les Llometes, out of 11 intact crania amenable to sexing techniques, in the one instance discriminant function sexing could be used, it agreed with impressionistic assessment.Three other sites gave one case each where both techniques were applicable although the results were equivocal: one instance of doubtful agreement and two of doubtful disagreement.

or non-metrical characters, could lead to exclusion of one-third from our purview, more may be lost than gained by taking such a step.

Male-female distinctions in Mediterranean skulls are often blurred. It may be wondered whether in fact the 60%:40% female: male ratio of El Argar skulls might not partly owe to application by Jacques of inappropriately narrow criteria of male largeness and robusticity and whether 40% might not have been better class- by him as sexually indeterminate.

It is admitted that gross sexual imbalance in some constituent series could distort our statistical results.Fusté identified as male almost three times as many skulls as those identified as female, at Cova del Camí Real d'Alacant, although our appraisal of the skulls suggests the sexes were equally represented. Fusté concluded the sexes were balanced in the Cova de Beni Sid skulls, whereas our evaluation of them* points to rather more than three times as many females as males. There is some convergence between the conclusions of Fusté of male predominance in the Cova de la Pastora skulls and our own, although discriminant function sexing offers hints that our impressions of "maleness" may be unwarranted, having perhaps been unduly influenced by the large size of Pastora skulls. It will be shown below that morphological aspects other than sex and overall size play an important part in defining the difference between Beni Sid and Pastora skulls. These aspects seem to reflect inherited differences between communities in distinct, but proximate, geographical areas. While sexual dimorphism could have exaggerated the differences, as regards the two caves named, it does not suffice to explain them because other sites share in the two patterns detected.

In short, there are no convincing grounds for believing that marked craniological sexual dimorphism was present in prehistoric S.E. Spain to such a degree as to jeopardise inter-community comparisons. These comparisons assume a fundamentally "androgynous" craniology, in which clear-cut sexual dimorphs are for the most part conspicuous by their absence. Inspection of the univariate craniometrical statistics for each series points less to dispersals (which might have been anticipated if, let us say, males were larger overall than females) than to "bunched" distributions of values, when there are numbers of skulls sufficient to favour the drawing of inferences at all with regard to a given variable at a particular site. It would appear that morphological characteristics of particular skull series, and morphological differences between series, cannot adequately be explained by an appeal to inequalities of sexual representation.

* It should be pointed out that, unlike Fusté, we have not tried to designate each and every skull as either male or female, and hence the proportions claimed by us refer only to those skulls whose sex is beyond question, whereas those of Fusté refer to his entire cranial series. Consequently, our respective conclusions are not wholly comparable and they could even have more in common than they appear to have at first sight.

3. Age at Death

Quite apart from the intrinsic interest of patterns of prehistoric mortality, the biological age of the skulls of this study must be considered from the standpoint of our concern with the strictest comparability of the cranial assemblages under review. It is preferable to confine statistical analysis of cranial measurements to skulls in which growth is complete to all intents and purposes. However it would be unwise to ignore the variation which is well-documented, in both time and space, in the human adolescent growth curve. In Classical Antiquity (and, indeed, in the Middle Ages) menarche in European girls may have occurred at an age not too far removed from its late twentieth-century range. The age-ranges frequently proposed for craniological features, such as sutural obliteration and eruption of permanent teeth, may be misleading if they are drawn from dissected series of cadavers of nineteenth- or early twentieth-century young adults analysed at European or American medical schools. Spatio-temporal fluctuations in the attainment of developmental milestones may be quite marked - for example, in some East African communities the wisdom tooth may erupt as early as at thirteen years of age.

A prudent approach to S.E. Spanish prehistoric cranial age is one which confines itself to relative biological age categories."Mature adult" crania were identified as those which had both the obliteration of the spheno-occipital suture and erupted wisdom teeth - owing to the fragmentary state of most of the skulls only 4 met both criteria. Altogether spheno-occipital obliteration could be defined for only 7 skulls. Of these, 2 showed no obliteration of calvarial vault sutures, but 5 showed varying degrees of obliteration. In none of them were the cusps of the molars and premolars sharp; tooth wear ranged from flattened occlusal surfaces, through exposure of dentine, to teeth worn down to the neck (one of the skulls with visible vault sutures had a wisdom tooth worn down to the neck). That vault sutures are a poor guide to biological age is well-established from studies on human cadavers (see Comas 1966:359-60 for a succinct review of the matter). Wisdom teeth seem to have erupted in our series before spheno-occipital sutural obliteration took place, but not long before, to judge from the relatively unworn state of the molar cusps in the other skulls of this group. It is interesting to note that in 11 El Argar skulls with unerupted wisdom teeth, sutural obliteration had nevertheless begun (Jacques 1887:314)*.

* Lately, 5 well-preserved skulls from Cueva del Barranco de la Higuera (Fortuna, Murcia) have become available for study (see also Campillo 1980; Font 1980; García del Toro and Lillo 1980). 3 skulls with obliterated spheno-occipital sutures show vault sutures in part obliterated, though one has an unerupted wisdom tooth and unworn molar and premolar cusps. 2 other skulls with obliterated spheno-occipital sutures show no vault sutural obliteration - at least one has erupted wisdom teeth and the occlusal molar and premolar tooth surfaces all worn flat. (Mutilation of some teeth is present in 2 or 3 skulls: Campillo 1980).

These considerations provide the starting point for assigning age categories to the rest of the skulls. As far as vault sutures were concerned, they were simply divided between skulls with all sutures visible and unobliterated on the one hand, and skulls with some degree of obliteration (from slight to total) on the other. In the absence of other criteria,the first group might be "juvenile", "young adult" or "mature adult". The second group may be regarded as "adult" ("young" or "mature")*.

Each tooth was inspected for degrees of occlusal wear, viz.:

sharp cusps
flattened cusps
exposure of dentine
tooth worn down to neck.

Particular consideration was paid to the order in each quadrant in which these stages of wear were present. Adult maturity was regarded as probably present where several premolars and molars displayed dentine or were worn down to the neck, especially if in vivo tooth loss and alveolar resorption and/or extensive periodontal pathology were recorded**.

By contrast, skulls with less worn cheek teeth, and without any obliteration of vault sutures, were assigned to the category of "young adult" provided that a wisdom tooth had erupted. Where none had done so, the term "juvenile" was used - a broad category

* This explains why in the statistical breakdown there are columns for "Total Adults" (= "Young" + "Mature") and "Other Crania with Unobliterated Sutures" (which are those where criteria did not exist to separate "Juveniles" from "Young" or from "Mature Adults").

** Of 253 cases open to inspection, 29 had carious teeth (5 with periodontal lesions) and a further 29 had ante mortem tooth loss and/or periodontal lesions. Four old mandibular abscesses and 2 maxillary antral fistulae were seen. The type of caries was noted in 15 skulls: 3 mesio-occlusal, 6 occlusal, 5 interproximal, 2 buccal and 1 lingual - only one lesion was on the tooth neck, the rest were on the crowns. In a new series from Cueva del Barranco de la Higuera (Fortuna, Murcia), out of 5 skulls three show no infectious pathology (one with impacted upper second premolar teeth however). Of the two with signs of infectious processes, one has two instances of premolar caries (on buccal and lingual aspects of the crowns respectively) and the other maxillary resorption with fistula formation. In general terms the pattern differs from that of Anglo-Saxon caries as described by Miles (1969). There is often fair correspondence between attrition of a given tooth crown and presence of dental/periodontal lesions associated with the tooth. In about one-in-five of the cases studied pathological signs and advanced crown attrition go hand in hand. It is perhaps worthwhile recalling that Jacques (1887:313) observed that among 45 Argar skulls, 25 had lost at least one tooth ante mortem and that 8 had carious teeth, figures similar to our own on prehistoric S.E. Spanish skulls.

incorporating those skulls with any permanent teeth whatsoever, regardless of the presence of milk teeth, in which the permanent dentition was incomplete. The only remaining category was that of "young children and infants", in which the permanent dentition had not begun to erupt.

The breakdown recalls many prehistoric distributions (though at Cova de Beni Sid immature skulls seem unusually common - which also attracted the attention of Fusté). Comparative information from El Argar was lacking. The overall breakdown is presented as well as that of 4 cave series:-

	Young Children	Juven-iles	Young Adults	Mature Adults	Total Adults	Other Crania Unobliterated Sutures
Overall	18	44	39	36	163	55
Pastora		4	9	7	34	14
Palanqués		1	8	7	16	4
Camí Real	1		8	2	12	6
Beni Sid	7	13	6	2	9	3

4. Pathology and Selection of Cases

It is necessary to consider those pathological malformations of the cranium which might be thought to influence craniometrical statistics, not only so as to enquire as to whether or not they do, but also because in the Discussion it will be proposed that those involving sutural synostoses may represent the other - recessive - side of a hemidominant phenotypic coin, so to speak, which seems to be indicated by the craniometrical statistical analysis which will be presented in the next section.

It might have been anticipated that malformations, such as platybasia, would have been highlighted by cluster analysis if they had really exerted a distorting influence on craniometrical statistics, whereas in fact they do not stand out in cluster analyses.

The purpose of this study is not to list all the pathological observations made on the skulls, which are detailed elsewhere (Walker 1973). Several observations about cranial pathology of S.E. Spanish skulls exist in the literature (Jacques, 1887:313-7; Lebzelter, 1946; Rincón de Arellano and Fenollosa, 1950; Riquet, 1953; Fusté 1957; Campiloo 1976, 1977). However, we have had the opportunity to record pathological features of skulls not hitherto studied from this standpoint, notably those in the museums at Alicante (e.g. Cova del Morro de la Barsella, Cova de Montgó), Villena (e.g. Cueva de las Lechuzas, Cabezo Redondo), Murcia and Almería (e.g. La Bastida, Los Blanquizares).

Where pathology might influence morphology, however, it is

necessary to draw attention to individual cases. Mention may be made of W-36* and W-44 from Cueva de las Lechuzas which show generalised hyperostosis. The heavy, massive skull, W-149. from Cova del Palanqués may be similar. Also from Palanqués is W-157 which shows platybasia and basal impression. W-153 from the same cave is scaphocepahlic with sagittal sutural synostosis but without coronal or lambdoid sutural obliteration. W-130 and W-198 from Cova de la Pastora appear to have thickening of the anterior part of the vault. W-202 from the same site also has thick vault bones and W-117 from Cova Frontó a vault which attains a thickness of 10 mm. From La Bastida, W-62 has a degree of cleft bony palate. At the same site, W-61 has a right parietal larger than the left and there is complete synostosis of the left coronal and lambdoid sutures, notwithstanding full visibility of all other vault sutures. Among El Argar skulls, Jacques (1887:Table XXVI and 322-4) observed 3 instances of scaphocephaly, one of which manifested platybasia and right-sided plagycephaly (coronal sutural synostosis)**.

3.

CRANIOLOGICAL RESULTS

1. Univariate and Bivariate Craniometrical Statistics

For the 9 major series, one-way statistics were calculated by the SPSS (Statistical Package for the Social Sciences) on an IBM 370/155 computer at the Edinburgh Regional Computing Centre in 1972. The statistics are given in Tables 3-11 together with information on numbers of skulls in each series on which given measurements could be taken (sometimes skulls were too incomplete for all measurements to be made). Although not compared until after measurements had been taken, the craniometrical data of Fusté were found to agree well with our measurements, those of Riquet (1953) less well. The tables refer to craniometrical measurements

* For Q-mode analysis (cluster analysis) it was necessary to number the skulls, and an arbitrary enumeration was used. Numbers introduced by W are those studied by us. J refers to Jacques.

**Mention may also be made of the peculiar Cueva de los Tiestos mandible which has very large teeth and a ramus which forms almost a rectangle with the body. In the new Cueva del Barranco de la Higuera series, one skull, without any vault sutural obliteration, has the left parietal larger than the right (with mandibular ramus compensation), sagittal keeling with parasagittal gutters, and steep inclination of the basi-occiput. The skull seems both elongated and heavy. Another skull shows basi-occipital inclination and yet another some sagittal keeling together with temporal (mainly mastoid process) disproportion. It is possible these represent congenital aspects of morphology. Also, six skulls had been trepanned, namely W-59 from Los Blanquizares (with two trepanations), W-103 from Cova d'En Pardo, and W-182, W-183, W-185 and W-186 from Cova de la Pastora.

taken between clear-cut anatomical landmarks. The only computed measurement is auriculo-bregmatic height.

Several of the more common craniological "indices" were also calculated, but they are not published because the unequal covariances of the measurements which contribute the numerators and denominators render exceedingly unclear just what meaning is to be attributed to "indices", both as regards the morphological information they may or may not contain and as regards their appropriateness in statistical comparison of skulls. The implication of our principal components analyses is that to invoke "indices" is to engage in craniological obscurantism. They obfuscate rather than illuminate the object of study.

Bivariate statistics were computed in order to find out if, for any pair of major assemblages, a particular measurement might be regarded as statistically-speaking homogeneous in all probability. The SPSS was used for computing Student's t and Snedecor's F, as well as the probability attributable to t. The measurements for which there is only a ±2.5% probability of homogeneity are regarded as dissimilar and are tabulated in Table 12. Also shown are those where the probability os ±5%; they are placed in brackets because it is not customary in biological statistics to admit a clear indication of homogeneity at the ±5% level.

Where F did not meet the conditions for meaning to be attributable to t, the SPSS computations were replaced by the Behrens-Fischer statistic (used where small numbers of individuals preclude use of t); these cases are flagged with a superscript dagger in Table 12. After each entry in the table, the number of crania on which the comparison was made is given in brackets. The entries refer to the mean value of the measurement for the assemblage belonging to the site named at the head of the column in every case. The site names against the rows facilitate recognition of the comparison under review in each case.

It should also be pointed out that the comparisons with El Argar are arranged peripherally in Table 12 because, as has been mentioned earlier, the full range of measurements taken by us on the other assemblages was not available in Jacques' (1887) study. The interpretation of El Argar comparisons should be approached with that in mind therefore.

The greatest disparity which the table highlights is between the skulls from Cova de la Pastora and those from Cova de Beni Sid (both in Alicante province) and inspection of the differences affords an initial impression that a gross size difference is involved. That matters are more complicated may perhaps be inferred from considering the neighbouring Cova del Morro de la Barsella cells of the dissimilarity table, which show no clear-cut pattern attributable to overall size difference vis-à-vis the other two sites just mentioned, notwithstanding several differences indicated by the t-tests. In order to clarify these and other matters, principal components analyses of the major assemblages were performed.

2. Principal components analyses of craniometrical data

Principal components analysis is used in two quite different ways in craniology at present. It is important to distinguish between them. On the one hand, it is used, as here, to find out about the internal structures of assemblages, and especially about possible inequalities of covariances of variables as between different series (R-mode use). On the other, it is often used with the presumption that any such inequalities may safely be ignored in portraying relationships between different assemblages on the basis of a a "common yardstick" of the same, arbitrarily chosen, variables (Q-mode use).

The results to be presented below suggest that to make the presumption is unwise, and even that the interpretations drawn when it is made may be misleading in the extreme. They carry similar implications also for all other "common yardstick" approaches to craniometry, from "indices" to linear discriminant functions and Penrose's coefficients, as well as for those taxonomic clustering algorithms which compute relationships in terms of common measures for different assemblages but which fail to allow for inequalities of covariance.

The SPSS principal components analyses (Nie, Bent and Hull 1970: 210-1) were performed on correlation coefficient matrices of the variables for each assemblage separately (with diagonal values = 1). The solution is of the form

$$z_j = a_{j1}F_1 + a_{j2}F_2 + \ldots + a_{jn}F_n$$

where each skull measurement is described linearly in terms of n new uncorrelated components F_1, F_2, ... F_n, each of which is in turn defined as a linear combination of the n original measurements. An iterative solution and varimax rotation were performed.

The components are orthogonal mathematical solutions in hyperspace, each accounting for a diminishing proportion of the within-group variance. The loadings of the skull measurements on them (see the eigenvalue matrices, Tables 13-21 and accompanying graphical plots) may therefore be regarded as independently assorting groups of data. Arbitrary cut-off points, of at least 2% for the total within-group variance and of eigenvalues of at least 0.6 for loadings of variables on components, are customarily taken as suggesting significance. Departure from this practice has only occasionally been suggested here in the interpretation of the matrices, which are in any case published so as to allow alternative opinions to be formed.

If, for any assemblage, the high eigenvalues of a particular principal component seem to reflect, in some degree, the craniometrical measurements of a well-known and discrete anatomical structure, such as an osteological element of the skull, and if, in other assemblages, they reappear in a principal component, together with high eigenvalues of measurements of a different bony element, it is possible that the mathematical arrangements of the variances point to an independent assortment of discrete elements analogous to that of, for instance, hemidominant characters. The assortment of the eigenvalues need not, after all, have suggested any particular structure in the craniometrical data - and that, indeed, is just what the Null Hypothesis presumes.

Let there be no misunderstanding about what such characterisation of bony elements signifies. It most certainly does not signify a return to a comparative morphology construed in terms of ostensibly different "forms" of the various bony elements. It is doubtful whether any such "forms" exist, and unclear what biological interpretation would be appropriate to them even were they to be capable of demonstration. R-mode principal components analysis does not define "formal" groups, rather it may or may not point to independence of structural elements within assemblages of whatever morphological kinds (and even when different assemblages ostensibly are of the same formal type).

Because of this, the analogy with phenotypic assortment cannot be stretched to the self-evident absurdity of equating the osteological elements (inferred from the eigenvalues) with alternative hemidominant phenotypes. Rather, the variety of assortment suggests alternative outcomes of the genetical control (or lack of control) in a quasi-hemidominant manner of the association of putative osteological elements (regardless of their ostensive form). In other words, the assortments may reflect second- or third-order genetical effects, not excluding linkage and pleiotropism. The data do not reflect morhpological structural types; they reflect variation in the structures of human populations.

At the risk of oversimplification, a tentative shorthand summary of the independently assorted groups of measurements may be offered for each of the major assemblages in order to facilitate discussion. The symbols refer to those groups which define cranial areas which sometimes assort independently on different principal components. (The areas are either comprehended by the craniometrical measurements or else they are projections - thus sagittal chords from the basion or opisthion to the skull vault are often strongly correlated with B and/or O.) The symbols are:

B	basi-occiput	E	orbit
F	frontal	M	mandible
N	nasal aperture	P	parietal
O	squamous occiput above inion	S	squamous occiput below inion
T	temporal	X	maxilla-hard palate

Z bizygomatic breadth.

Where a group of craniometrical measurements seems to point towards a cranial area, because the eigenvalues in a principal component, while below the threshold value, are yet noticeably above those of other measurements, the group is indicated by a question mark. Numerals indicate the principal components in order of extraction - higher numbers refer to components which accounted for a proportion of the within-group variance only trivially over the 2% threshold and which at times lacked significant eigenvalues >6

Assortment of Osteological Areas of the Skull in the Principal Components of 9 Cranial Series

ARGAR	BASTIDA	BENI SID	LECHUZAS	PALANQUES
1. F+P+S+O	1. E+N+X	1. E+N+X	1. E+N+X+B	1. E+N+X+B
2. E+N	2. T+S+?B	2. P+S	2. P+S	2. Z+S+O+?B
3. M	3. F+P	3. Z+B	3. M	3. T
4. X+?Z	4. M	4. O	4. O	4. M
5. S	5. Z	5. M	5. T	5. P+S
		6. F	6. F	6. S+?B
		7. ?	7. ?P+?O+?S	7. F
			8. E	
			9. O	

LLOMETES	PASTORA	CAMI REAL D'ALACANT	MORRO DE LA BARSELLA
1. F+P+S+?M	1. F+P+S	1. F+P+S	1. F+P+S+O
2. E+N+X+?M	2. E+N+X	2. N+X	2. E+N+X+B+F
3. M	3. O+?B	3. Z+E+S	3. M
4. B	4. M	4. B+X	4. F
5. O	5. B+?T	5. O	5. T
6. T	6. M	6. M	6. ?P
7. Z+E	7. ?F	7. B	
8. F		8. M	

That the table oversimplifies matters is seen by attentive scrutiny of Tables 13-21. For instance, the two mandibular components of Pastora and Camí Real d'Alacant respectively reflect maximum length-bicondylar breadth on the one hand, and all other mandibular measurements (including bigonial breadth) taken by us on the other. At Llometes, by contrast, the distinction appears thrice over between maximum length + bicondylar and bigonial breadths vis-à-vis the remaining measurements (symphysial and ramus heights, minimum ramus breadth and mandibular angle). Again, at Llometes and Lechuzas orbital height and breadth load most heavily on different components, in contrast to their covariance at other sites. Even more complicated appear to be the relationships between the basi-occiput and the inion-opisthion region of the occiput; sometimes the foramen magnum dimensions and projections in the sagittal plane on the basion and opisthion are associated with the basi-occiput, sometimes with the inion-opisthion region of the squamous occiput.

Perhaps the Beni Sid, Palanqués and Lechuzas skulls share elements of a common configuration somewhat different from that which appears from inspection of the Pastora, Llometes, Morro de la Barsella and Camí Real d'Alacant skulls. Argar and Bastida, however, on the one hand neither look particularly alike, nor yet like either of the aforementioned groups of sites, on the other. Considered in the light of the dissimilarity Table 12, these tentative proposals suggest that more than mere size underlies the marked dissimilarity between Pastora and Beni Sid, highlighted by the t-tests.

The t-tests also suggest some dissimilarity between Pastora and Lechuzas, and between Beni Sid, on the one hand, and Pastora, Llometes, Barsella and Camí Real d'Alacant, on the other. They do not, however, suggest a contrast between Pastora and Palanquès but they do point to differences between it and Barsella. It may be pointed out also that even where t-tests do not demonstrate inter-assemblage heterogeneity (e.g. with regard to the Pastora and Bastida bizygomatic breadths) principal components analysis can show the measurement to have very different effects on assemblage structure. Further comment on similarities and dissimilarities between the assemblages must be deferred until the epigenetical characteristics have been presented below.

It is worth noting at this point that there is no indication at all that the first (or for that matter any other) principal component of the respective skull assemblages reflects overall cranial size. This it is sometimes said to do when skulls are compared in terms of a "common yardstick" by principal components analysis of a common list of measurements arbitrarily chosen without any prior attempt to find out if there might exist inequalities of covariances - the results presented above therefore tell strongly against the advisability of using principal components analysis in that way.

3. Principal factor analysis of craniometrical data

A comparison of this technique with principal components analysis was undertaken. It differs fundamentally because the solution is of the form (Nie, Bent and Hull 1970:211-2):

$$z_j = a_{j1} F_1 + a_{j2} F_2 + \ldots + a_{jm} F_m + d_j U_j$$

where U is a unique factor presumed to exist with reference to skull measurement j and a_{ji} is the standardised multiple regression coefficient of j (the "factor loading", as it were) on the i-th hypothetical factor F_i. U_j is assumed orthogonal to all the common factors and unique factors associated with other skull measurements.

This means that the unique portion of a skull measurement is not related to any other skull measurement or to that part of itself which is due to the common factor. Consequently if there is any correlation between skull measurement j and k, let us say, it is assumed to be due to the common factors. If the common factors are assumed to be orthogonal to each other, the correlation between them may be expressed by:

$$r_{jk} = \sum_{i=1}^{m} a_{ji} a_{ki} .$$

If only one common factor be assumed, the partial correlation between j and k = 0.

In factor analysis a minimum number of common factors is specified (conveniently taken as not less than the number of cranial measurements used) such that after controlling for them the remainig partial correlations between the variables = 0. There is therefore an assumption of the existence of a residual variance which is not accounted for by the common factors and which does not contribute to the intercorrelations between the variables. It is an unknown quantity which must be calculated from the data - the communalities reflect this and after calculation are inserted in the diagonal of the reduced correlation matrix. They are replaced iteratively by recalculation following the extraction of each factor in turn until the difference between successive communality estimates is negligible.

For the Beni Sid and El Argar skull assemblages (Tables 22, 23, and corresponding graphical plots) the principal factor matrices, and the numbers of principal factors accounting individually for at least 2% of the within-group variance, are virtually identical to the principal components analysis solutions.

The technique was applied to a somewhat reduced list of cranial measurements of the La Bastida skulls (Table 24 and corresponding graphical plots) after removal of measurements that only infrequently could be recorded in the assemblage. Again, correspondence with the principal components analysis solution was quite good, although some condensation is observable, with two principal components "condensed", so to speak, on a single principal factor in one instance.

For the rest of the cranial assemblages, further reduced variable lists were used, with correspondingly increased condensation. The results are briefly summarised at the foot of each of the principal components matrices for the major assemblages.

It is concluded that there is little to choose between R-mode principal components and R-mode factor analyses in practical terms, from the point of view of describing the composition of cranial However, the assumptions which have to be made for factor analysis make it less appealling than principal components analysis, and probably inappropriate for comparing assemblages in Q-mode, if a "common yardstick" of craniometrical measurements, where inequalities of covariances and correlations are unknown, is imposed on them at the outset.

4. Epigenetical characterisation

Taking all of the southeastern Spanish crania, 23 had complete metopic sutures and a further 7 a minor degree of metopism, usually abour 5 mm. The incidence of metopism is more than 10% of frontal bones on which information was available. However, the incidence varies remarkably between the major series. Thus there was no instance at Cova del Morro de la Barsella, only a single instance (of incomplete metopism) at La Bastida, and a single instance (of complete metopism) at Cova del Palanqués. One complete and one incomplete metopic suture were seen in the Cueva de las Lechuzas skulls, two complete and one incomplete in the Çova de Les Llometes crania, and one complete and two incomplete in those from Cova del Camí Real d'Alacant. In stark contrast to these sites are Cova de la Pastora with six instances of complete metopism and Cova de Beni Sid with four complete and three incomplete metopic sutures. At El Argar ten out of 64 skulls showed metopism (Jacques, 1887:309).

However, the contrasts previously remarked on between Pastora and Beni Sid have their epigenetical counterpart in the contrast between the dearth of lambdoid intrasutural ossicles at Pastora and their presence in no less than six crania (out of 9 appropriate for inspection) from Beni Sid. Lambdoid intrasutural ossicles were well represented at Palanqués (multiple in three cases) but not at Lechuzas, the two sites with which Beni Sid was tentatively related craniometrically. While they were also infrequent on the Barsella skulls, they were well represented on those from both Camí Real d'Alacant and Les Llometes, with all of which a tentative craniometrical relationship was proposed for Pastora. Jacques (1887:309) remarked that out of 63 El Argar skulls, 23 had intrasutural ossicles, usually in the lambdoid suture or at the pterion.(At other sites pterionic ossicles are not noticeably frequent.)

The traits suggested by Berry (1968) were sought, but their usefulness was at times restricted owing to the fragmentary state of many skulls, with consequent problems about the comparability of particular skulls with regard to clusters of traits, and even, indeed, about whether traits are present uni- or bilaterally, not to mention about the incidences of left-sided versus right-sided unilateral traits and of differing numbers of left- versus right-sided multistate traits (such as zygomatic foramina, ossicles in the coronal and lambdoid sutures, etc.).

The following are among the more frequently observable traits. For each there are given four rows of numbers as follows:

a the number of cases with the trait observed on both sides of the skull
b the number of cases where the trait was observed on just one side of the skull
c the number of skulls on which bilateral inspection could be undertaken
d the number of skulls on which only one side of the skull was available for inspection, for the trait in question.

Skulls from the Cova Frontó are included here in addition to the other major series. El Argar is omitted because comparable data were not published by Jacques. Because of some of the problems of comparability mentioned above, chi-square and probability determinations have not been calculated. Only incidences are given.

Incidences of some of the more frequently observed epigenetical traits in 9 cranial assemblages

		BAS-TIDA	LLOM-ETES	BARS-ELLA	LECH-UZAS	FRON-TO	PAS-TORA	PALA-NQUES	CAMI REAL	BENI SID
Total cases allowing inspection of at least one trait		14	25	15	11	6	39	6	13	9
FRONTAL NOTCHES	a	7	16		7	6	20	3	5	5
	b	1	1		1	0	10	2	5	2
	c	13	25		11	6	28	5	11	9
	d	0	0		0	0	10	1	2	0
SUPRAOR-BITAL FORAMINA	a	1	7	4	1	2	7	1	2	5
	b	3	1	4	0	1	7	3	9	3
	c	12	24	13	11	5	25	4	10	9
	d	0	1	0	0	0	7	2	3	0
ZYGOMATIC FORAMINA	a	7	1	6	4	0	6	0	1	5
	b	2	3	0	2	1	6	1	2	3
	c	11	12	11	10	1	9	2	3	5
	d	0	0	0	0	1	3	1	1	3
ACCESSORY LESSER PALATINE FORAMINA	a	4	5	4	2	1	1	1	0	2
	b	0	0	0	0	0	2	1	1	1
	c	11	13	9	10	1	9	3	1	6
	d	0	0	0	0	0	2	0	0	0
ANTERIOR ETHMOIDAL FORAMINA EXSUTURAL	a	3	0	0	0	0	3	0	0	0
	b	0	1	0	0	0	4	1	0	0
	c	10	6	7	9	0	4	3	1	4
	d	0	0	0	0	0	6	0	0	1
POSTERIOR CONDYLAR CANAL PATENT	a	5	0	2	2	0	5	3	3	3
	b	0	2	1	0	1	2	1	3	1
	c	11	12	10	9	1	6	4	4	6
	d	0	0	0	0	2	1	0	1	1
MASTOID FORAMINA ABSENT	a	3	5	2	0	5	3	3	4	3
	b	1	2	0	0	0	3	1	4	3
	c	10	13	12	9	5	12	4	6	7
	d	0	0	0	0	0	6	2	4	0
MASTOID FORAMEN EXSUTURAL	a	3	5	2	0	5	3	3	4	3
	b	1	2	0	0	0	3	1	4	3
	c	10	13	12	9	5	12	4	6	7
	d	0	0	0	0	0	7	2	4	0

The data presented here suggest similarity between Pastora and Beni Sid; nevertheless, there are differences between them not only as regards lambdoid sutural ossicles (see above) but also as regards the bilateral multiple nature of the zygomatic foramina at Beni Sid, contrasting with the usually bilateral single ones of Pastora skulls.

Two Pastora crania each had the unusual configuration of bilaterally patent posterior condylar canals, left-sided double anterior condylar (hypoglossal) canals, zygomatic facial foramina, and frontal notches. Close genetic relationship might perhaps have been supposed, but single-link cluster analysis does not demonstrate the pair (W-133, W-134) to be particularly close vis-à-vis other skulls (see below).

Frontal notches, exsutural mastoid foramina and lambdoid ossicles are well represented at Cova Frontó. They are all well represented at Cova del Palanqués as are patent posterior condylar canals and supraorbital foramina, seen all together on some skulls and (apart from frontal notches on one of them) together with double hypoglossal canals on two (W-148, W-150) - once again however this pair is not especially close when cluster analysis of skulls is inspected (see below).

At Camí Real d'Alacant lambdoid intrasutural ossicles (often multiple) and asterionic ossicles are quite common along with exsutural mastoid foramina, supraorbital foramina, frontal notches, and patent posterior condylar canals. Accessory lesser palatine foramina are more strongly represented at Morro de la Barsella vis-à-vis other cave asemblages but accessory ossicles are conspicuous by their absence; supraorbital and zygomatic foramina are well represented however.

Only zygomatic foramina and frontal notches show any noteworthy incidence among the Lechuzas skulls. The Bastida skulls show a moderate representation of most of the anomalies involving foramina along with a low incidence of lambdoid sutural ossicles, but 6 crania have patent posterior condylar canals, bilaterally absent mastoid foramina, zygomatic foramina, and frontal notches (W-60, W-63, W-64, W-66, W-69, W-70) - only two (W-63, W-66) seem to be particularly well linked by cluster analysis (see below).

The use of epigenetical traits, for characterising the major series* on the assumption of independent assortment of characters, is limited by the fragmentary nature of the remains, should advan-

* Since carrying out the bulk of the study, five remarkably well preserved skulls from the Cueva del Barranco de la Higuera (Fortuna, Murcia) became available for study. They show neither metopism and almost no accessory ossicles. All have zygomatic foramina, three have patent posterior condylar canals, three have exsutural anterior ethmoidal foramina (the other two have the foramina at the suture), four have accessory lesser palatine foramina and there is a reciprocal relation between frontal notches (in 3 skulls) and supraorbital foramina (1 skull) and between their left- and right-sided presentation in the fifth skull. The mastoid foramen is absent in 2 out of 10 possibilities but exsutural in only three of these.

ced statistical analysis be proposed, not to mention by the difficulty of posing valid questions about the independence of unilateral from bilateral representation, or about different multistate values, when incidences of metopism, let us say, are compared with zygomatic facial foramina or lambdoid sutural ossicles. It can be concluded from the results presented here that the major cranial series considered all differ from one another, even if it is unclear how the relative differences might best be expressed.

5. Cluster analyses

Craniology does not seem to have at its disposal any measurements appropriate for assessing the relationships between the assemblages in terms of the twin criteria of

(a) within-group orthogonality

and (b) capacity to account for the full range of between-group compositional orthogonality.

A possible, although incomplete, answer might be the higher-order analysis of principal component z-scores from R-mode analyses. It is hoped to attempt this in the future, provided certain difficulties can be overcome. Given some of the aforementioned problems presented by non-metrical observations, it might be prudent to eliminate redundancy within them by R-mode principal components analysis in non-parametric dimensions as a first step, or even to exclude them from comparative procedures altogether.

However, the problems inherent in any such exercise go far beyond such practical considerations. There are two quite different kinds of theoretical problems to be faced, concerning mathematical and anthropological priorities, respectively. The mathematical difficulty concerns the variation in the numbers of components above the arbitrary threshold level of the within-group variance to which they respond. If it be a requirement of algorithms for higher-order comparison that identical numbers of components be taken, then the proportions being compared of the within-group variances become increasingly disparate while at the same time use cannot be made of some of the intrinsic differences in the characterisations of the respective assemblages. The anthropological problem is quite different. It is that the characterisation of cranial assemblages is but a step on the road to exploring the biological structure of earlier human communities. Among other matters, the exchange of sexual partners between communities, and also with communities represented by only isolated skulls, is one which should receive high priority. If comparisons are limited to the more numerous skull assemblages and defined in terms of higher-order analysis, not only is it extremely difficulty to detect internal anomalies ("likelihood" analysis offers a way out in part), but it is impossible to investigate the relation to the assemblages of other, isolated crania which come from communities whose R-mode components are both unknown and unknowable.

In view of these daunting obstacles to moving from R-mode analysis of assemblage structure to Q-mode taxonomic analysis of forms, and in view of the anthropological priority which has just been mentioned, an appropriate prelude to higher-order analysis may be a simple Q-mode taxonomy of craniological forms which uses an algorithm incurring fewest assumptions about possible within-series structure and which also admits all cases, regardless of missing data. The algorithm of first resort therefore is single-link cluster analysis.

The results of single-link cluster analysis are shown in Dendrograms 1-9, the legends to which are self-explanatory. The collaboration is gratefully acknowledged of G. Newell at the University Computing Centre of The University of Sydney, who ran the GENSTAT hierarchical single-link cluster programs in 1979-80 on the following combinations of assemblages (which included that from Cova Frontó so that use could be made of the representation of non-metrical traits there) and of variables*:

Argar, Barsella, Bastida, Beni Sid, Camí Real d'Alacant, Frontó, Lechuzas, Llometes, Palanqués, Pastora

1 only metrical data; all crania; loose mandibles excluded

2 metrical and non-metrical data; all crania; loose mandibles excluded

3 only metrical data; loose mandibles and very fragmentary crania excluded

4 metrical and non-metrical data; loose mandibles and very fragmentary crania excluded

Barsella, Bastida, Beni Sid, Camí Real d'Alacant, Frontó, Lechuzas, Llometes, Palanqués, Pastora

5 only non-metrical data; loose mandibles excluded

6 only non-metrical data; loose mandibles and very fragmentary crania excluded

All sites (major series and other assemblages) except El Argar

7 only non-metrical data; all crania; loose mandibles excluded

8 only metrical data; all crania and all loose mandibles included

Argar, Barsella, Bastida, Beni Sid, Camí Real d'Alacant, Frontó, Lechuzas, Llometes, Palanqués, Pastora

9 only metrical data; all crania and all loose mandibles (loose mandibles removed en bloc from Dendrogram where they formed a single chain as a "tail").

The analyses show the "chaining" effect which is a common result of single-link clustering, especially when there are many missing data which leave empty the same set of variables for many cases (e.g. El Argar,where several craniometrical variables used by us but not by Jacques had therefore no entries; again, loose mandibles generated vast zero entries for the missing crania they represented). Apart from specific instances (such as some already mentioned, e.g. W-63, W-66) where particular criteria point towards a close morphological relationship, most "chains" at P>90% may be attributed to the missing data effect and consequently ignored.

However, some small, tight groups are suggestive, particularly as regards some Llometes skulls, some others from Bastida, and perhaps as regards sporadic Argar-Bastida similarities. The frequent absence of low splits hints at a fundamental similarity between all of the cases over and above the missing data correlations (the one dendrogram with a low split sems to be due to the arbitrary starting point, which happened to be among some very disparate and incomplete cranial fragments). The analysis of cranial measurements on major assemblages other than El Argar, and from which especially fragmentary crania were excluded, does not lead to any greater discrimination but merely to a shallow chain. This is in line with the overall similarity of most of the major assemblages in Table 12 and with the metrical conclusions of Fusté (1957) about the fundamental homogeneity of S.E. Spanish skulls. Given the absence of the most rudimentary discrimination between major assemblages, it is hardly surprising that incorporating outlying skulls from other stations is uninformative.

Analysis of the major assemblages (other than Argar), with exclusion of the more fragmentary crania, perhaps hints at some small clusters, but as has already been mentioned by no means all of the skulls with ostensibly similar epigenetical traits are clearly picked out. Thus not identified by cluster analysis were possible pairs from Cova de la Pastora (W-133, W-134) and from Cova Frontó (W-148, W-150). Some further comments on possible relationships will be made in the Discussion section below, in connexion with possible archaeological interpretations, but it should be clearly understood that they are speculative rather than founded on firm statistical argument.

It must be concluded that, while "it may well be worth attempting single-linkage with any new set of data" (Doran and Hodson 1975:176), it would seem indicated now to begin to formulate hypotheses which incorporate assumptions which we may wish to draw from the bivariate, principal components and epigenetical inquiries into our skulls, so that other Q-mode taxonomic procedures can be tried. It is also desirable to consider the possibility, mentioned above, of comparing different assemblages from the standpoint of differences in the structure of their R-mode principal components analyses. (The information these provide, about differences in assemblage characterisation, would be at once lost if we were simply to revert to a "common yardstick" of variables, using principal components analysis for Q-mode comparisons.)

4.

Discussion

It may be asked, whether the results of the enquiry provide statistically valid characterisation of prehistoric communities in terms of their craniology; if so, whether that characterisation appears to have meaning in terms of human biology; whether that characterisation and that biological interpretation offer insights into some of the problems of S.E. Spanish prehistory indicated in the Introduction; and, finally, whether the approach followed here offers useful insights for physical and biological anthropology in general.

Any one of these four matters is worthy of a full-length review. In order not to stray too far from the stated aim of pressing physical anthropology into the service of southeastern Spanish prehistory, this Discussion will be limited to aspects intrinsically related to the enquiry.

The matter of the validity of the characterisation of prehistoric communities in terms of their craniology goes beyond their comparison with respect to a "common yardstick", such as is customarily used as the basis for that comparison. It is first of all incumbent on craniologists to enquire whether there are grounds for accepting a "common yardstick" with respect to the assemblages under review.

The strength above all of principal components analysis lies in its ability to effect such a preliminary enquiry. It is particularly appropriate for R-mode within-group analyses. Not only is it an effective data reduction technique, which identifies that "redundancy" in the osteological data which has long been a source of anxiety to craniologists (e.g. Corruccini, 1975), but also it can reduce the within-group data to orthogonal components of singular interest from the standpoint of the differing characteristics of different biological communities.

The assumptions required for R-mode analysis concern the representativeness or otherwise of the cases included with respect to the populations from which they come. When it is believed that different populations are, indeed, being compared, it does not matter that one (or more) of them may be hybrid, although the technique cannot indicate it to be so - other statistical techniques must be used to do this.

Might there exist cultural or biological factors which could cause foreseeable intercorrelations between groups of variables, and hence influence the R-mode results, in one or more assemblage ? As a starting point, it is probably reasonable to assume that small, relatively isolated, prehistoric communities are reflected more or less, as regards their morphology, in the skeletal remains which have come down to us. Where burial vaults (such as caves) were used, it is not unreasonable to assume that these were part of the patrimony of discrete communities sharing a cultural tradition. Where burial took place at settlements an analogous pattern within a perhaps somewhat different tradition may be inferred. There are no overwhelming archaeological grounds for believing the major assemblages to be unrepresentative of local communities to which the deceased probably had belonged. Nor does it appear that sexual dimorphism is likely to be a hidden factor capable of distorting craniometrical comparability. As regards sexual dimorphism, biological age and pathological features, the assemblages do not, by and large, show deviations which demand particular attention. The possibility of a contrast in sexual representation between Cova de la Pastora and Cova de Beni Sid can neither explain all of the differences between their craniological statistics nor yet why other assemblages share in their resive statistical compositions.

Given the absence of obvious extraneous influences, which might have prejudged the assortment of the within-group variances of particular assemblages, there is no good reason for avoiding R-mode principal components analysis of each, even if it be used only for data-reduction as a preliminary to numerical taxonomy (so that heavy biasses may be pared down and so that programs may run faster after removal of redundant data).

However, there is no a priori reason to assume that R-mode principal components should reflect morphological elements and it is surprising that it seems to do so. It might, for instance, have reflected observer-induced variation, by identifying values according to categories of overall size. Instead, it is interesting that values very different in size, but which relate to anatomical areas of the skull, are, more often than not, found in association on one component (e.g. symphysial height/mandibular length). Alternatively, it might have been anticipated that at least some components of at least one or two assemblages might have offered a meaningless and random distribution of variables with high eigenvalues, yet such is not the case.

It would seem, therefore, that R-mode principal components analysis of craniometrical measurements contains interesting information about groups of measurements which repeatedly reflect anatomical entities and which sometimes, moreover, assort in an orthogonal manner. These elments are not seen when principal components analysis is used for Q-mode enquiry in craniology.

Quite apart from the intrinsic interest of the R-mode findings, they imply not only that a given investigator need not always use a full list of measurements for the componential characterisation of an assemblage to be comparable with that of another studied by that investigator, but also that different land-marks may be tolerated, both for different, and for supposedly similar, measurements, provided that in the latter case landmarks are not mixed within the same assemblage. This means that the data of different investigators may be used for comparative characterisation (in this study, my own and those of Jacques).

Q-mode principal components analysis has been used frequently in recent years in comparative craniometry. When it is performed there is a well-known tendency for the first principal component (or, if factor analysis be used, the first factor) to reflect somewhat diffusely overall vault and/or facial size. The matter is not wholly resolved by carrying out a prior double standardisation, by variable and by case. This procedure may lead to a valid discrimination between species, which tend to have different mean values for measurements, (e.g. Homo sapiens sapiens, Homo sapiens neanderthalensis, Homo erectus - see Habgood and Walker, in press), where attention is focussed on overall cranial form.

When, however, it is a matter of trying to characterise biological groups within a single species, the approach is less than adequate. It can no longer be taken for granted that size differences are a morphological adaptation to natural selection of species. And while sexual dimorphism may account for a part of the observed size differences in a population, it is by no means the only cause - other genetic influences, and perhaps nutritional influences on growth, cannot be discounted.

With regard to the present study it is not denied that sexual differences contribute to the Pastora-Beni Sid difference. Yet the R-mode analyses lead to the inference that sexual imbalances account for only part of the difference, as has been argued earlier. The R-mode principal components analyses point to other assemblages sharing their respective characteristic structures, and it is hard to sustain the view that sexual imbalance is at the root of this divergence, particularly as some size differences seem to exist at times within the two groups of assemblages according to the t-tests, and sometimes they fail to be discerned by these tests between the two.

If such distinctions are not highlighted by the Q-mode clustering algorithm used, this may be due in part to inherent shortcomings in single-link clustering, commented on above. It should be borne in mind that our aim with single-link clustering was the identification of anomalous cases within series and the relating of isolated cases to major series. It is quite likely that limiting a future clustering attempt to the major series considered in terms of those measurements, which are not only critical for the osteological elements identified by principal components analysis but also have a high incidence of occurrence, discrimination between the major series may be reproduced. Such a reproduction can hardly be regarded as independent confirmation, since it involves preselection in terms of the characterisation already attained in order to overcome the shortcomings generated by spurious correlations.

In the R-mode principal components analyses presented above. the first principal component usually accounts for a large proportion of the within-group variance. It also usually reflects different permutations and combinations of intercorrelated cranial measurements. Consequently comparison of different assemblages in terms, let us say, of the z-scores of the first components (e.g. in a graphical, Q-mode display which purports to show separation of different assemblages) involves a loss of the information which R-mode analysis identified in the first components. The loss is greater when double standardisation precedes Q-mode comparison.

Given the discriminatory power of R-mode principal components analysis to reduce correlation and covariance matrices, the outcome of such a reversion to Q-mode comparison is to throw out the anthropological baby with the bathwater. It reveals the unthinking conflation of anatomical form with the characterisation of population structure by reference to anatomy. This is manifested by its presumption that inequalities of correlation and covariance do not exist (or at any rate are of small account), such that a "common yardstick" of craniometrical measurements is regarded as a perfectly acceptable basis on which to propose comparisons.

The results of our enquiry are in conflict with this presumption. They therefore put in jeopardy Q-mode comparisons of cranial series in terms of principal component scores. It cannot be affirmed too strongly that principal components analysis is far better suited to defining within-group intercorrelations and covariances of variables than to specifying between-group relations*. Nor is the first time doubts have been raised concerning the presumption that inequalities of correlation and covariance need not worry anthropologists. Howells (1972) raised the matter, though in his monograph on cranial variation (Howells, 1973) it was passed over, as we remarked at the time (Walker, 1975**). Lately, the issue has been aired by Utterschaut and Wilmink (1983) in an important critique.

The unwisdom in palaeoanthropological enquiries of relying on a "common yardstick", whether raw measurements, whether transforms such as "indices" or even distance statistics, shape coefficients or linear discriminant functions, is more than hinted at by the present study. Cluster algorithms suffer from precisely the same drawback (not to mention other shortcomings such as spurious correlations due to missing variables and missing values, especially in bilateral multistate characters). Even the clustering of principal component z-scores presents severe theoretical difficulties as regards the relative desirability of comparing

* It may be that when individual skulls are considered in respect of a given series the working hypothesis may be put forward that they will probably not share craniometrical product-moment correlation coefficients with the series, and that if they do a provisional hypothesis of similarity to the series may be admitted; if not, nothing can be inferred, since the individual could have come from a population with quite different structural characteristics.

**The sense of the remark was marred by an unfortunate typographical misprint: "disturbing" was transformed into "distributing" the similar numbers of components or similar proportions of the within-group variances, as has been remarked earlier.

If these problems can be overcome there may be much to be said for attempting higher-order clustering in joint non-metric-parametric hyperspace. First, however, R-mode principal components analysis on non-metrical variables must be undertaken so as resolve for each assemblage such matters (about which poorly substantiated assertions abound in the literature) as independent/non-independent assortment with regard to sidedness, differing ordinal values of multistate characters, and even whether some ostensively different traits may not in fact be ordinal variants* and if so how they should be scored. These problems, together with the fragmentary nature of the skull series, render extremely difficult the calculation of chi-square for the various incidences and it has been prudently avoided therefore. Nevertheless, attention has been drawn to some aspects of epigenetical distinctiveness which, together with the principal components characterisations, offer clues about the intrinsic circumscription of some human communities in prehistoric southeastern Spain.

The impression gained from both types of characterisation is that there may exist permutations and combinations of craniometrical data and, independently of these, permutations and combinations of epigenetical phenomena. The former seem to reflect cranial osteological areas in discrete anatomical relationship - whole bones, parts of bones, and groups of bones. There is clear indication of discrete components.

It is not fanciful to propose that they reflect inherited aspects of osteogenesis of cranial bones and of the mandible, at times in inherited association, at times assorting independently. The impression given by the non-metrical observations is that assortment of metopism and intrasutural ossicles may show similar behaviour, likewise the assortment of foramina - as might indeed be anticipated if foramina are the consequence of perineurial histogenesis and hence quite unconnected with the osteogenetical control of bony dimensions.

Although the non-metrical observations point towards the distinctiveness of each of the major skull assemblages considered here, both principal components analysis and bivariate craniometrical comparisons seem to indicate some degree of difference between the skulls of El Argar and those of La Bastida, as well as between both sites and the two groups of cave burial assemblages. The first group comprises stations in a short N.-S. line from Albaida (Valencia) to Jijona (Alicante) passing through Alcoy (Camí Real d'Alacant; Cova de la Pastora; Cova de Les Llometes; Cova del Morro de la Barsella). The second group lies peripherally, to the W., N., and E., and comprises the Cueva de las Lechu-

* See earlier footnote on the Cueva del Barranco de la Higuera skulls with regard to supraorbital foramina and frontal notches. Another case may be the various absence, intrasutural presence and exsutural occurrence of the mastoid foramen.

zas (Villena, Alicante), the Cova del Palanqués (Navarrés, Valencia), and the Cova de Beni Sid (Vall d'Ebo, Alicante). It is perhaps somewhat less homogeneous, craniologically speaking.

The first group includes assemblages which contain both 3rd millennium pottery and also Bell Beakers (e.g. Cova de la Pastora) and thus may belong to the archaeological phase characterised by Bell Beakers dated ca. 3900 - 3800 b.p. at Cerro de la Virgen (Orce, Granada) where Argaric elements appear around 3750 b.p.. While it is quite possible that the archaeological assemblages in burial caves accumulated over several generations there exists some possibility that at least a part of the assemblages was contemporaneous with a date as late as 3750.

What this might imply is that, even were demographical movements to have taken place further South, the communities in northern Alicante may have represented at a late date the remnants of a more widespread antecedent population.

The Cova del Morro de la Barsella also belongs to the first group. Here the excavator identified two phases of burials, of which one, at least, had associated Argaric material inter alia. In short, there seems to be good evidence for a degree of chronological overlap between a tradition of cave burial/vault burial on the one hand, and the appearance of the Argar Culture of Almería, Granada and Murcia on the other.

Even if some of the human skeletal remains from the caves span several centuries, the likelihood that others are close in time to the Argar Culture permits comparison to be made of human remains from vault burials and from Argaric settlements. It is somewhat surprising that the latter do not show striking differences from the supposedly antecedent population represented by the former, such as were to have been anticipated had demographical shifts occurred. Rather, the most striking differences seem to lie within the northern Alicante-southern Valencia area of cave burials itself. This finding is hard to square with a hypothesis of maximum heterogeneity to the South, in Almería-Granada-Murcia. The hypothesis must be regarded as not substantiated.

Mention has been made earlier of some minor craniological differences between Cova de la Pastora and Cova del Morro de la Barsella, however. It is possible that these reflect changes taking place within one or both communities over time. Some of the archaeological remains at Morro de la Barsella are clearly Copper Age and not Argaric.

A "double-anchor" pendant from Morro de la Barsella has its parallel at the Cueva de los Blanquizares, where a trepanned individual was found, in addition to Copper Age, Bell Beaker and perhaps early Argaric artefacts, and where an alabaster vessel has painted motifs similar to those on potsherds from Cueva de los Tiestos (where the burial assemblage seems somewhat older than 3800 - 3600 b.p.) and from Cova Montgó. Decorated bone items from Cova de la Pastora are parallelled at Ereta del Pedregal (Navarrès, Valencia) where a date of 3930±250 b.p. (M-753) marks an advanced stage of the Copper Age sequence.

It is beyond the scope of this study to give a detailed account of the southeastern Spanish Copper Age, which has been presented elsewhere (Walker, 1984). Rather, attention is drawn to the likelihood that one of the two groups of cave burials may contain skeletal remains which are not necessarily any earlier than 3900 - 3700 b.p.. The other group does not offer particular clues about its chronological situation within the Copper Age.

Nor is it necessary to regard as particularly different in time the settlements of El Argar and La Bastida (Lull 1983: 323-4). Lull feels that the archaeological evidence points to the beginning of La Bastida around 3650 - 3600 b.p., i.e. perhaps only a century later than that of El Argar itself. His view may receive support from a comparison between a metal dagger from La Bastida and English Wessex Culture examples (Walker 1973). It is possible that the cluster analyses hint at some similarities in the skulls between the two sites, though it must be pointed out that neither the bivariate analysis nor the principal components analyses point towards similarity.

It is likely, therefore, that some of the skulls in the major series belong to the relatively brief span of time between 4000 and 3500 b.p., and without doubt most of the skulls in this study belong to the period 4500 - 3500 b.p.. (A detailed archaeological justification of the dates proposed for the sites in Map 1 would be out of place, given the difficulty we have referred to with regard to arranging their craniological similarity/dissimilarity to the major series by cluster analysis.) In short, they span both the geographical and chronological ranges in which some archaeologists have made claims of cultural discontinuities. It does not matter from the standpoint of biological anthropology whether these be envisaged as exotic cultural groups or simply a consequence of spatio-temporal inequality in the development of new social structures (e.g. social stratification).

From the perspective of physical anthropology what matters is whether the biological findings may or may not corroborate the archaeological theories. Generally speaking, these theories imply a greater heterogeneity in the southern (Almería-Granada-Murcia) area than in the northern one (northern Alicante-southern Valencia) where Copper Age traditions are strongly marked in the so-called Valencian Bronze Age of the 2nd millennium and where proto-urban development is slight with respect to the southern area.

The craniological findings, however, point in a quite different direction, namely, to a striking heterogeneity represented by two proximate groups in the northern area. Nor do the univariate statistics suggest that at El Argar or La Bastida the populations were internally heterogeneous.

They do not support the assertion of three craniological

"types" in the El Argar skulls, which was made by Jacques (1887: 325-8) on the basis of a wholly inadequate nineteenth century approach to statistics. The kurtosis and skewness statistics do not point to major deviations from normality. Nor do the cluster dendrograms correspond in any way to Jacques' categories when the individual skulls of the clusters are inspected from the standpoint of the criteria on which Jacques affirmed the supposed types. Fusté (1957) failed to find these in his study of the Alicante-Valencia skulls and manifested a healthy scepticism about their existence. It can be stated categorically that they exist neither in the northern nor in the southern parts of south-eastern Spain.

Fusté concluded that the Alicante-Valencia skulls resemble other Spanish cranial series in general terms. He insisted, nevertheless, on assigning individual skulls to the "types" of the French school of craniology, namely, "Upper Palaeolithic Cro-magnon", "Upper Palaeolithic Combe-Capelle", "Eurafrican", "Mediterranean Gracile", "Brachycephalic" and, a local invention this, "Western Pyrenaean." These designations were based on comparison with an arbitrary check-list of measurements and indices, the deviations of which, beyond one standard deviation from the mean, were regarded as of significance by Fusté, following the classical French approach. Since it has been argued above in this study that the "common yardstick" approach to craniology has little to commend it, his particular assignations may be disregarded.

Nevertheless, Fusté's general conclusion of the existence of a broad similarity among the skulls is borne out by the present enquiry. At first sight this seems contradicted by the heterogeneity of the two Alicante-Valencia cave burial groups to which repeated mention has been made in this study. While "indices" are not given in this study (because their value as criteria on which to base skull comparisons is put in doubt by the results of R-mode principal components analysis) they do not show marked patterns of differences between assemblages. While Table 12 indicates that some series differ markedly for particular measurements, it is important to remark that of the 81 site-wise comparisons only 8 show clear-cut heterogeneity ($P \geq \pm 2.5\%$) for ten or more cranial measurements.

It is no less important to point out that, even where such a dissimilarity occurs, the differences in mean values for a given measurement may be so slight as to have gone undetected by a classical approach (the significant difference between the nasal breadths of Cova de la Pastora and Cova de Beni Sid is of only 2.6 mm with respect to the respective mean values, while that between the maximal frontal breadths is only 4.6 mm). It is perhaps also worth remarking that not even such chronologically disparate specimens as those from the Barranco de las Ovejas or the Cova de El Parpalló stand out in cluster analyses from the southeastern skulls which particularly concern this enquiry. In brief, there is a high degree of overall homogeneity and only by resorting to powerful multidimensional analytical procedures can further discrimination be achieved within it.

Before leaving the matter of discrimination between individual skulls and sites in the context of archaeological theories, mention may be made of some possible clues offered by cluster analysis of non-metrical traits, notwithstanding the danger of perhaps overinterpreting a singularly weak aid to seeking order in the data. Of particular interest is the possible similarity between a skull from Isleta de Campello (Campello, Alicante) and two from Cova del Morro de la Barsella (Torremanzanas, Alicante).

This possible similarity may lend support to an archaeological theory about the "penetration" from the South of Argaric cultural traits. Isleta de Campello is a coastal settlement on a headland, cut off from the mainland at high tide, which was inhabited in the 2nd and 1st millennia B.C.. It is the object of extensive aarchaeological excavations under the direction of Dr. E. Llobregat. In its early phase there were simple grave burials not unlike those of the Argar Culture further South. Unfortunately it is not known whether the Cova del Morro de la Barsella skull came from the burial phase at the cave characterised by Argaric metal objects.

Attention has been drawn elsewhere (Walker, in press) to the extraordinary, and unique, resemblance of a dentate, tubular bone object from Isleta de Campello and the well-known "sceptre-mounts" of the English Wessex Culture Bush Barrow burial. There is also some similarity between miniature "weapons" in that culture and items from Cova del Morro de la Barsella (Walker, 1973). Some contemporaneity between the cave burial and the early phase of settlement at Isleta de Campello might not be cause for undue surprise therefore.

The two sites are but 20 kilometres apart and natural routes of communication between them present no special obstacles. If Isleta de Campello were to have represented a northern outpost of the Argaric cultural phenomenon, it is possible that it enjoyed relations with nearby communities practising multiple burial in cave vaults.

At the northern end of the axis, whose southern end is marked by Cova del Morro de la Barsella, and which passes through Cova de la Pastora, Cova de Les Llometes and Cova del Camí Real d' Alacant, lies the Cova (del) Frontó (Castellón de Rugat, Valencia). Some cluster analyses suggest that various skulls from this cave are similarity to some from Pastora as regards non-metrical traits. Such a resemblance comes as no surprise. It suggests a local population in a restricted geographical area, perhaps made up of close-knit communities.

If this area was approached in the South by members of quite different communities (e.g. at Cova del Morro de la Barsella) with Argaric cultural artefacts, it is also possible that the existence of such artefacts well away from the coast in the upper Vinalopó valley, at Cabezo Redondo near Villena, may have engendered contacts at more northerly points along the axis occupied by the cave burials just mentioned.

Clustering of non-metrical traits hints at some similarity between a skull from Cova del Morro de la Barsella, two from Cova de la Pastora and various skulls from Villena, namely three from Cueva de las Lechuzas, one from Covacha del Alto and one from the Argaric settlement at Cabezo Redondo, as well as with one from La Bastida (Totana, Murcia) which is another Argaric settlement. The settlement at Cabezo Redondo has given dates of around 3600 and 3300 b.p.. Moreover, Covacha del Alto contained an assemblage in which there were perforated bone buttons of a kind known from Bell Beaker and Argaric stations elsewhere in S.E. Spain.

The anthropological data, although tenuous, do not contradict archaeological interpretations about a 2nd millennium zone of contact, extending from the upper Vinalopó basin to the coast near Alicante, between the Argar Culture and the highlands of northern Alicante-southern Valencia in cultural transition from the Copper Age to the so-called Valencian Bronze Age*.

Nor does this conflict with the findings that, on the one hand, there are two groups in the northern Alicante area of different population structure, viewed from the standpoint of craniology, while on the other the major series each show rather restricted, as opposed to wide ranges of craniometrical measurements (which might have suggested heterogeneity). In any case the largest number of skulls in the cluster comes from the Villena neighbourhood, which perhaps suggests continuity between the population which effected the cave burial in Cueva de las Lechuzas and the 2nd millennium community (Cabezo Redondo; Covacha del Alto), rather than an influx of newcomers from further South.

* It is not necessarily the case that Copper Age elements vanished without trace outside the northern Alicante-Valencia area. Quite the contrary. Indeed, the argument which has raged over whether the appropriate classification of the Cabezo Redondo pottery should be "Argaric" or "Valencian Bronze Age" is precisely the basis for viewing it as a cultural admixture. In a different study (Walker, 1973) carried out with Dr. J.D. Wilcock, multidimensional scaling (using the Renfrew-Sterud MDSCAL program for ceramic profiles) was carried out on pottery from Argaric sites in the lower Segura valley near Orihuela and Callosa de Segura, in southern Alicante, thanks to the collaboration of the custodians of Fr. Furgús' excavation collections at the Orihuela Public Library, the Murcia Archaeological Museum and the Jesuit Colegio de la Imaculada Concepción at Alicante, who kindly allowed us to draw the materials in 1970. The MDSCAL study suggested that the pottery belongs to 5 distinct series. These, however, did not separate clearly into baggy Copper Age and carinated Argaric forms. Rather, representatives of both were grouped together in each of two series. Perhaps the Copper Age-Argaric transition was less abrupt and discontinuous than some prehistoric archaeologists have preferred in the past to believe. If the cultural traditions are less clear-cut than subjective classification would suggest, it is comes as no surprise to find that craniological boundaries are not hard and fast either.

It is perhaps noteworthy that it is precisely a geographically intermediate group (at Villena) which seems to relate on the one hand to the central group of the Alicante-Valencia highlands and on the other to Murcia.

Unfortunately it is not at present possible to undertake craniological comparisons of the Cueva del Barranco de la Higuera skulls from Fortuna (Murcia), not far distant from Villena*. It may be surmised that they also will occupy an intermediate place, perhaps between the Villena skulls and those of Murcia and El Argar.

The possible relations of the Villena-centred cluster, and the inclusion in it of both Copper Age and Argaric sites, lend force to those arguments drawn from material cultures which attribute the "Argaric 'phenomenon'" (Walker, 1973) or the "El Argar 'culture'" (Lull, 1983) more to internal change than to external implantation.

In discussing the possible significance of the results presented in this study for the prehistoric archaeology of southeastern Spain, caution has been repeatedly enjoined. The conclusions are tentative rather than definitive. Even so, it is possible the craniological findings have been overinterpreted.

Prudence must also be shown with regard to an undue desire to regard the craniological findings of this investigation as putting in jeopardy other palaeoanthropological enquiries into skulls and ancient communities in other parts of the world, which have used statistical approaches different from that regarded as the most appropriate for enquiring into the relationships between communities in prehistoric S.E. Spain. The relation between aims, methods and conclusions in those enquiries is not necessarily the same as that on which the present study was predicated.

This study is not so much a veiled criticism of them, as an indirect warning, drawn from the somewhat unexpected findings of a particular case-study, about the pitfalls which may lie in the path of the unwary craniologist.

* Only in January 1985 have we had the opportunity to carry out a detailed study of these skulls. The paucity of Wormian ossicles in these crania recalls those from the Cueva de las Lechuzas at Villena. A preliminary impression is that the cranial measurements resemble El Argar means, but the comparative statistical enquiries are yet to be undertaken. It must be emphasised that while bivariate analyses show no very great differences between El Argar, La Bastida and Lechuzas, R-mode principal components analysis suggests the Cueva de las Lechuzas belongs more with other cave burials than with the Argar or Bastida. Although the new site has only 5 skulls, they are remarkably complete and it would seem worthwhile attempting bivariate and multivariate comparisons in the near future with the major series of this study.

It is always unwise to argue general propositions from particular cases. This Discussion is not a general theoretical critique of analytical procedures and priorities in craniological statistics; the topic is so large that it would demand a separate monograph.

Under the influence of the Harvard school, there has been an increasing use of multivariate statistical procedures in craniology over the past forty years. It is less a cause for surprise that some of them have presented practical and theoretical difficulties, than that even now there are young craniologists who can still publish studies based on the antiquated, not to mention simple-minded, comparison of "indices" by visual reference to the standard deviation of some other cranial series, without even so much as bothering to test the validity of the comparisons by resort to elementary squared statistics (chi-square, Student's t, Behrens-Fischer statistic, etc.)!

Nevertheless, both the old-fashioned and the multivariate statistical approaches usually take as a common starting point the view that craniological analysis is above all one of form, that it can be reduced to morphometrical analysis.

Certainly there is small chance of comparing the variations in population structure of palaeontological remains, and, as has been mentioned earlier, multivariate comparison of these tends to be morphometrical, faute de mieux. However, when they are dispersed in time and space it is parsimonious to explain variety in terms of phylogenetical separation due to natural selection of species. An osteological "common yardstick" of measures is all that can be applied to palaeontological species, given inadequate samples in which to investigate the possibility that there might exist inequalities in the covariances and correlations of the chosen measurements.

Regrettably, the phyletic model of relative separation of morphometric types has tended to predominate even in comparative investigations of recent Homo sapiens. Perhaps when groups widely dispersed in time, and from different continents, are considered, the model still has utility (e.g. in interpreting later Upper Pleistocene human dispersal around the world). In comparing communities closer in time and space (e.g. in regions of Western Europe during the past few thousand years) its applicability seems less appropriate.

The reason is that morphological variation is no longer governed solely by a natural environment to which adaptation is a sine qua non for group survival. Disturbances other than natural selection now affect genetic equilibria. These will be mentioned presently. Suffice it to say that variation in population structure lies at the root of these disturbances.

This variation presupposes a more complex model of polymorphic diversity than one which assumes the equal interrelatedness of morphological responses in respect of different selection pressures (working in consort in direction or another achieve maximum fitness). The "common yardstick" approach to measures underlies Q-mode statistical comparisons. More complex models in which morphological adaptation does not override other causes of polymorphic diversity cannot take for granted harmonious morphometrical proportionality. If skull measurements from different assemblages show inequality of correlation and covariance, this is hardly a cause for astonishment. Rather, it should have been not unexpected. Where it were to have been anticipated, R-mode principal components analysis could easily have detected its presence. It is a reflection of the intellectual poverty of craniologists that such analysis has been conspicuous by its absence.

There is little point in comparing the present enquiries in a detailed manner with those other studies which have used quite different statistics (such as Mahalanobis' distance statistic, Penrose's coefficient and linear discriminant functions), or even those principal components and factor analyses which are published with the presumption of equality of covariances in Q-mode comparisons of series and/or individual cases, be they principal components studies or be they cluster analyses.

These studies are founded on a "common yardstick" approach to the cranial assemblages into which they enquire. Consequently there is a fundamental theoretical difference between them and the enquiry presented here. They are incompatible with it because have taken too much for granted and have set out from a starting point which carries the risk of predetermining the end result. It is not necessarily the case that the results are wrong, simply that there is no way of knowing, short of carrying out R-mode analysis of the original raw cranial data*.

None of the published studies commonly cited takes sufficient account of the possibility (dare one say probability?) that in geographical regions craniometrical covariances may be unequal when different assemblages of skulls are investigated. Statistical conclusions can never improve on the data and the premisses on which their computation rests. In the worst case, "nonsense in is nonsense out." Perhaps many enquiries have been saved from the worst consequences of cavalier disregard of those premisses by the robusticity of the craniological data themselves. Unfortunly this does little to advance making relative comparisons between different approaches to different data sets - particularly when the multivariate methods are ostensibly similar.

In the final analysis, however, the goals of craniology have less to do with prehistoric archaeology than with biological anthropology. Craniology is not a branch of archaeological taxon-

* Regrettably, some Q-mode studies, particularly those which use principal components, are not based on raw data from different assemblages, but rather on assemblage means for each measure. This usually renders it quite impossible to check the validity of the conclusions. The same problem can also arise, of course, with some other statistical approaches.

omy. Nor are there overwhelming reasons to think that cultural or linguistic boundaries correspond to any in human biology, except in such broad terms as to be of scant use to detailed inquiry into any of the three disciplines. It is simply superstitious to seek enlightenment by trying to attach to craniological assemblages labels in terms of archaeological cultures or linguistic families.

The other side of the coin of simple-mindedness is a touching faith in Darwinist rationalisations, post hoc propter hoc, of gross morphology as the outcome of selective adaptation to natural habitats. Since human groups are not dominated by natural habitats but, on the contrary, dominate a wide variety of them, as well as moving readily betwen some of them, this faith is no less superstitious.

It demonstrates a singular confusion of mind, which assumes that, because some human polymorphisms confer selective advantage on groups in a precise and demonstrable manner, the imprecise characteristics of gross anatomy must represent the transcendence of the whole over the sum of its parts, as a comparable outcome of natural selection. Unlike polymorphisms such as haemoglobinopathies (where selective fitness can be expressed in terms of precise gene frequencies), conclusions about the possible significance of gross morphology are mere assertions, which are irrefutable by further internal investigation because they are fundamentally incommensurable with the procedures of morphological research, being drawn, instead, from supposed analogies with particular, selected examples of anatomical adaptation taken from natural history.

These analogies are no closer to the genetic processes which underlie the biological structure of human communities than are analogies drawn from archaeological cultures or linguistic families for explaining craniological variation.

All of them rely on comparison of cranial forms defined on the supposition of a "common yardstick" of equally invariant metrical parameters between which comparisons and contrasts are licit. If the supposition is false, the results may at times be highly misleading.

In that case, it is necessary to go back to first principles and to ask whether, in fact, there might not exist more obvious and commensurable analogies, capable of explaining both the inequalities detected and the anatomical arrangement which nonetheless is also detected. It will be proposed that these alternative analogies not only do indeed exist, but also that they interpret our findings in a more parsimonious fashion than do the analogies just mentioned, and moreover that they do so in a fashion wholly commensurable with known biological mechanisms in human populations.

The Hardy-Weinberg equilibrium of gene frequencies can be disturbed by effects other than natural selection. Among them may be mentioned:

positive assortative mating (brought about by factors which may be geographical, social, professional, economic, cultural, religious, or kinship, in any combination or permutation - with endogamy and consanguinity as extreme outcomes)

variation in mutation rates between communities (possibly due local environmental causes)

genetic drift (unequal loss of individuals from small communities)

founder effect (establishment of communities by small, unrepresentative samples of other communities)

hybridisation of communities (e.g. increased contact between adjacent communities, by absorption of sporadic emigrants from other communities, or by massive immigration) with both short-term effects (heterosis) and long-term consequences of unequal genetic penetrance.

It is self-evident that most of these effects owe much more to cultural responses of human societies than to external circumstances to which the only responses could be morphological adaptation or extinction.

This is not to say that at times cultural responses may not foster conditions to which a morphological adaptation may take place. It has been proposed that plant cultivation may have brought in its train an increase in breeding grounds for the malarial mosquito, which, in turn, may have favoured a rise in recessive gene frequencies for polymorphisms inviable in the homozygote but offering a selective advantage to the heterozygote via-à-vis the homozygous dominant.

Angel (1966, 1971) has even gone so far as to suggest that generalised cranial porotic hyperostosis could be a consequence of abnormal haemopoiesis, were this to have been the consequence of an anaemia (such as thalassaemia) provoked in heterozygotes by an increase in recessive gene frequencies.

Mention has been made above of hyperostosis of crania from areas notorious for their swamps even in recent times (e.g. Villena and Navarrés). Whether these ought really to be attributed to the pathological process just referred to is a matter that only radiological and histological studies may one day resolve.

Processes such as this are possible outcomes of dominant-recessive, or "balanced", polymorphisms. By contrast, polymorphisms due to hemidominant (or codominant) genes, such as blood groups A, AB or B, tend to be relatively less influenced by direct environmental or ecological circumstances (although it is well known that such genes may be indirectly associated with particular pathological tendencies, in a complex manner).

There are many blood group systems and hemidominant alleles play a large part in determining the phenotypes. However, it is not necessary that all of the systems be present in a given individual for it to be capable of a viable existence. Very different would be the case of genetic systems working in harmony in order to produce some complex morphological structure out of many components whose respective morphologies were to be determined in part, at least, by genetic mechanisms - let us say, the skull and its constituent bones. Complete absence of one system responsible for the development of an constituent bone would be incompatible with a viable existence.

Such a complex structure, it would be anticipated, should be even more stable than are serological or biochemical polymorphic systems. All the same, some polymorphic variation ought to be detectable. As with the serological and biochemical polymorphisms, there might even be sporadic recessive genes with particular homozygotic phenotypes. Moreover, it could also be envisaged that the alleles might exert their effects, less in isolation, at the respective centres of ossification, than at a second, or even third order of morphological organisation and its control. Finally, it would be anticipated that phenomena, such as foramina, which are determined by polymorphisms of non-osteological tissues (nerves, blood vessels, connective tissue), should be represented by epigenetical characters quite uncorrelated with osteometrical patterns of correlation.

To come to the point, let us suppose that the R-mode principal components analyses presented above reflect variations in polymorphic hemidominant assortment in different communities with regard to organisation and control of development of the skull in terms of differently associated bony elements. The epigenetical traits may or may not demonstrate a consistent pattern of correlation with respect to those. It should not be expected that they would, nor is there overwhelming evidence from our results that they do.

Of particular interest is an aspect to which scant reference so far has been made. This concerns the sporadic occurrence of anomalous phenotypes in recessive homozygotes. Just as recessives coexist with a variety of hemidominants in some blood groups systems (e.g. Rhesus), so also might they occur in osteological systems. In the skull they may well be represented by abnormal synostoses.

In some 230 crania investigated from southeastern Spain, the examples were identified: platybasia (W-157), scaphocephaly with sagittal synostosis (W-153), left coronal synostosis and left lambdoid synostosis (W-61)*. The number of crania rises to almost 300 if Jacques' series from El Argar is added. He cited 3 cases of scaphocephaly (Jacques 1887:Table XXVI and 322-4) of which one showed platybasia and right coronal synostosis. The frequency of the anomalies is between 0.3% and 1%, which suggests gene frequencies between 0.55 and 0.1 on the assumption that recessive homozygotes are identified. This would be of an order of magnitude comparable with, for example, albinism or phenylketonuria**.

* The presentation of this skull strongly recalled that from the Menorca talayot pf Biniadris (Campillo 1977:85-92) which shows widespread craniosynostosis without platybasia.

Other congenital anomalies include a third occipital articular surface (at the anterior margin of the foramen magnum) observed in one skull from El Argar by Jacques and also present in one skull from the Cueva del Barranco de la Higuera. Jacques also observed an exostosis or spur at the basion of an El Argar skull, a feature we have also observed on another cranium. Mention may also be made of a skull (W-62) with an incomplete cleavage of the bony palate. W-153 showed an accessory tubercle between the digastric fossa and the occipital condyles (possibly a direct response associated perhaps with an enlarged sternomastoid muscle in this scaphocephalic cranium). W-137 had a congenitally absent left upper incisor. Jacques mentioned a skull with a supplementary right incisor. In short, the more noticeable anomalies have a similarly low frequency of occurrence to the different varieties of synostosis (0.3% to 1%).

Consequently it is less than wholly convincing to interpret the synostoses as due to pathological processes (e.g. osteomalacia). Given the variety of synostoses, the frequency of each kind is quite similar to that of other congenital traits. The view expressed by Comas (1965) that synostoses are in large part of congenital origin seems reasonable, notwithstanding opinions to the contrary.

The force of those opinions in part derives from the absence of a coherent genetic interpretation of patterns of cranial osteogenesis and development. Cranial morphology has been viewed too often in terms of an overall adaptive moulding to exigent circumstances. Malformations have consequently been seen in the same light. The model proposed here to explain parisimoniously the inequalities of correlations between craniological measurements, when different assemblages of skulls are considered, seems adequate not only to interpret the craniometrical statistical results of the present enquiry, but also to take account of synostotic malformations.

It is a model which focusses attention not so much on craniological form or shape, as on the possible expression, in the variance within the morphometrical data, of the assortment of anatomical elements in differing associations. These differences call to mind genetical differences in population structure. It is proposed that these are more useful for characterising archaeological communities than are direct morphometrical comparisons between assemblages.

It may be asked if the findings correspond to one or another deviation from hypothetical genetic equilibria. Perhaps the N.-S. group of cave burials (Cova Frontó, Cova del Camí Real d'Alacant, Cova de Les Llometes, Cova de la Pastora, Cova del Morro de la Barsella) represents a geographically restricted population within which positive assortative mating took place. This may have led to increasing differentiation with respect to surrounding populations (e.g. Cueva de las Lechuzas, Cova del Palanqués, Cova de Beni Sid), which may have taken place not in space, but also over time, for it will be recalled that there is greater reason to regard some, at least, of the former group of skulls as relatively late in the Copper Age than there is for the latter group.

Possibly there was a relatively greater loss of individuals from the former group to the latter, than the other way round. It is certainly the case that the latter is somewhat more diverse in its assortment of component elements. It also represents a much wider geographical area.

Even so, one assemblage, that from the Cova de Beni Sid, is from a location difficult of access. It has been remarked that in respect of metopism it shares a high incidence with Cova de la Pastora, vis-à-vis the other cave assemblages to which the two were respectively associated by metrical analysis. Sporadic anomalies in gene frquencies, such as these might imply, are attributable to genetic drift. They can leave a community standing out from those, with which it is otherwise associated biologically, by chance loss to them of individuals who bear a particular allele. It is a result of the unequal sampling (drawing off of individuals) of small communities.

Its effects are very limited with regard to the overall genetic composition of the populations to which the communities belong. This may be illustrated perhaps from our data by the contrast between the dearth of Wormian and Inca bones in the lambdoid suture at Cova de la Pastora and their noteworthy incidence at Cova de Beni Sid. These assemblages have quite different associations with regard to craniometrical composition, of course. Nevertheless, the ossicles seem to be relatively well-represented at other caves with which Pastora is in metrical association, as was stated earlier.

Of the assemblages in metrical association with Cova de Beni Sid, they were well represented at Cova del Palanqués but not at Cueva de las Lechuzas. In this case, however, it may be there is some relationship with the Cueva del Barranco de la Higuera (Fortuna, Murcia) where intrasutural ossicles are also uncommon. (It is also possible that the Lechuzas skulls are somewhat earlier in time.)

Mention has already been made of the valley of the River Vinalopó and the low-lying coastal zone of Alicante, from Campello in the North to the lower reaches of the River Segura at Orihuela in the South, as one of greater demographical mobility. Perhaps this was especially so during the 2nd millennium (see above). Yet from Villena sites in the upper Vinalopó valley, there are hints that there was some degree of biological continuity from earlier times.

The lower Segura, and its longest tributary, the River Guadalentín, offer the natural route South to northern Almería and consequently to El Argar. La Bastida is in the valley of the Guadalentín. Unfortunately it has not been possible to inspect El Argar skulls for epigenetical traits. They appear to have had high incidences of metopism and of intrasutural ossicles (at the pterion and in the lambdoid suture) and are therefore not altogether like those from La Bastida.

The principal components analyses of the two sites show some resemblance but it is not overwhelming. It is probable that there was contact between the sites but it is no less likely that indigenous genetic differentiation played a part in defining their biological composition. From the standpoint of bivariate metrical analysis, neither is so strikingly different from the other, or from most of the other assemblages considered, as to render obligatory the view that their communities were fundamentally incompatible with indigenous communities. They do not even show differences of an order comparable to that between Cova de la Pastora and Cova de Beni Sid, for instance. Nor do the univariate statistics lead us to believe that there may have been sub-groups at El Argar which could either have been foreigners or highly differentiated social groups.

The most parsimonious working hypothesis to explain the biological structure of the communities from the Vinalopó to El Argar, vis-à-vis those North of the Vinalopó in the highlands of northern Alicante and southern Valencia, is that which regards them as somewhat less constrained by positive assortative mating limited by geographical obstacles and as somewhat less subject to the vagaries of genetic drift and founder effect. There are no grounds for thinking that any particular community may have comprised sufficient numbers of disparate individuals as to render likely their attribution to hypothetical exotic populations or to render likely an interpretation of heterosis following on their arrival.

The emphasis throughout has been laid on the identification of biological structure of populations, as opposed to morphometrical classification which fails to take account of differences in internal structure. An attempt has also been made to escape from the confines of discourses, in which acceptable analogies are limited to those wherein considerations of overall cranial form override all others, e.g. quasi-archaeological or linguistic classification, or quasi-phyletic morphological adaptation. Such discourses tend to revolve in a circular fashion around propositions not open to refutability. Alternative interpretations of palaeoanthropological findings, in terms of the structures of biological communities, may not be any more capable of refutation by the findings presented. However, they try to take account of the diversity of association of the craniological measures and to refer it to alternative discourses about biological mechanisms, the existence of which is not mere inference, but rather is firmly grounded in the empirical findings of the genetical workings of living human populations. Consequently the working hypotheses put forward to explain the results are more parsimonious and therefore to be preferred.

5.

Conclusion

In this study of prehistoric crania from S.E. Spain, the principal finding is of their fundamental homogeneity, both overall and as regards individual assemblages. Some important differences between even geographically close assemblages (e.g. between those of Cova de la Pastora and Cova de Beni Sid) can be detected by careful bivariate statistical analysis. This may exceed differences with respect to more distant assemblages. It is to be remarked that important differences detected by t-tests can occur even between values which lie within particular categories of description of classical craniology in terms of numerical values of measurements and indices. Because of this, the underlying homogeneity of the cranial series must be stressed.

Carrying the analysis further, it is found that there may exist measurements which assort in different ways in R-mode principal components analyses of different assemblages. Sometimes a particular craniometrical measurement may vary in its orthogonal association even where t-tests cannot show its values to be heterogeneous for the assemblages concerned.

Even more important is the finding that the different ways in which skull measurements assort are not random or meaningless. Rather, in each major assemblage investigated, they clearly refer to discrete and recognisable anatomical aspects of the skull.

This extremely interesting and unexpected discovery of order in the inequality of correlations and covariances of craniological measurements suggests what may be a novel way to characterise cranial assemblages.

It offers an alternative to comparative morphometrical studies which take for granted the availability of a "common yardstick" of measures. If such a "common yardstick" does not always exist, then it is unwise to use it, unless prior correlation analysis of the raw values of the measurements of each assemblage has established its existence.

Where it does not exist, the alternative is to compare the patterns of independence and of association of the identifiable anatomical elements on the orthogonal principal components of the respective assemblages. These patterns offer a way of characterising assemblages in a fashion other than comparison of their cranial form. It is to compare the biological structure of the assemblages from the standpoint of the variances of morphological elements.

From this general conclusion, there may be drawn three sets of inferences concerning, respectively, interpretation of morphological skull elements as the outcome of genetic polymorphic variations, the dangers inherent in any statistical comparison of assemblages (whether of biological material, man-made artefacts, natural phenomena, or whatever) performed with the assumption of comparability of correlations and covariances of the observations chosen, and finally, concerning the light cast by the findings on prehistoric southeastern Spanish communities.

With regard to the first matter - the interpretation of the cranial morphological elements as the outcome of genetic polymorphic variations - it is appreciated that this is a novel and perhaps risky speculation. It is not suggested that such variations directly exert their effects at the primary and secondary centres of ossification of cranial bones. Rather, it is suggested that the effects may be exerted in the manner of control of osteogenesis during foetal and post-natal development.

The assortment of the elements on independent aspects of the variance of each assemblage, at times manifesting associations of elements and at other times independence, is consonant with what is known about some hemidominant polymorphic systems. The model provides, moreover, an intelligible interpretation of certain malformations of the skull, notably the craniosynostoses, as sporadic recessive polymoprhic manifestations. Furthermore, there are hints that the assortments may be independent of those of cranial features determined by soft-tissue histogenesis and its genetic control mechanisms.

In any event, the model appears to offer a more parsimonious explanation of many, diverse kinds of craniological data than do theories that purport to explain cranial morphometrical variation either by invoking gross morphological adaptation to external circumstances or else by assumimg that somehow it reflects ethnographical categories. These circumstances and categories are post hoc propter hoc rationalisations which rarely correspond to findings made in living human communities today. By contrast, the model proposed is not only more comprehensive, but conforms to the known aspects of present-day human biology.

With regard to the second matter - the perils of avoiding the investigation of correlations between observations within assemblages as a prerequisite to performing comparisons between assemblages - it is one which has very wide ramifications, that go far beyond osteology. Indeed it is possible to hazard a guess that several of the applications of advanced statistical comparison and taxonomy attempted in recent years in archaeology, linguistics, life sciences, and other disciplines, may be less robust than they are claimed to be.

The point at issue concerns morphometrical comparisons based on a "common yardstick", be they performed in terms of distance measures, shape coefficients, discriminant functions, some clustering algorithms, or Q-mode principal components and factor analyses. The results can be no better than the data submitted. They assume those data to be equally comparable. If they are not, then the results may distort the relationships between the data.

Particularly disquieting is the widespread use of Q-mode principal components comparisons between assemblages. It purports to offer the threefold advantage of ease of use, particularly as regards smaller computers (because it does not require all of the original measurements, only means and univariate statistics), ease of discrimination (in terms of graphical displays), and the prospect of explanatory power (because the components are orthogonal).

Yet to by-pass R-mode principal components analyses demonstrates a failure to understand where the real power of the technique lies. Among multidimensional procedures it is pre-eminently suited to investigate whether inequalities of correlations or of covariances might occur in the observations. When they do, further attempts at multivariate statistical comparisons should take cognisance of them. Nowhere is this more necessary than in Q-mode principal components and factor analyses, because of the temptation to refer orthogonal aspects of the results to separate explanatory frames of reference. These are a flimsy house of cards if they are erected on the basis of comparing essentially non-comparable assemblages. Certainly, when such is the case, there are practical and theoretical difficulties to be surmounted, to in the present study. The point to be stressed is that they cannot blithely be ignored by craniologists (and others) keen to make a gesture towards twentieth-century science.

The third and final matter concerns the inferences which may be drawn for southeastern Spanish prehistoric communities from the enquiry into the prehistoric skulls of the region. It may be concluded that there is no pressing reason to perceive intruders from afar as having exerted any particular influence over the biological structure of the prehistoric communities of S.E. Spain in the Copper and Bronze Ages. However, there is some evidence that geographical factors influenced the biological structure of human communities in the region, within the broad framework of biological homogeneity. The variations which may be observed permit the characterisation of some communities and offer hints with regard to likely palaeodemographical relationships. The discrimination perceived is compatible with known genetic mechanisms at work in small communities and does not demand recourse to special theories for its explanation.

M.J. Walker
Dept. of Anthropology
University of Sydney

Acknowledgements

I wish to thank the following for kindly allowing me to investigate skull collections: Dr. Domingo Fletcher Valls at the Museo de Prehistoria de Valencia, Dr. Enrique Llobregat Conesa at the Museo Arqueológico de la Diputación Provincial de Alicante, Sr. Manuel Jorge Aragoneses at the Museo Arqueológico Provincial de Murcia, Sr. Francisco García Jiménez at the Museo Arqueológico Provincial "Luis Siret" de Almería, Sr. Vicente Pascual Pérez and Dr.Federico Rubio Gomis at the Museo Arqueológico Municipal "Camilo Visedo Moltó" de Alcoy, Sr. José María Soler García at the Museo Arqueológico Municipal de Villena, Sr. Jerónimo Molina García at the Museo Arqueológico Municipal de Jumilla, Sr. Antonio Sancho Santamaría at the Museo Arqueológico de Gandía, Dr. Amparo Font of the Depto. de Antropología of the Facultad de Ciencias de la Universidad Autónoma de Barcelona.

I also wish to thank Mr. David Muxworthy of the Edinburgh Regional Computing Centre at the University of Edinburgh and Mr. Gary Newell of the University Computing Centre at the University of Sydney, for their assistance to me, and to Dr. John D. Wilcock of the Dept. of Computing at the North Staffordshire Polytechnic for his collaboration in studying prehistoric ceramic profiles.

Appreciation must also be mentioned of the assistance with radiocarbon dating provided by Dr.M. Barbetti of the N.W.G. Macintosh Centre for Quaternary Research at the University of Sydney and in particular for facilitating the hitherto unpublished date from the Cova del Moro at Agres (Alicante). I am also obliged to Dr. R.L. Otlet of the Atomic Energy Research Centre at Harwell in England for dating remains for me from the Cueva de los Tiestos at Jumilla (Murcia).

It is appropriate to offer my thanks to the Provost and Fellows of The Queen's College of the University of Oxford, and in particular to the late Lord Howard Florey, F.R.S., for enabling me to commence this work under the terms of the Randall MacIver Studentship in Archaeology. My thanks must also go to Professor George Romanes of the Dept. of Anatomy at the Edinburgh University Medical School for enabling me to continue the research in his Department, and to the Senate of the University of Edinburgh for apportioning funds for computing and a Gilchrist Travelling Fellowship. I am also grateful to the support given by Professor Richard V.S. Wright of the Dept. of Anthropology at the University of Sydney and for financial support given by the University with regard to computing and field research.

My gratitude goes also to the following bodies for their interest and financial support with respect to my prehistoric researches in S.E. Spain: the Australian Research Grants Scheme and Committee, the Committe for Research and Exploration of the National Geographic Society, the Carnegie Fund for the Universities of Scotland, and the Emslie Horniman Trust Committee of the Royal

Anthropological Institute.

Mention must without doubt be made of the encouragement I have continually received from Professor John D. Evans, F.B.A., F.S.A., the Director of the London University Institute of Archaeology. I also wish to thank Professor G. Ainsworth Harrison of the Dept. of Biological Anthropology at the University of Oxford for his encouragement and for his helpful comments about the manuscript. It is also fitting to thank Professor Ana María Muñoz Amilibia of the Depto. de Arqueología y Prehistoria at the Universidad de Murcia for encouraging my research in southeastern Spain.

I am appreciative of the advice and help offered to me by my many friends over the years, among whom may be mentioned: Sr. Artemio Cuenca at the Instituto de Geografía de la Universidad de Alicante and Dr. Pedro Lillo at the Depto. de Arqueología y Prehistoria de la Universidad de Mucia. I am please to have had many fruitful conversations with Dr. Manuel García Sánchez at the Laboratorio de Antropología de la Facultad de Medicina de la Universidad de Granada, Dr. Miguel Botella of the Delegación de Estudios Arqueológicos de la Cueva del Agua de la Diputación Provincial de Granada, Dra. María Eugenia Aubet, Dr. Vicente Lull and Dr. Jordi Esteve at the Depto. de Arqueología y Prehistoria de la Universidad Autónoma de Barcelona, Dra. Amparo Font at the Depto. de Antrpología of the same university, Dr. Jaume Bernarpetit at that of the Universidad de Barcelona, Dres. Mauro Hernández Pérez and Dr. Alfredo González Prats at the Depto. de Arqueología y Prehistoria de la Universidad de Alicante, Dr. Martín Lillo of the Depto. de Geografía de la Universidad de Murcia, Dr. Gratiniano Nieto Gallo and Dr. José Sánchez Meseguer at the Depto. de Arqueología y Prehistoria de la Universidad Autónoma de Madrid.

I must also thank my students, particularly Dr.Cheryl Swanson and Mr. Phillip Habgood, whose interests in craniological research has allowed a fruitful cross-fertilisation of ideas to take place.

It is also appropriate to recognise the forebearance of my wife, María Teresa Pina Velasco, over the many inconveniences provoked by the exigencies of my research, in particular as regards frequent changes of residence and absences in addition to the usual exigencies of research.

My thanks go to Mr.E. Roper of the Department of Archaeology at the University of Sydney, for technical assistance in photographic reduction of the principal component matrices and dendrograms.

I am grateful to the following for having read the manuscript and for their comments: Dr.A.E. Mourant, F.R.S., Professor G.A. Harrison (University of Oxford) and Professor W.W. Howells (Harvard University).

References

Almagro Gorbea, M. 1976 "La espada de Entrambasaguas. Aportación a la secuencia de las espadas del Bronce en el Norte de la Península Ibérica" XL Aniversario del Centro de Estudios Montañeses pp. 455-77 (Santander)

Angel, J.L. 1966 "Porotic hyperostosis, anaemias, malarias, and marshes in the prehistoric Eastern Mediterranean" Science 153 (3737):760-3.

Angel, J.L. 1971 Lerna II. The People. (Princeton: Princeton University Press).

Arribas, A. 1976 "Las bases actuales para el estudio del eneolítico y de la edad del bronce en el sudeste de la Península Ibérica" Cuadernos de Prehistoria de la Universidad de Granada 1:139-55.

Berry, R.J. 1968 "The biology of non-metrical variation in mice and men" in D.R. Brothwell (ed.) The Skeletal Biology of Earlier Human Populations, pp. 103-33 (Oxford: Pergamon, Symposiia for the Study of Human Biology VIII).

Campillo, D. 1976 Lesiones Patológicas en Cráneos Prehistóricos de la Región Valenciana (Valencia: Servicio de Investigación Prehistórica, Trabajos Varios No. 50, 96 pp.).

Campillo, D. 1977 Paleopatología del Cráneo en Cataluña, Valencia y Baleares (Barcelona: Montblanc-Martin, Colección de Monografías Locales, Serie B, No. 17, 630 pp.).

Campillo, D. 1980 "Lesiones paleopatológicas en los individuos de la Cueva del Barranco de la Higuera (Baños de Fortuna, Murcia)" Anales de la Universidad de Murcia, Filosofía y Letras 37 (3):201-9.

Comas, J. 1965 "Crânes méxicains scaphocéphales" L'Anthropologie 69:273-302.

Comas, J. 1966 Manual de Antropología Física (México, D.F.: Universidad Nacional Autónoma de México, 710 pp.).

Corruccini, R.S. 1975 "Biological anthropology, some considerations" Journal of Human Evolution 4:1-19.

Doran, J.E. and Hodson, F.R. 1975 Mathematics and Computers in Archaeology (Edinburgh: Edinburgh University Press,381 pp.).

Font, A. 1980 "Estudio antropológico de los esqueletos de la Cueva del Barranco de la Higuera (Baños de Fortuna, Murcia)" Anales de la Universidad de Murcia, Filosifía y Letras 37 (3):267-90

Fusté, M. 1957 Estudio Antropológico de los Pobladores Neo-Eneolíticos de la Región Valenciana (Valencia: Servicio de Investigación Prehistórica, Trabajos Varios No. 20, 128 pp.).

García del Toro, J.R. and Lillo, P.A. 1980 "Un nuevo enterramiento colectivo eneolítico en la Cueva del Barranco de la Higuera (Baños de Fortuna, Murcia)" Anales de la Universidad de Murcia, Filosofía y Letras 37 (3):191-9.

Giles, E. and Elliott, O.1963 "Sex discrimination by discriminant function analysis of crania" American Journal of Physical Anthropology 21:53-68.

Habgood, P. and Walker, M.J. (in press) "Principal components and cluster analyses on Upper Pleistocene crania" in H. and M-A. de Lumley (eds.) Actes du Premier Congrès de Paléontologie Humaine,Nice Septembre 1981.

Howells, W.W. 1972 "Analysis of the patterns of variation in crania of recent Man" in R. Tuttle (ed.) The Functional and Evolutionary Biology of Primates pp.23-151 (Chicago: Aldine)

Howells, W.W. 1973 Cranial Variation in Man. A Study by Multivariate Analyis of Patterns of Difference among Recent Populations. (Cambridge, Mass.: Harvard University, Papers of the Peabody Museum 67, 259 pp.).

Jacques, V. 1887 "Ethnologie, Le Peuple de L'Argar" in H. and L. Siret (eds.) Les Pemiers Ages du Métal dans le Sud-Est de l' Espagne pp.239-404 (Antwerp).

Lebzelter, V. 1946 "Sobre algunos cráneos eneolíticos del este de España" Archivo de Prehistoria Levantina (1945) 2:143-9.

Lull, V. 1983 La "Cultura" de El Argar (Madrid: Akal, 487 pp.).

Martin, R. 1906 Lehrbuch der Anthropologie in systematischer Darstellung mit besonderer Berücksichtigung der anthropologischen Methoden (Jena: Fischer).

Miles, A.E.W. 1969 "The dentition of the Anglo-Saxons" Proceedings of the Royal Society of Medicine 62:1311-5.

Nie, N.H., Bent, D.H. and Hunt, C.H. 1970 SPSS Statistical Package for the Social Sciences (New York: McGraw-Hill, 343pp.).

Rincón de Arellano, A. and Fenollosa, J. 1950 Algunos consideraciones acerca de los cráneos trepanados hallados en la Cueva "La Pastora" (Alcoy) (Valencia: Diputación Provincial de Valencia and Consejo Superior de Investigaciones Científicas "Instituto Diego Velázquez", 11 pp.).

Riquet, R. 1953 "Analyse anthropologique des crânes énéeolithiques de la grotte sepulcrale de 'La Pastora' (Alcoy)" Archivo de Prehistoria Levantina 4:105-22.

Utterschaut, H.T. and Wilmink, F.W. 1983 "The assumption of equality of variance - covariance metrics in the sex and racial diagnosis of human skulls" American Journal of Physical Anthropology 60:347-59.

Vogel, J.C. and Waterbolk, H.T. 1972 "Groningen radiocarbon dates" Radiocarbon 14(1):6-110.

Walker, M.J. 1973 Aspects of the Neolithic and Copper Ages in the Basins of the Rivers Segura and Vinalopó, South-East Spain (MS, D.Phil. thesis, University of Oxford).

Walker, M.J. 1975 Man (n.s.) 10:627-8 Review of Cranial Variation in Man by W.W. Howells.

Walker, M.J. 1984 "3. The Site of ElPrado (Murcia) and the Copper Age of South-East Spain" in T.F.C. Blagg, R.F.J. Jones Jones and S.J. Keay (eds.) Papers in Iberian Archaeology pp. 47-78 (Oxford: BAR International Series 193, 740 pp.).

Walker, M.J. (in press) "Un interesante paralelo con el Bush Barrow (Inglaterra) procedente de la Isleta de Campello (Alicante)" Helike 2.

Table 2

Craniometrical measurements and landmarks as defined in R. Martin *Lehrbuch der Anthropologie* vol. 3, 3rd. edition revised by K. Saller (Stuttgart: Fischer, 1957) pp. 453-87. Values are given for 9 sites (Argar data taken from Jacques 1887). n = number of cases. m = number of missing instances at the site. $\bar{x}$ = mean value. s = standard error. σ = standard deviation. V = variance. k = kurtosis. sk = skewness. Maximum and minimum values are also shown.

g-op (chord) Glabella-Opisthokranion (Martin: 1)
eu-eu (chord) Euryon-Euryon (Martin: 8)
ft-ft (chord) Frontotemporale-Frontotemporale (Martin: 9)
co-co (chord) Coronale-Coronale (Martin: 10)
zy-zy (chord) Zygion-Zygion (Martin: 45)
ast-ast (chord) Asterion-Asterion (Martin: 12)
au-au (chord) Auriculare-Auriculare (Martin: 11)
ms-ms (chord) Mastoideale-Mastoideale (Martin: 13)
ba-b (height) Basion-Bregma (Martin: 17)
po-b H (height) Porion-Bregma (calculated by Pythagoras' theorem; Martin: 20)
n-pr (height) Nasion-Prosthion (Martin: 48)
ba-pr (chord) Basion-Prosthion (Martin: 40)
n-ns (height) Nasion-Nasospinale (Martin: 55)
NB breadth of nasal aperture (Martin: 54)
mf-ek orbital breadth from Maxillofrontale to Ektokonchion (Martin: 51)
OH height of orbital cavity (Martin: 52)
mf-mf breadth from Maxillofrontale to Maxillofrontale (Martin: 50)
n-ba (chord) Nasion-Basion (Martin: 5)
pr-alv length Prosthion-Alveolon (Martin: 60)
ekm-ekm breadth from Ektomolare to Ektomolare (Martin: 61)
ol-sta length from Orale-Staphylion (Martin: 62)
enm-enm breadth from Endomolare to Endomolare (Martin: 63)
FMB breadth of Foramen Magnum (Martin: 16)
ba-o length from Basion to Opisthion (Martin: 7)
g-op-g* (arc) Glabella-Opisthokranion-Glabella (Martin: 23)
po-b-po* (arc) Porion-Bregma-Porion (Martin: 24)
n-gn (height) Nasion-Gnathion (Martin: 47)
pr-M3 distance from Prosthion to posterior margin of the tuberosity of the dental arcade behind the third molar (not in Martin)
MM minimum vertical height of zygomatic process of maxilla (not in Martin)
ba-sphba (length) Basion-Sphenobasion (Martin: 6)
OPBB breadth of Pars Basilaris Occipitalis (Martin: 15)
n-o (chord) Nasion-Opisthion (Martin: 1d)
n-b (chord) Nasion-Bregma (Martin: 29)
b-l (chord) Bregma-Lambda (Martin: 30)
l-i (chord) Lambda-Inion (Martin: 31(1))
i-o (chord) Inion-Opisthion (Martin: 31(2))
g-n (chord) Glabella-Nasion (not in Martin)
g-b (chord) Glabella-Bregma (not in Martin)
g-l (chord) Glabella-Lambda (Martin: 3)
g-i (chord) Glanella-Inion (Martin: 2)
g-o (chord) Glabella-Opisthion (not in Martin)
n-o (chord) Nasion-Opisthion (not in Martin)
n-b* (arc) Nasion-Bregma (Martin: 26)
b-l* (arc) Bregma-Lambda (Martin: 27)
l-o* (arc) Lambda-Opisthion (not in Martin)
g-b* (arc) Glabella-Bregma (not in Martin)
g-l* (arc) Glabella-Lambda (not in Martin)
g-i* (arc) Glabella-Inion ((g-i) - (g-n) = Martin 25a)
g-o* (arc) Glabella-Opisthion ((g-o) - (gn) = Martin 25)
kdl-kdl external breadth Kondylion-Kondylion (Martin: 65)
go-go breadth Gonion-Gonion (Martin: 66)
ML mandibular length (Martin: 68)
gn-id (height) Gnation-Infradentale (Martin: 69)
MRH height of mandibular ramus (Martin: 70)
MRB minimum breadth of mandibular ramus (Martin: 71)
MA mandibular angle (Martin: 79)

There may be some discrepancy between some of the measurements in Jacques (1887) and those defined in the above list because Jacques was working before the Monaco Convention had been established. Also it should be noted that in order to maximise use of fragmentary skulls we have departed from the conventional usage in averaging orbital heights and breadths from both sides of the skull where both were available for measurement and by using whichever side was available when averaging was not possible because of skull damage.

TABLE 3: UNIVARIATE STATISTICS: EL ARGAR

	n	m	$\bar{x}$	s	σ	V	k	sk	max	min
g-op	63	20	179.873	0.761	6.044	36.532	12.945	-0.170	193	165
eu-eu	61	22	138.098	0.641	5.007	25.067	2.191	0.270	150	129
ft-ft	65	18	94.862	0.511	4.123	16.998	3.074	0.054	105	85
co-co	65	18	114.862	0.639	5.154	26.561	2.897	-0.243	126	99
zy-zy	38	45	125.316	0.924	5.696	32.443	1.969	0.204	139	115
ast-ast	58	25	108.000	0.753	5.734	32.877	4.576	1.256	131	97
ms-ms	53	30	99.736	0.801	5.835	34.047	0.601	-0.042	111	87
au-au	62	21	118.839	0.659	5.186	26.892	0.680	0.358	133	109
ba-b	61	22	129.885	0.721	5.628	31.673	1.220	-0.021	142	115
n-ns	52	31	48.269	0.427	3.081	9.495	1.598	0.976	59	42
NB	48	35	23.313	0.334	2.317	5.368	0.659	0.611	30	19
mf-ek	58	25	39.603	0.296	2.255	5.087	-0.141	0.585	46	36
OH	60	23	31.467	0.299	2.318	5.372	1.731	-0.232	38	24
mf-mf	51	32	20.039	0.250	1.788	3.198	-0.721	0.192	24	17
n-ba	62	21	96.468	0.579	4.559	20.781	2.689	0.262	106	87
pr-alv	39	44	50.103	0.505	3.152	9.938	-0.077	-0.304	57	43
enm-enm	35	48	37.829	0.519	3.073	9.440	-1.103	0.014	43	32
ba-o	55	28	34.418	0.335	2.485	6.174	-0.253	0.523	40	30
FMB	50	33	28.760	0.318	2.246	5.043	1.388	0.957	36	25
g-op-g*	62	21	510.742	1.775	18.979	195.410	41.382	-0.496	546	482
po-b-po*	62	21	297.839	1.195	9.410	88.541	12.879	0.142	322	276
g-i	63	20	168.651	0.933	7.402	54.790	3.172	-0.287	187	151
n-o	58	25	368.879	1.363	10.379	107.719	11.116	-0.555	386	344
n-b*	65	18	125.862	0.707	5.701	32.499	0.569	0.038	140	114
b-1*	63	20	123.571	0.956	7.588	57.573	-0.205	-0.064	142	105
1-o*	56	27	118.946	0.949	7.103	50.455	0.664	-0.353	133	101
kdl-kdl	25	58	118.560	1.250	6.252	39.091	0.374	-0.097	130	105
go-go	31	52	97.839	1.590	8.855	78.408	-1.242	-0.163	112	82
gn-id	34	49	30.971	0.500	2.918	8.514	0.135	0.097	38	24
MRH	35	48	59.571	0.747	4.421	19.548	-0.890	-0.213	68	51
MRB	40	43	31.075	0.391	2.474	6.122	-0.362	-0.273	36	25
MA	31	52	55.742	0.869	4.837	23.398	-0.809	0.134	65	46

TABLE 4: UNIVARIATE STATISTICS: LA BASTIDA

	n	m	$\bar{x}$	s	σ	V	k	sk	max	min
g-op	9	19	177.778	2.543	7.629	58.195	-0.789	0.201	190	169
eu-eu	8	20	130.875	2.255	6.379	40.696	-0.375	-0.546	138	120
ft-ft	13	15	93.615	1.439	5.189	26.927	0.099	0.525	105	85
co-co	7	21	112.100	1.609	5.087	25.882	0.491	-0.523	120	102
zy-zy	4	24	122.750	1.436	2.872	8.250	-16.373	-0.374	126	119
ast-ast	7	21	106.429	1.999	5.288	27.958	-2.236	0.234	115	99
ms-ms	5	23	95.600	1.631	3.647	13.301	-2.096	-0.686	99	90
au-au	5	23	100.400	2.135	4.775	22.801	-1.307	0.277	107	95
ba-b	7	21	131.286	0.680	1.800	3.240	-50.430	-0.278	133	128
po-b H	10	18	120.900	1.130	3.574	12.771	-0.675	0.411	126	115
n-pr	11	17	67.909	1.282	4.253	18.091	2.281	1.777	79	64
ba-pr	9	19	89.222	0.795	2.386	5.695	2.549	0.351	93	86
n-ns	11	17	48.727	0.574	1.902	3.618	-1.790	0.747	53	46
NB	12	16	22.500	0.557	1.931	3.727	-0.823	0.515	26	20
mf-ek	12	16	37.833	0.474	1.642	2.697	-2.346	0.117	40	36
OH	11	17	32.182	0.658	2.183	4.764	-0.620	0.125	36	29
mf-mf	11	17	20.091	0.368	1.221	1.491	-0.427	-0.522	22	18
n-ba	9	19	97.000	1.683	5.050	25.500	-0.841	0.857	107	90
pr-alv	12	16	47.500	0.909	3.148	9.909	0.781	-0.868	52	40
ekm-ekm	12	16	58.000	1.624	5.625	31.636	0.901	-0.099	67	49
ol-sta	12	16	43.250	1.553	5.379	28.932	0.606	-0.056	54	32
enm-enm	12	16	33.667	0.865	2.995	8.970	-0.781	-0.385	38	28
ba-o	7	21	35.714	0.644	1.704	2.905	0.042	0.909	39	34
FMB	6	22	30.500	0.342	0.837	0.700	4.347	1.122	32	30
g-op-g*	8	20	477.875	17.159	48.534	2355.571	2.139	-1.808	520	364
po-b-po*	5	23	295.200	3.569	7.981	63.703	5.832	-0.158	304	285
n-gn	3	25	113.667	1.856	3.215	10.334	-3.000	-0.516	116	110
pr-M^3	11	17	53.091	1.385	4.592	21.091	0.371	-0.602	60	43
MM	12	16	21.167	0.672	2.329	5.424	-0.769	0.287	25	18
ba-sphba	9	19	25.778	1.011	3.032	9.195	0.179	0.652	32	22
OPBB	9	19	20.778	0.547	1.641	2.694	-0.734	-0.167	23	18
n-b	11	17	109.727	0.992	3.289	10.819	-1.316	0.273	115	105
b-l	10	18	112.400	1.869	5.911	34.938	-0.825	0.343	123	104
l-i	6	22	83.333	4.402	10.783	116.267	-0.809	-0.113	98	67
i-o	6	22	27.500	5.602	13.722	188.300	-1.826	0.125	43	14
g-n	12	16	13.083	0.723	2.503	6.265	0.987	-0.171	17	9
g-b	11	17	101.636	1.302	4.319	18.656	0.398	0.662	110	95
g-l	9	19	172.11	2.424	7.271	52.867	2.358	0.596	187	161
g-i	6	22	155.000	4.297	10.526	110.800	-0.728	-0.003	170	140
g-o	7	21	137.571	1.888	4.996	24.958	-3.000	-0.485	144	129
n-o*	6	22	368.333	7.486	18.338	336.275	-0.496	0.191	393	345
n-b*	11	17	126.455	1.436	4.762	22.675	5.215	-1.181	133	115
b-l*	9	19	128.222	3.045	9.135	83.445	0.118	0.941	147	118
l-o*	5	23	115.600	3.710	8.295	68.813	-1.074	0.655	128	108
g-b*	12	16	112.917	1.485	5.143	26.449	-0.169	-0.637	120	105
g-l*	9	19	242.667	4.233	12.698	161.250	0.478	0.494	267	223
g-i*	6	22	327.833	8.064	19.753	390.175	-0.314	-0.428	355	295
g-o*	6	22	357.500	7.261	17.785	316.300	-1.113	-0.030	380	335
kdl-kdl	6	22	114.167	2.213	5.420	29.375	-1.861	0.138	120	109
go-go	5	23	94.600	3.586	8.019	64.301	-1.220	0.352	106	87
ML	0	28								
gn-id	12	16	29.083	1.282	4.441	19.720	-1.328	0.046	36	23
MRH	12	16	59.917	1.515	5.248	27.538	0.434	-0.164	70	49
MRB	13	15	30.231	0.709	2.555	6.526	-1.247	0.109	34	27
MA	13	15	56.692°	1.759	6.343	40.231	-0.249	-0.672	66°	43°

TABLE 5: UNIVARIATE STATISTICS: COVA DEL PALANQUES

	n	m	$\bar{x}$	s	σ	V	k	sk	max	min
g-op	4	31	178.250	5.186	10.372	107.583	-0.405	-0.243	190	165
eu-eu	7	28	131.429	3.545	9.379	87.958	-1.385	0.611	141	118
ft-ft	6	29	98.167	1.851	4.535	20.567	-1.112	-0.491	103	91
co-co	7	28	120.143	3.693	9.771	95.479	-1.575	-0.290	130	107
zy-zy	1	34	112.000	0	0	0	0	0	112	112
ast-ast	4	31	106.250	1.493	2.986	8.917	4.155	-0.752	109	102
ms-ms	3	32	96.333	0.667	1.155	1.334	84.664	1.590	97	95
au-au	5	30	100.000	1.761	3.937	15.500	-1.335	0.742	106	97
ba-b	3	32	124.333	10.713	18.556	344.334	-1.500	-0.164	142	105
po-b H	6	29	123.500	2.907	7.120	50.700	0.059	-0.782	132	111
n-pr	3	32	66.000	3.512	6.083	37.000	-1.510	-0.686	70	59
ba-pr	1	34	89.000	0	0	0	0	0	89	89
n-ns	3	32	47.333	1.764	3.055	9.334	-1.407	-0.391	50	44
NB	3	32	22.333	0.333	0.577	0.333	1.218	0.584	23	22
mf-ek	3	32	38.333	1.202	2.082	4.334	-0.964	0.556	40	36
OH	3	32	31.333	1.202	2.082	4.333	-1.962	-0.526	33	29
mf-mf	3	32	22.667	2.404	4.163	17.333	-1.498	-0.528	26	18
n-ba	1	34	91.000	0	0	0	0	0	91	91
pr-alv	3	32	47.000	0	0	0	0	0	47	47
ekm-ekm	3	32	55.000	2.646	4.583	21.000	-1.503	-0.382	59	50
ol-sta	3	32	42.667	1.202	2.082	4.334	-0.285	0.518	45	41
enm-enm	3	32	32.000	1.528	2.646	7.000	-1.500	0.595	35	30
ba-o	3	32	32.667	2.603	4.509	20.333	-1.511	-0.135	37	28
FMB	3	32	29.333	0.667	1.155	1.333	-2.156	-0.721	30	28
g-op-g*	6	29	528.500	8.978	21.991	483.600	0.363	0.432	565	499
po-b-po*	6	29	310.667	5.536	13.560	183.875	0.954	-1.487	322	284
n-gn	0	35								
pr-M^3	3	32	54.333	0.334	0.578	0.334	-3.000	0.595	55	54
MM	3	32	21.667	1.202	2.082	4.333	-1.535	0.525	24	20
n-o	1	34	122.00	0	0	0	0	0	122	122
n-b	4	31	106.500	3.862	7.724	59.667	-1.050	0.580	117	99
b-l	7	28	111.143	4.616	12.213	149.146	-0.856	-0.351	127	91
l-i	6	29	74.000	2.556	6.261	39.200	-0.346	-0.225	83	64
i-o	3	32	29.667	4.372	7.572	57.333	-0.501	-1.652	35	21
g-n	4	31	9.000	0.913	1.826	3.333	-1.640	0	11	7
g-b	5	30	103.000	3.899	8.718	76.000	-1.587	0.251	114	94
g-l	4	31	172.750	5.542	10.905	118.917	-1.037	0.442	187	162
g-i	4	31	165.250	8.440	16.879	284.917	-0.886	-0.351	184	143
g-o	1	34	128.000	0	0	0	0	0	128	128
n-o*	1	34	350.000	0	0	0	0	0	350	350
n-b*	4	31	123.750	4.973	9.946	98.917	-1.465	-0.065	135	112
b-l*	7	28	123.857	5.483	14.508	210.479	-0.892	-0.316	142	100
l-o*	2	33	120.000	2.000	2.828	8.000	-3.000	0	122	118
g-b*	5	30	117.400	4.611	10.311	106.313	-1.627	0.033	130	105
g-l*	3	32	244.000	12.490	21.633	468.000	-1.457	-0.471	262	220
g-i*	4	31	339.250	11.940	23.880	570.250	-1.074	0.682	372	321
g-o*	1	34	342.00	0	0	0	0	0	342	342
kdl-kdl	0	35								
go-go	0	35								
ML	0	35								
gn-id	3	32	28.333	0.667	1.155	1.333	-0.047	-0.696	29	27
MRH	1	34	61.000	0	0	0	0	0	61	61
MRB	0	35								
MA	3	32	58.333°	1.667	2.887	8.334	-1.791	-0.711	60°	55°

TABLE 6: UNIVARIATE STATISTICS: CAMI REAL D'ALACANT

	n	m	$\bar{x}$	s	σ	V	k	sk	max	min
g-op	10	30	184.600	1.462	4.624	21.382	-0.7888	0	191	178
eu-eu	10	30	137.100	1.980	6.262	39.215	0.494	-0.114	147	128
ft-ft	10	30	94.500	0.619	1.958	3.833	-33.111	-0.218	97	91
co-co	10	30	116.600	1.301	4.116	16.938	0.966	0.709	125	111
zy-zy	1	39	127.000	0	0	0	0	0	127	127
ast-ast	11	29	107.455	1.885	6.251	39.075	-0.621	-0.479	116	95
ms-ms	8	32	99.375	3.168	8.959	80.268	-1.404	0.584	113	90
au-au	9	31	102.444	2.364	7.091	50.281	0.190	0.808	117	93
ba-b	2	38	138.000	2.000	2.828	8.000	-59.000	0	140	136
po-b H	13	27	124.231	1.277	4.604	21.193	3.432	-0.142	131	116
n-pr	2	38	67.500	1.500	2.121	4.500	4.901	0.037	69	66
ba-pr	1	39	97.000	0	0	0	0	0	97	97
n-ns	2	38	47.500	5.500	7.778	60.500	-1.995	0	53	42
NB	3	37	22.667	0.882	1.528	2.333	-1.373	-0.387	24	21
mf-ek	1	39	37.000	0	0	0	0	0	37	37
OH	2	38	30.000	2.000	2.282	8.000	-2.000	0	32	28
mf-mf	3	37	23.333	1.856	3.215	10.333	-1.496	0.631	27	21
n-ba	3	37	100.667	2.186	3.786	14.334	-0.197	0.711	105	98
pr-alv	5	35	49.400	1.470	3.286	10.801	-1.628	-0.106	53	46
ekm-ekm	3	37	60.000	2.082	3.606	13.000	-1.509	0.470	57	64
ol-sta	0	40								
enm-enm	3	37	35.000	2.517	4.359	19.000	-1.463	0.665	40	32
ba-o	2	38	35.500	0.500	0.707	0.500	-107.00	0	36	35
FMB	2	38	29.000	1.000	1.414	2.000	-2.000	0	30	28
g-op-g*	8	32	522.000	3.505	9.914	98.286	41.305	0	537	510
po-b-po*	8	32	300.750	11.389	32.212	1037.643	2.610	-2.053	322	223
n-gn	0	40								
pr-M3	4	36	53.500	1.323	2.646	7.000	-1.404	-0.509	56	50
MM	5	35	19.800	0.663	1.483	2.200	-0.736	0.366	22	18
ba-sphba	4	36	26.750	1.377	2.754	7.583	-1.617	0.187	30	24
OPBB	5	35	21.200	1.497	3.347	11.200	-0.058	1.283	27	19
n-o	4	36	136.000	1.581	3.162	10.000	-6.413	0.389	140	133
n-b	12	28	111.917	0.917	3.176	10.085	8.981	1.138	118	108
b-l	15	25	113.867	1.582	6.128	37.554	-0.055	-0.622	122	101
l-i	11	29	75.909	1.604	5.319	28.291	-1.100	0.051	84	68
i-o	5	35	28.000	4.393	9.823	96.500	-1.259	-0.138	40	15
g-n	12	28	9.750	0.993	3.441	11.841	0.767	1.256	18	6
g-b	12	28	106.167	1.093	3.786	14.335	2.189	0.686	113	100
g-l	11	29	177.727	1.579	5.236	27.419	7.788	0.269	186	171
g-i	9	31	164.889	1.752	5.255	27.617	6.818	0.438	174	158
g-o	4	36	141.500	1.708	3.416	11.667	17.062	0.618	146	138
n-o*	5	35	382.000	6.473	14.474	209.500	0.266	-0.566	395	360
n-b*	12	28	129.167	2.351	8.145	66.335	-0.369	0.307	143	116
b-l*	13	27	130.538	1.821	6.565	43.104	2.150	-1.319	137	115
l-o*	5	35	117.800	0.861	1.924	3.703	-102.175	0.314	120	115
g-b*	13	27	120.077	2.438	8.789	77.245	-1.102	0.370	135	110
g-l*	12	28	249.417	3.611	12.508	156.449	-0.311	-0.046	269	230
g-i*	10	30	332.900	6.711	21.221	450.333	-1.284	0.169	362	307
g-o*	5	35	372.800	7.067	15.802	249.703	-1.029	-0.695	388	348
kdl-kdl	1	39	113.000	0	0	0	0	0	113	113
go-go	2	38	102.500	10.500	14.849	220.500	-1.986	0	113	92
ML	1	39	99.000	0	0	0	0	0	99	99
gn-id	7	33	33.429	1.020	2.699	7.286	-0.740	0.387	38	30
MRH	3	37	58.333	3.667	6.351	40.334	-1.510	-0.707	62	51
MRB	5	35	31.800	0.200	0.447	0.200	113.959	-1.365	32	31
MA	5	35	58.6°	0.748	1.674	2.801	-4.912	0.757	60°	56°

TABLE 7: UNIVARIATE STATISTICS: CUEVA DE LAS LECHUZAS

	n	m	$\bar{x}$	s	σ	V	k	sk	max	min
g-op	12	2	181.833	2.611	9.044	81.790	-0.450	-0.435	195	165
eu-eu	14	0	132.357	2.223	8.317	69.173	-0.731	-0.178	146	119
ft-ft	14	0	92.429	1.912	7.155	51.188	-0.378	0.088	107	80
co-co	14	0	111.500	2.313	8.654	74.885	0.978	0.406	132	96
zy-zy	3	11	118.333	6.173	10.693	114.334	-1.502	-0.695	125	106
ast-ast	2	12	106.833	4.269	14.788	218.699	1.833	0.737	143	79
ms-ms	12	2	95.417	2.950	10.220	104.449	0.414	-0.014	116	75
au-au	11	3	103.909	3.709	12.300	151.294	-0.616	-0.070	125	83
ba-b	7	7	130.571	3.108	8.223	67.625	0.211	1.099	147	122
po-b H	13	1	122.462	1.352	4.876	23.771	0.313	-0.024	130	115
n-pr	9	5	59.556	3.920	11.759	138.278	-0.334	-1.091	68	36
ba-pr	8	6	93.625	3.784	10.703	114.554	-0.006	0.221	113	76
n-ns	9	5	43.667	2.128	6.384	40.750	-0.333	-0.912	51	31
NB	8	6	21.750	0.921	2.605	6.786	-0.709	-0.797	24	17
mf-ek	10	4	34.700	0.883	2.791	7.789	-0.709	-0.835	38	30
OH	11	3	30.455	0.578	1.917	3.673	1.387	1.012	35	28
mf-mf	11	3	23.727	0.954	3.165	10.018	-0.350	0.341	30	19
n-ba	7	7	98.429	6.347	16.792	281.958	0.456	0.564	130	73
pr-alv	8	6	48.125	2.142	6.058	36.696	-0.672	-0.078	58	39
ekm-ekm	7	7	59.857	1.805	4.775	22.810	-1.116	-0.828	64	53
ol-sta	6	8	37.500	3.695	9.050	81.900	-1.490	-0.607	46	26
enm-enm	6	8	30.833	1.400	3.430	11.767	-1.021	0.154	36	27
ba-o	6	8	34.000	1.095	2.683	7.200	0.333	1.089	39	31
FMB	6	8	27.500	1.057	2.588	6.700	-0.519	-0.910	30	23
g-op-g*	14	0	499.071	5.852	21.895	479.385	-0.260	-0.134	535	460
po-b-po*	12	2	301.167	3.466	12.008	144.182	2.628	1.137	331	285
n-gn	2	12	115.500	1.500	2.121	4.500	72.852	0.296	117	114
pr-M^3	8	6	54.375	2.228	6.301	39.696	-1.084	-0.581	62	44
MM	11	3	20.909	1.013	3.360	11.291	-0.741	0.563	27	17
ba-sphba	6	8	25.167	2.522	6.178	38.167	-0.275	0.832	36	18
OPBB	7	7	20.000	0.690	1.862	3.333	1.550	-1.775	21	16
n-b	2	12	107.583	1.351	4.680	21.903	1.128	-0.582	114	97
b-l	13	1	111.462	1.338	4.824	23.271	2.207	-1.001	116	100
l-i	10	4	71.500	3.110	9.835	96.722	-0.504	0.081	87	54
i-o	8	6	33.625	3.595	10.169	103.411	-0.673	0.186	51	19
g-n	17	9	11.929	0.650	2.433	5.918	0.497	1.151	17	9
g-b	13	1	101.000	1.396	5.033	25.333	0.025	-0.431	108	90
g-l	13	1	172.462	2.825	10.187	103.771	0.777	-0.877	184	149
g-i	9	5	171.667	4.368	13.105	171.750	0.495	0.828	199	153
n-o*	10	4	369.800	3.893	12.311	151.556	1.227	-0.289	387	347
n-b*	14	0	125.929	1.408	5.269	27.764	-0.497	0.402	135	119
b-l*	14	0	125.857	1.941	7.263	52.750	0.757	-0.437	138	110
l-o*	10	4	117.500	3.745	11.844	140.278	-0.597	-0.427	135	98
g-b*	14	0	114.000	1.191	4.455	19.846	2.384	0.607	123	108
g-l*	14	0	240.000	2.353	8.806	77.538	-0.291	0.419	255	228
g-i*	11	3	330.091	8.016	26.588	706.900	3.117	1.920	402	308
g-o*	10	4	357.900	3.943	12.468	155.444	2.358	-0.232	376	336
kdl-kdl	2	12	119.000	13.000	18.385	338.000	-2.001	0	132	106
go-go	3	11	89.667	6.836	11.060	122.334	-1.489	-0.217	100	78
gn-id	3	11	34.667	1.856	3.215	10.333	-1.630	-0.630	37	31
ML	0	14								
MRH	3	11	59.333	1.667	2.887	8.334	-1.791	-0.709	61	56
MRB	2	12	32.000	0	0	0	0	0	32	32
MA	3	11	61°	3.786	6.557	43.000	-1.494	0.274	68°	55°

TABLE 8: UNIVARIATE STATISTICS: COVA DE LES LLOMETES

	n	m	$\bar{x}$	s	σ	V	k	sk	max	min
g-op	24	8	182.333	1.329	6.512	42.408	1.857	-0.582	193	168
eu-eu	25	7	135.120	0.889	4.447	19.779	2.908	-0.039	145	126
ft-ft	24	8	93.917	0.899	4.403	19.386	1.265	0.416	104	86
co-co	23	9	117.391	0.973	4.669	21.795	1.507	-0.490	125	107
zy-zy	2	30	121.500	8.500	12.021	144.500	-1.970	0.001	130	113
ast-ast	20	12	104.800	1.135	5.074	25.750	1.406	0.701	116	98
ms-ms	18	14	97.833	1.258	5.339	28.500	4.224	1.910	115	93
au-au	18	14	101.611	1.237	5.249	27.548	0.908	0.877	112	95
ba-b	10	22	132.600	1.470	4.648	21.604	3.230	0.336	141	126
po-b H	22	10	124.091	1.000	4.690	21.994	3.336	0.068	134	116
n-pr	10	22	68.900	1.804	5.705	32.545	-0.695	0.098	79	60
ba-pr	8	24	92.875	2.295	6.490	42.125	0.910	1.379	107	86
n-ns	11	21	48.636	1.081	3.585	12.855	-0.561	-0.687	54	42
NB	9	23	22.667	0.850	2.550	6.500	-1.446	-0.182	26	19
mf-ek	8	24	37.250	0.840	2.375	5.643	1.307	-1.352	40	32
OH	10	22	30.900	0.482	1.524	2.322	-0.322	-0.618	33	28
mf-mf	10	22	21.300	0.790	2.497	6.234	0.317	-0.586	25	16
n-ba	9	23	98.667	1.472	4.416	19.500	-1.769	-0.376	104	92
pr-alv	11	21	50.273	0.945	3.133	9.818	-0.426	-0.678	54	44
ekm-ekm	9	23	61.222	1.267	3.801	14.445	2.241	-1.691	65	52
ol-sta	10	22	41.500	0.734	2.321	5.389	-0.347	0.536	46	38
enm-enm	9	23	33.667	1.225	3.674	13.500	0.005	-1.114	37	26
ba-o	7	25	35.857	0.595	1.574	2.477	0.582	-0.583	38	33
FMB	7	25	30.143	0.670	1.773	3.143	-0.461	-0.616	32	27
g-op-g*	24	8	510.583	3.303	16.184	261.913	-0.226	-0.842	532	470
po-b-po*	18	14	298.889	2.903	12.315	151.647	2.147	-0.216	320	275
n-gn	0	32								
pr-M^3	11	21	55.545	0.609	2.018	4.073	1.244	-0.408	58	52
MM	11	21	19.727	0.982	3.259	10.618	0.999	-1.073	24	12
ba-sphba	8	24	27.125	1.493	4.224	17.839	-1.344	0.126	33	22
OPBB	9	23	20.444	0.766	2.297	5.278	-0.228	0.863	25	18
n-b	24	8	109.042	1.186	5.812	33.783	0.002	0.510	118	97
b-l	24	8	114.042	1.504	7.369	54.304	-0.050	0.101	127	99
l-i	23	9	70.696	1.851	8.875	78.767	-0.649	0.528	90	57
i-o	14	18	36.429	2.717	10.166	103.341	-0.410	-0.564	51	15
g-n	21	11	9.619	0.485	2.224	4.984	1.242	1.193	16	7
g-b	27	5	103.111	1.208	6.278	39.411	0.068	-0.515	111	89
g-l	25	7	176.240	1.478	7.390	54.615	3.079	-0.749	188	157
g-i	15	17	136.400	1.460	5.654	31.973	0.986	0.242	146	127
n-O*	13	19	379.077	3.970	14.315	204.917	2.636	-1.552	396	340
n-b*	21	11	126.333	2.939	13.470	181.434	3.931	1.567	171	108
b-l*	23	9	129.435	3.013	14.450	208.804	3.264	-1.390	150	82
l-o*	15	17	117.800	2.096	8.117	65.888	-0.486	-0.100	130	102
g-b*	25	7	116.520	2.336	11.680	136.427	6.026	1.927	160	100
g-l*	25	7	246.120	2.595	12.973	168.292	1.921	-0.454	270	210
g-i*	23	9	322.696	3.496	16.766	281.091	-0.083	-0.086	350	295
g-o*	15	17	367.667	3.321	12.873	165.714	7.593	-1.295	385	332
kdl-kdl	0	32								
go-go	0	32								
ML	0	32								
gn-id	10	22	29.200	0.917	2.898	8.400	0.653	-0.526	34	23
MRH	2	30	58.000	2.000	2.828	8.000	-2.000	0	60	56
MRB	4	28	31.250	2.175	4.349	18.917	-1.984	-0.026	35	27
MA	5	27	54.8°	1.715	3.834	14.700	-1.126	0.168	60°	50°

TABLE 9: UNIVARIATE STATISTICS: COVA DEL MORRO DE LA BARSELLA

	n	m	$\bar{x}$	s	σ	V	k	sk	max	min
g-op	12	11	182.167	2.194	7.602	57.790	-0.567	0.045	195	171
eu-eu	12	11	136.250	1.620	5.610	31.477	0.690	0.189	146	128
ft-ft	9	14	95.222	0.795	2.386	5.695	-1.890	-0.185	98	91
co-co	13	10	117.077	1.529	5.515	30.411	-0.301	-0.348	126	108
zy-zy	2	21	125.500	6.500	9.192	84.500	-1.924	0.002	132	119
ast-ast	10	13	111.800	2.323	7.346	53.958	-1.437	-0.098	121	101
ms-ms	5	18	102.200	1.158	2.588	6.700	4.128	-0.741	105	98
au-au	7	16	108.286	1.304	3.451	11.906	-4.405	1.187	115	105
ba-b	8	15	134.625	2.719	7.689	59.125	-1.278	-0.365	143	123
po-b H	9	14	120.889	1.483	4.315	18.617	0.947	0.059	127	115
n-pr	9	14	66.000	0.898	2.693	7.250	0.810	1.100	72	63
ba-pr	6	17	92.167	1.759	4.309	18.567	-0.327	0.249	99	86
NB	7	16	23.143	0.508	1.345	1.810	-0.862	-0.273	25	21
mf-ek	8	15	35.375	0.754	2.134	4.554	1.157	1.265	40	33
OH	8	15	30.000	1.376	3.891	15.143	1.887	-1.679	34	21
mf-mf	10	13	22.700	0.616	1.947	3.789	-1.332	0.445	26	21
n-ba	6	17	101.833	2.971	7.278	52.967	-0.569	0.070	113	91
pr-alv	8	15	47.750	0.996	2.816	7.929	-0.881	-0.263	51	43
ekm-ekm	7	16	60.286	0.969	2.564	6.752	0.530	0.748	65	58
ba-o	7	16	34.857	0.937	2.479	6.143	-1.022	0.672	39	33
FMB	6	17	31.167	0.749	1.835	3.367	-1.370	-0.264	33	29
g-op-g*	12	11	514.417	4.503	15.597	243.273	-3.000	-0.346	535	485
po-b-po*	7	16	305.571	3.287	8.696	75.625	0.899	-0.175	315	292
n-gn	1	22	105.000	0	0	0	0	0	105	105
pr-M^3	7	16	54.00	0.951	2.517	6.333	-1.1759	-0.203	57	50
ba-sphba	6	17	27.000	1.438	3.521	12.400	-1.530	-0.361	30	22
OPBB	6	17	19.333	1.116	2.733	7.467	-1.070	-0.704	22	15
n-b	9	14	110.889	0.857	2.572	6.617	16.732	-1.114	114	105
b-l	12	11	109.083	2.661	9.219	84.994	-0.796	-0.310	124	93
l-i	10	13	70.700	2.011	6.360	40.456	-0.511	0.055	82	60
i-o	10	13	39.300	1.789	5.658	32.011	2.243	-1.692	45	25
g-n	11	12	8.455	0.545	1.809	3.273	-1.240	0.024	11	6
g-l	11	12	175.182	2.486	8.244	67.969	0.023	-0.210	186	161
g-i	10	13	171.000	1.856	5.869	34.444	2.541	0.093	180	163
n-o*	7	16	373.000	6.908	18.276	334.000	0.313	-0.672	392	342
n-b*	10	13	126.400	2.778	8.784	77.160	-1.386	-0.299	137	112
b-l*	11	12	123.273	3.242	10.753	115.619	0.417	-0.760	140	100
l-o*	8	15	125.125	3.847	10.882	118.411	-0.985	-0.332	140	108
g-b*	13	10	117.846	2.097	7.559	57.146	-0.905	-0.315	126	105
g-l*	13	10	239.077	3.509	12.652	160.078	1.185	-0.516	260	210
g-i*	10	13	331.100	4.428	14.004	196.111	0.997	-0.469	353	303
g-o*	9	14	363.222	5.416	16.248	264.000	-0.355	-0.301	385	335
kdl-kdl	2	21	108.500	0.500	0.707	0.500	-3.000	0	109	108
go-go	4	19	95.750	2.983	5.965	35.583	-0.754	-1.008	100	87
ML	0	23								
gn-id	9	14	30.889	1.073	3.219	10.361	-0.896	0.750	36	28
MRH	5	18	58.000	1.140	2.550	6.500	-3.118	0	61	55
MRB	5	18	30.200	1.393	3.115	9.700	-1.662	0.294	34	27

TABLE 10: UNIVARIATE STATISTICS: COVA DE LA PASTORA

	n	m	$\bar{x}$	s	σ	V	k	sk	max	min
g-op	23	34	183.826	1.384	6.638	44.060	4.219	0.109	198	172
eu-eu	24	33	137.125	0.895	4.387	19.245	2.519	-0.362	144	129
ft-ft	22	35	94.909	0.887	4.163	17.327	2.189	-0.065	105	86
co-co	27	30	119.630	1.136	5.904	34.858	1.712	0.646	134	110
zy-zy	3	54	122.333	2.028	3.512	12.334	-5.524	0.297	126	119
ast-ast	17	40	108.353	1.331	5.488	30.121	1.103	0.561	121	100
ms-ms	9	48	97.778	1.770	5.310	28.195	-0.192	-0.156	107	88
au-au	15	42	100.400	1.077	4.172	17.402	0.429	0.691	108	95
ba-b	9	48	131.778	2.613	7.839	61.445	-0.693	0.167	145	120
po-b H	24	33	125.500	0.967	4.739	22.457	4.370	0.073	137	114
n-pr	10	47	68.200	1.849	5.846	34.178	-0.869	-0.227	77	59
ba-pr	5	52	86.400	1.600	3.578	12.801	-0.559	0.226	91	83
n-ns	12	45	49.250	0.930	3.223	10.386	0.089	-0.199	55	43
NB	11	46	23.364	0.691	2.292	5.255	-0.594	0.680	28	21
mf-ek	11	46	38.273	0.715	2.370	5.618	-0.602	0.464	43	35
OH	11	46	32.455	0.652	2.162	4.673	-1.182	-0.188	36	29
mf-mf	9	48	20.556	0.709	2.128	4.528	-1.127	0.291	24	18
n-ba	8	49	98.375	2.556	7.230	52.268	-1.868	0.439	107	91
pr-alv	10	47	48.800	1.373	4.341	18.845	-0.608	0.477	57	43
ekm-ekm	9	48	58.778	0.641	1.922	3.695	1.450	0.112	62	56
ol-sta	6	51	41.167	1.302	3.189	10.167	-1.366	-0.168	45	37
enm-enm	8	49	32.750	0.701	1.982	3.929	-1.138	0.603	36	31
ba-o	7	50	36.286	0.944	2.498	6.238	-0.747	-0.696	39	32
FMB	6	51	29.883	0.543	1.329	1.767	0.458	0.321	32	28
g-op-g*	22	35	517.364	3.142	14.736	217.143	4.766	0.277	554	490
po-b-po*	15	42	310.733	3.276	12.689	161.000	1.837	-0.148	335	282
n-gn	4	53	113.750	1.887	3.775	14.250	-0.759	-0.222	118	109
pr-M^3	11	46	54.636	1.106	3.668	13.455	-0.715	-0.206	60	48
MM	13	44	21.462	0.627	2.259	5.103	1.046	0.932	27	18
ba-sphba	7	50	24.286	0.865	2.289	5.238	-0.732	0.254	28	21
OPBB	7	50	19.143	0.508	1.345	1.810	-1.196	0.617	21	18
n-o	7	50	129.143	1.752	4.635	21.479	1.208	-0.456	134	122
n-b	21	36	110.524	1.178	5.400	29.162	0.255	-0.125	120	101
b-l	30	27	115.633	0.918	5.028	25.276	2.260	0.433	127	107
l-i	22	35	78.773	1.799	8.440	71.232	-1.115	0.133	92	65
i-o	10	47	32.400	2.197	6.947	48.267	1.245	-1.275	41	16
g-n	21	36	6.810	0.423	1.940	3.762	0.768	0.738	12	4
g-b	30	27	106.867	1.241	6.796	46.190	1.948	0.542	127	95
g-l	25	32	177.920	1.343	6.714	45.078	2.774	0.301	195	163
g-i	20	37	161.600	2.280	10.195	103.938	-0.416	0.327	184	147
g-o	8	49	135.875	1.737	4.912	24.125	1.021	0.619	145	130
n-o*	8	49	375.750	6.748	19.086	364.286	-0.984	-0.112	398	348
n-b*	17	40	125.235	1.930	7.957	63.316	-0.341	0.088	140	113
b-l*	23	34	130.522	1.915	9.184	84.352	1.213	-0.597	148	105
l-o*	9	48	119.889	4.686	14.058	197.617	-0.749	0.371	145	100
g-b*	30	27	120.300	1.449	7.936	62.976	-0.421	0.012	135	105
g-l*	27	30	250.852	2.603	13.525	182.923	1.850	0.187	280	229
g-i*	20	37	342.850	4.260	19.053	363.000	0.417	-0.384	375	306
g-o*	8	49	369.000	6.256	17.696	313.143	-0.709	-0.296	388	340
kdl-kdl	3	54	111.333	2.667	4.619	21.334	-1.734	-0.640	114	106
go-go	9	48	92.444	1.908	5.725	32.781	0.350	0.086	103	82
ML	3	54	96.333	0.667	1.155	1.334	84.664	1.590	97	95
gn-id	20	37	31.550	0.671	3.000	8.998	1.741	-1.377	36	23
MRH	13	44	59.769	1.868	6.735	45.539	0.369	-0.969	68	44
MRB	14	43	31.429	1.004	3.756	14.110	-0.856	-0.031	37	25
MA	17	44	59.412•	1.286	5.304	28.133	-0.071	-0.061	70•	48•

TABLE 11: UNIVARIATE STATISTICS: COVA DE BENI SID

	n	m	$\bar{x}$	s	σ	V	k	sk	max	min
g-op	11	29	174.455	2.229	7.394	54.675	0.014	0.025	185	164
eu-eu	10	30	133.60	0.654	2.067	4.271	14.327	-0.637	136	129
ft-ft	15	25	93.133	0.878	3.399	11.554	0.816	-0.286	98	88
co-co	14	26	115.143	1.128	4.222	17.827	3.873	-0.187	122	108
zy-zy	2	38	119.000	4.000	5.657	32.000	-2.000	0	123	115
ast-ast	9	31	104.667	1.581	4.743	22.500	-0.635	-0.152	110	97
ms-ms	8	32	97.250	2.226	6.296	39.643	-1.298	0.374	108	90
au-au	8	32	99.000	2.841	8.036	64.571	-1.226	-0.299	110	86
ba-b	5	35	126.800	3.513	7.855	61.703	-0.205	-0.855	135	114
po-b-H	11	29	119.909	0.768	2.548	6.494	41.074	0.406	124	117
n-pr	11	29	60.364	1.820	6.038	36.455	-1.368	0.254	69	52
ba-pr	3	37	90.667	1.453	2.517	6.334	11.955	0	93	88
n-ns	11	29	43.273	1.471	4.880	23.818	-0.490	0.492	53	37
NB	9	31	20.778	0.703	2.108	4.444	-0.757	-0.710	23	17
mf-ek	11	29	36.364	0.730	2.420	5.855	-1.768	-0.225	39	33
OH	11	29	31.364	0.509	1.690	2.855	-1.191	0.571	34	30
mf-mf	8	32	19.875	0.915	2.588	6.696	-0.724	0.305	24	16
n-ba	3	37	96.000	3.606	6.245	39.000	-1.485	-0.528	101	89
pr-alv	10	30	45.900	1.958	6.191	38.322	-1.042	-0.190	54	35
ekm-ekm	9	31	57.222	1.188	3.563	12.695	-0.487	-0.824	61	51
ol-sta	6	34	37.333	2.445	5.989	35.867	-1.810	-0.120	43	30
enm-enm	9	31	32.889	1.230	3.689	13.611	-1.436	-0.350	37	27
ba-o	2	38	36.000	0	0	0	0	0	36	36
FMB	5	35	31.000	0.316	0.707	0.500	7.000	0	32	30
g-op-g*	10	30	497.700	4.764	15.067	227.000	5.008	0.386	525	475
po-b-po*	7	33	300.143	3.210	8.494	72.146	2.815	-0.348	310	288
n-gn	3	37	103.333	9.171	15.885	252.334	-1.492	-0.703	113	85
pr-M^3	9	31	51.556	1.226	3.678	13.528	-1.033	-0.381	56	45
MM	10	30	18.600	0.670	2.119	4.489	-0.059	0.629	23	16
ba-sphba	4	36	27.250	1.548	3.096	9.583	-1.103	-0.657	30	23
OPBB	4	36	21.000	1.291	2.582	6.667	-1.360	0	24	18
n-o	4	36	126.500	3.524	7.047	49.667	-1.432	0.004	135	118
n-b	16	24	104.875	1.472	5.886	34.650	-0.347	-0.243	115	94
b-l	12	28	109.500	1.786	6.186	38.273	1.316	-1.290	116	94
l-i	11	29	75.545	2.425	8.042	64.673	-0.428	-0.294	88	60
i-o	5	35	31.400	2.379	5.320	28.301	-1.443	-0.071	38	25
g-n	15	25	8.867	0.336	1.302	1.6950	-0.345	-0.350	11	6
g-b	16	24	98.500	1.255	5.020	25.200	0.469	-0.833	105	86
g-l	10	30	168.800	2.289	7.239	52.403	-0.238	-0.390	177	157
g-i	12	28	153.417	3.585	12.420	154.267	-0.576	-0.736	168	129
g-o	4	36	131.750	3.637	7.274	52.917	-0.846	-0.512	139	122
n-o*	5	35	358.200	6.499	14.533	211.203	-0.704	0.682	380	345
n-b*	15	25	123.133	1.781	6.896	47.554	0.708	-0.465	134	110
b-l*	13	27	123.462	2.289	8.253	68.104	0.797	-0.506	137	105
l-o*	5	35	111.600	2.272	5.079	25.801	-1.318	0.239	119	105
g-b*	16	24	115.125	1.873	7.491	56.117	0.099	-0.595	126	100
g-l*	12	28	237.250	2.978	10.314	106.386	-0.057	0.282	254	221
g-i*	12	28	321.667	4.646	16.093	259.000	0.294	-0.752	337	294
g-o*	5	35	349.400	6.838	15.291	233.813	-1.127	0.623	372	335
kdl-kdl	8	32	101.750	3.913	11.068	122.500	-1.298	0.514	119	89
go-go	14	26	81.786	2.677	10.017	100.337	2.534	1.561	110	70
ML	10	30	83.600	3.468	10.967	120.271	-1.414	0.095	98	68
gn-id	19	21	26.211	0.752	3.276	10.731	-0.660	0.500	33	21
MRH	16	24	50.813	2.537	10.147	102.962	-1.109	0.532	70	37
MRB	21	19	29.381	0.705	3.232	10.448	-0.672	0.048	35	23
MA	20	20	55.950°	1.428	6.386	40.787	0.224	0.792	70°	46°

Craniometrical measurements which are non-homogeneous

(9 assemblages are considered)

The non-homogeneous measurements in each cell correspond to the site which heads the corresponding column. Measurements are shown for that site which, when compared with the corresponding measurement of the site in which row the cell lies, have no greater probability of homogeneity than ± 2.5% when tested by Student's t (or, when Snedecor's F did not allow calculation of t, when tested by the Behrens-Fischer statistic - values indicated by ↑). Values in brackets are those with a probability of homogeneity between ± 2.5% and ± 5%.

	PALANQUÉS	CAMI REAL D'ALACANT	LECHUZAS	LLOMETES	BARSELLA	PASTORA	BENI SID

Please note that a full-size version of this page is available to download from www.barpublishing.com/additional-downloads.html
The original foldout has been reduced in size to match the A4 format of this book, the image is therefore not as clear as the original foldout. Please refer to the original foldout via the download for the original content.
Please also be aware that the image might be cut off or not complete in the printed book.

Table 13

		Comp.1 50.9%	Comp.2 13.4%	Comp.3 8.2%	Comp.4 4.4%	Comp.5 3.2%
1	g-op	0.87741	0.14332	-0.22011	0.17875	0.17649
2	eu-eu	0.80558	0.10652	-0.06931	0.16101	0.12078
3	ft-ft	0.75364	0.37855	-0.14208	0.10950	-0.09858
4	co-co	0.84723	0.26809	-0.12112	0.05982	-0.08740
5	zy-zy	0.35739	0.37231	0.18220	0.48505	-0.10249
6	ast-ast	0.77928	0.18483	-0.10341	-0.09336	0.35590
7	ms-ms	0.65262	0.39825	0.00596	-0.19005	0.21040
8	au-au	0.81257	0.36191	-0.06501	-0.12677	0.12482
9	ba-b	0.82836	0.24459	-0.09993	0.15378	0.17145
10	n-ns	0.23775	0.86008	0.04122	0.30563	-0.00641
11	NB	0.17715	0.85242	-0.01015	0.21291	0.01052
12	mf-ek	0.42330	0.73251	-0.11798	0.22568	0.08335
13	OH	0.45434	0.74370	-0.12574	0.19662	0.10166
14	mf-mf	0.29012	0.84104	-0.00787	0.03354	0.28745
15	n-ba	0.78369	0.30994	-0.12686	0.17236	0.14839
16	pr-alv	0.22538	0.36797	-0.02458	0.73098	0.28049
17	enm-enm	0.18480	0.39725	-0.01258	0.79784	0.15718
18	ba-o	0.58219	0.23594	-0.12141	0.20061	0.59068
19	FMB	0.47344	0.21692	-0.12382	0.25020	0.68633
20	g-op-g*	0.88515	0.15136	-0.05603	0.16945	0.12097
21	po-b-po*	0.86711	0.25472	-0.06465	0.12733	0.07660
22	g-i	0.83112	0.14741	-0.22091	0.25216	0.11875
23	n-o	0.73403	0.12204	-0.13694	0.15821	0.51054
24	n-b*	0.93670	0.20944	-0.15176	0.08688	0.07297
25	b-l*	0.89120	0.13317	-0.15192	0.19608	0.03481
26	l-o*	0.70249	0.05194	-0.17238	0.23346	0.47604
27	kdl-kdl	-0.09925	-0.02131	0.80390	-0.05125	-0.11798
28	go-go	-0.01953	0.03833	0.81300	0.06940	-0.15979
29	gn-id	-0.13017	-0.02988	0.77591	0.03627	-0.05690
30	MRH	-0.15642	-0.03495	0.92464	0.01532	-0.06284
31	MRB	-0.12062	-0.01071	0.90751	-0.00806	-0.00179
32	MA	-0.24223	-0.09735	0.82464	-0.09269	0.25322

Rotated principal component matrix (varimax rotation) for El Argar skulls (Jacques' data)

Loadings on the first 5 components are given and the percentage of the variance accounted for by each component is shown at the head of each column. The numbers 1-32 beside the variables is their key for the graphical presentations of the components (El Argar graphs 1-10). They represent the variables for which measurements by Jacques were compatible with those taken on other series by me and for which integer values were published. Some measurements of Jacques could not be used as the landmarks appeared non-comparable with those used by me while several other measurements I used on the collections which I measured were not recorded by Jacques.

Component 1 receives heavy loadings from frontal, parietal and occipital bones.
Component 2 receives heavy loadings from the upper face.
Component 3 receives heavy loadings from the mandible.
Component 4 appears to be associated with maxillary, palatal and zygomatic structure.
Component 5 receives heaviest loadings from measurements associated with the occiput.

Plots for Table 13

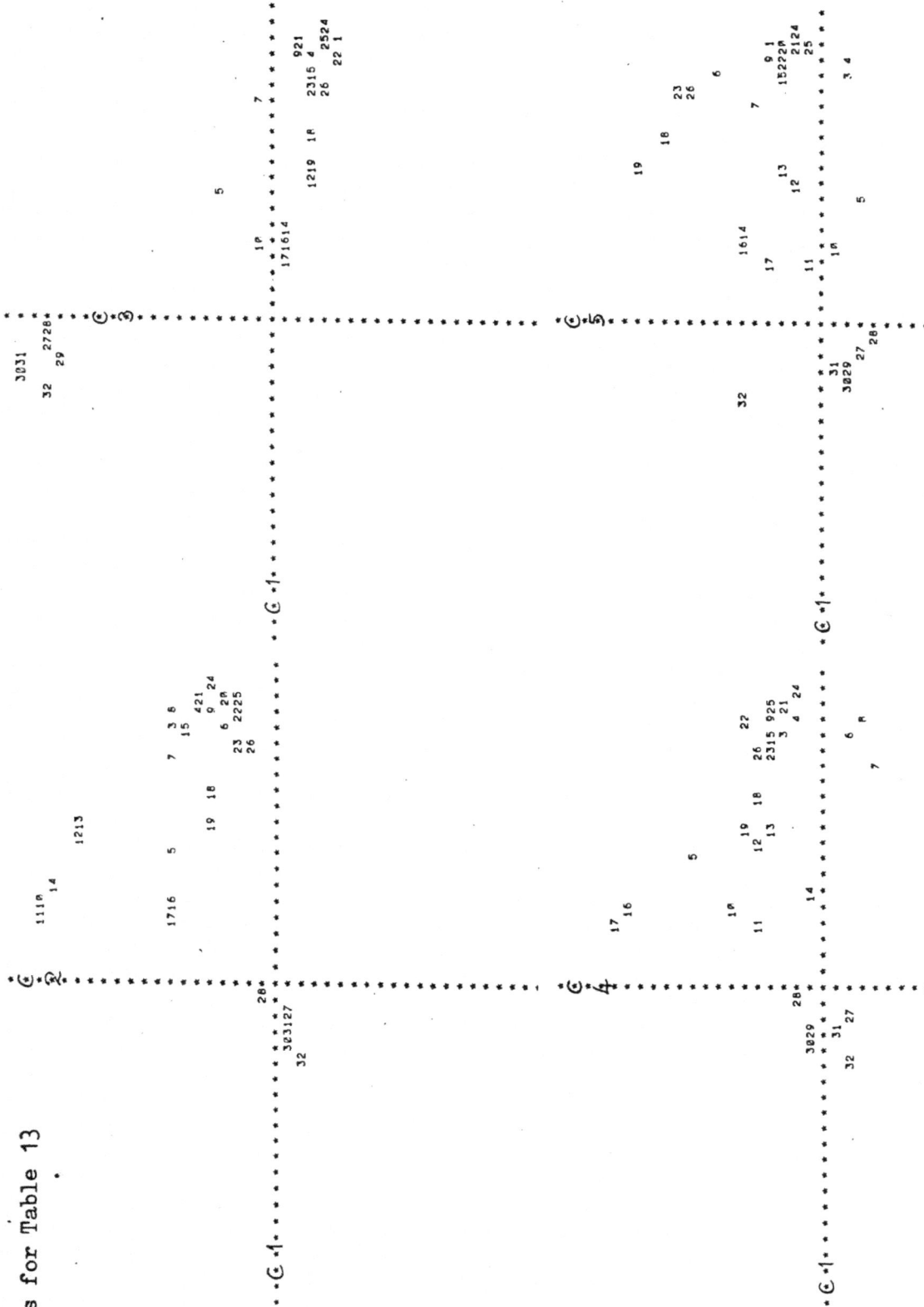

El Argar skulls

Plot of variables for the El Argar assemblage in terms of their loadings on principal components 1 - 5.

Plots for Table 13

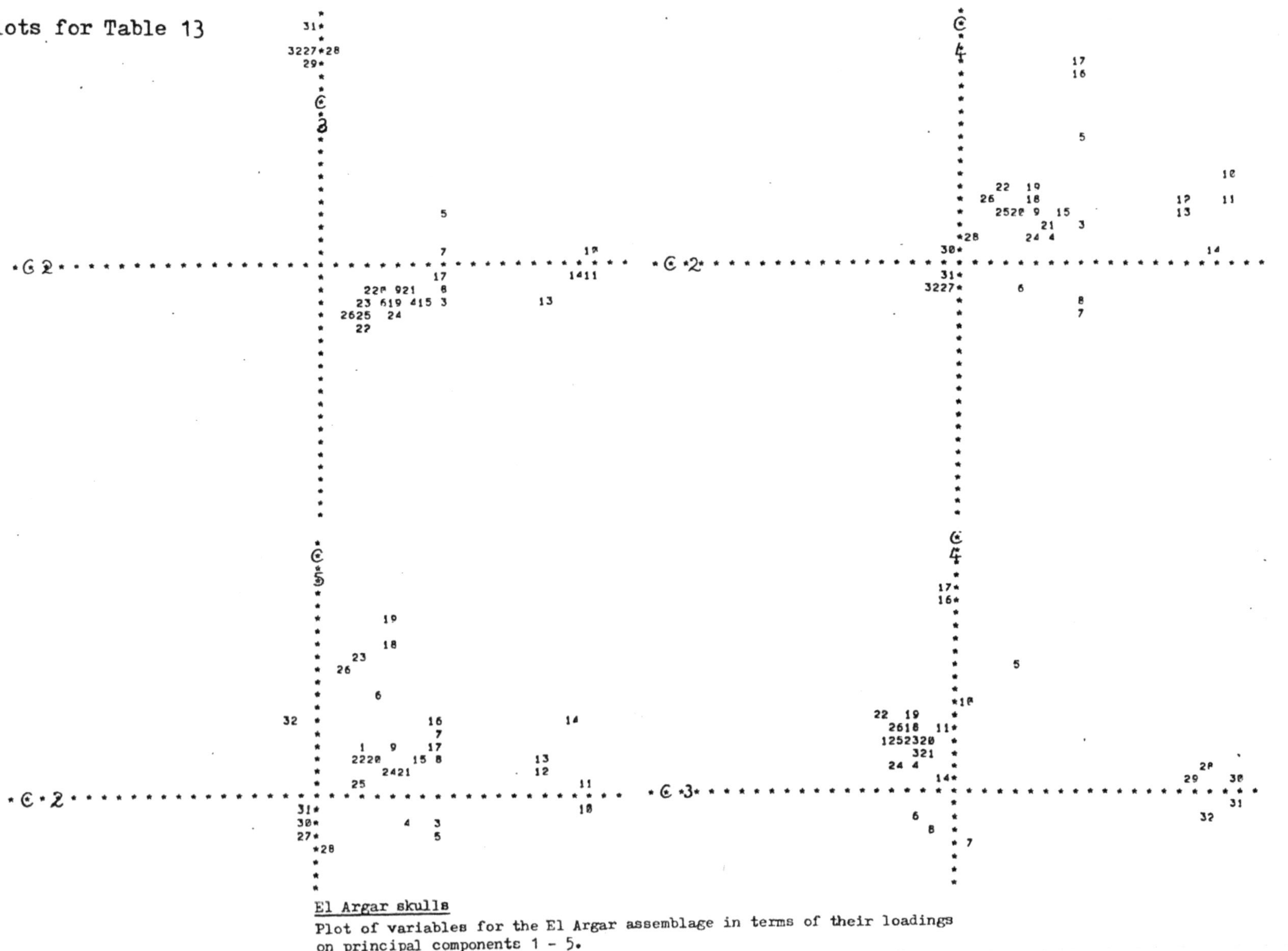

<u>El Argar skulls</u>

Plot of variables for the El Argar assemblage in terms of their loadings on principal components 1 - 5.

Plots for Table 13

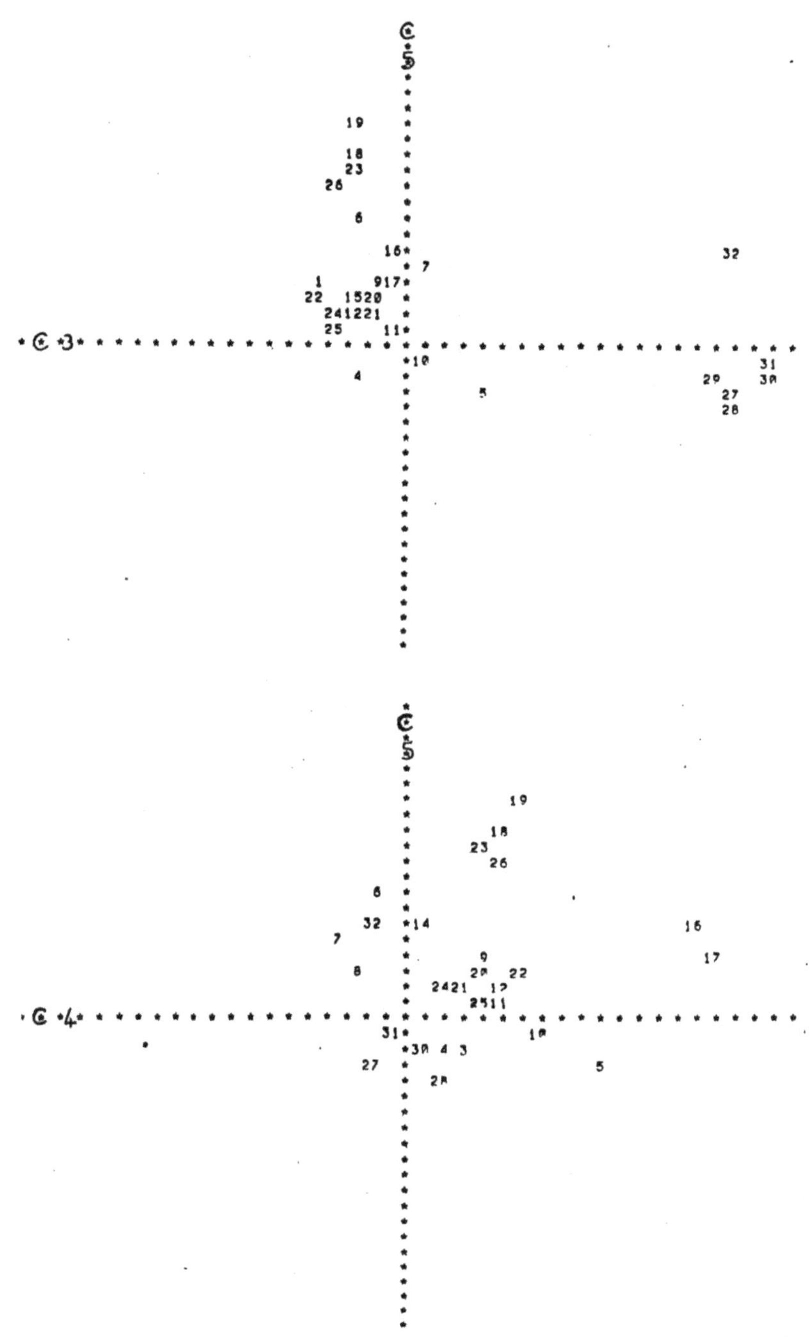

El Argar skulls

Plot of variables for the El Argar assemblage in terms of their loadings on principal components 1 - 5.

Table 14

		Comp.1 65.2%	Comp.2 12.8%	Comp.3 7.2%	Comp.4 6.5%	Comp.5 2.7%
1	g-op	0,57153	0,46103	0,59345	0,06499	-0,08278
2	eu-eu	0,30335	0,71302	0,46090	-0,06880	-0,10203
3	ft-ft	0,38955	0,23721	0.77773	-0,14561	0,22792
4	co-co	0,35449	0,22199	0.79761	0,02784	-0,20426
5	zy-zy	0,36216	0,42994	0,05752	0,02892	0,70331
6	ast-ast	0,38630	0.74469	0,43357	-0,00893	-0,04531
7	ms-ms	0,24633	0.83457	0,24236	0,07647	0,32427
8	au-au	0,24495	0,83671	0,24124	0,05679	0,32897
9	ba-b	0,41818	0,75226	0,33198	0,01719	-0,02196
10	po-b H	0,44755	0,40078	0,75616	0,01511	-0,03548
11	n-pr	0,86245	0,27963	0,36482	-0,03194	0,07026
12	ba-pr	0,71076	0,55486	0,09741	-0,05674	0,14240
13	n-ns	0,84517	0,32257	0,37014	-0,01020	0,06760
14	NB	0,88092	0,30472	0,31888	-0,05259	0,07139
15	mf-ek	0.90225	0,28570	0,27602	-0,05770	0,06519
16	OH	0.85713	0,29452	0,35747	-0,03951	0,07951
17	mf-mf	0.82908	0,33675	0,40133	-0,01441	0,04930
18	n-ba	0,71398	0,54211	0,09873	-0,05623	0,13113
19	pr-alv	0,90461	0,27070	0,26889	-0,06848	0,09861
20	ekm-ekm	0,89361	0,27133	0,30984	-0,04458	0,04191
21	ol-sta	0,89499	0,27386	0,32464	-0,07215	0,05419
22	enm-enm	0.87478	0,33026	0,30647	-0,06988	0,02360
23	ba-o	0,41857	0,74864	0,33404	0,02416	-0,01639
24	FMB	0,39196	0,68880	0,13535	0,02809	0,53582
25	g-op-g*	0,32265	0,72398	0,46185	-0,04381	-0,08733
26	po-b-po*	0,24647	0,83415	0,24332	0,06820	0,32268
27	n-gn	0,29241	0,15914	0,38308	0,55788	0,18986
28	pr-M^3	0,84961	0,30829	0,35964	-0,03521	0,10686
29	MM	0,90613	0,28703	0,27458	-0,06317	0,06019
30	ba-sphba	0,47145	0,56250	0,21964	-0,09692	-0,13070
31	OPBB	0.71598	0,53547	0,09105	-0,08190	0,13335
32	n-o	0,66313	0,64606	0,57875	0,83522	0,20143
33	n-b	0,34721	0,33308	0.83958	-0,02701	0,07736
34	b-l	0,23520	0,39670	0.82408	0,02908	0,13699
35	l-i	0,29561	0,89396	0,29321	0,03720	0,00564
36	i-o	0,26133	0,80944	0,25332	0,18034	0,22996
37	g-n	0,43638	0,18255	0.70304	-0,06374	0,36982
38	g-b	0,36707	0,35664	0,79682	-0,05554	-0,09083
39	g-l	0,33102	0,48003	0.74009	0,06451	0,03291
40	g-i	0,29822	0.89237	0,29814	0,08356	0,05472
41	g-o	0,42129	0,74339	0,33221	0,02260	-0,02536
42	n-o*	0,30040	0.88954	0,30184	0,06952	0,03468
43	n-b*	0,34150	0,31638	0,84797	-0,02962	0,08686
44	b-l*	0,34192	0,48563	0,73193	0,06767	0,03586
45	l-o*	0,26929	0,81314	0,26392	-0,03387	-0,12173
46	g-b*	0,27898	0,30299	0,88017	-0,09301	0,02035
47	g-l*	0,33673	0,48096	0,73721	0,06267	0,03468
48	g-i*	0,30103	0,88754	0,30339	0,05826	0,01919
49	g-o*	0,30000	0,89048	0,30111	0,06844	0,03781
50	kdl-kdl	-0,06930	0,16823	-0,06033	0,76553	0,15225
51	go-go	-0,11580	0,01177	-0,09372	0,73665	0,21181
52	ML	0,66314	0,64605	0,57875	0,83522	0,20142
53	gn-id	-0,17395	-0,10817	-0,08066	0,88479	0,12191
54	MRH	-0,14949	-0,05862	-0,08266	0,99853	0,00876
55	MRB	-0,10483	0,09158	-0,04968	0,96992	-0,22868
56	MA	-0,10992	0,05074	-0,04902	0,97667	-0,21449

Rotated principal component matrix (varimax rotation) for La Bastida skulls.

Loadings on the first 5 components are given. Each accounted for at least 2% of the total variance. A sixth component which accounted for 2.3% is not shown because no loading on it exceeded the cut-off taken for interpreting osteometrical measurements of 0.6. The variance accounted for by each component is given as a percentage of the total variance at the head of each column. The numbers 1-56 beside the variables is their key for the graphical presentations of the components (Bastida principal components graphs 1 - 8).

Component 1 receives heavy loadings from the upper face (including maxillary and palatal measurements) and the breadth of the basi-occiput as well as projection of the face in the midline on the basion. Mandibular length and nasion-opisthion distance load on this component.

Component 2 receives heavy loadings from temporal and squamous occipital bones including the foramen magnum, and although less strongly the basi-occiput. Mandibular length and basi-bregmatic distance load on this component.

Component 3 receives heavy loadings from sagittal and coronal dimensions of the frontal and parietal bones and, less strongly, from mandibular length.and nasion-opisthion distance.

Component 4 reflects all mandibular dimensions and mandibular length loads more strongly than on any of the previous components. Nasion-opisthion distance and total facial height are represented on this component.

Component 5 receives a heavy loading from the bizygomatic breadth and a weak one from foramen magnum breadth.

Plots for Table 14

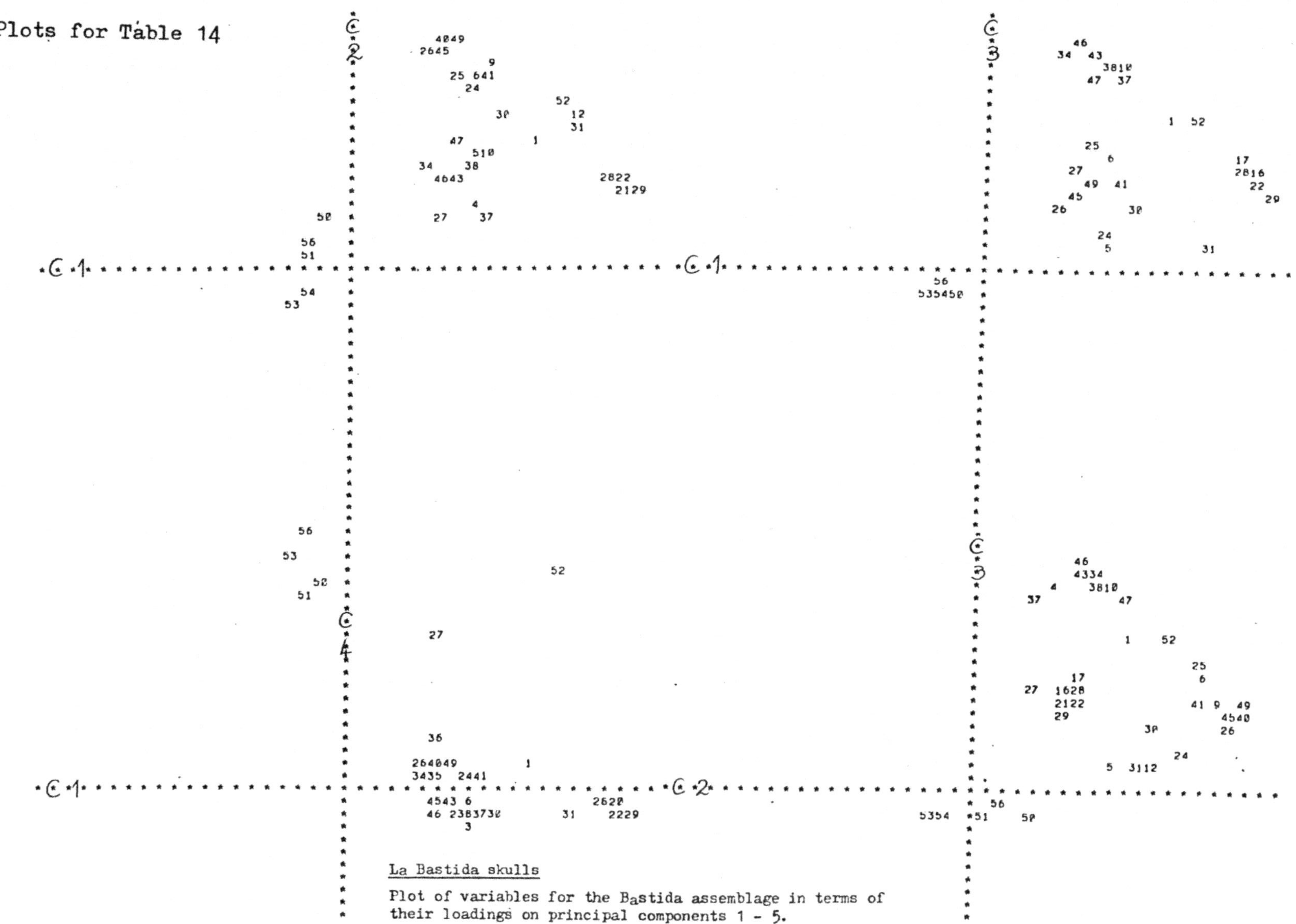

La Bastida skulls

Plot of variables for the Bastida assemblage in terms of their loadings on principal components 1 - 5.

Plots for Table 14

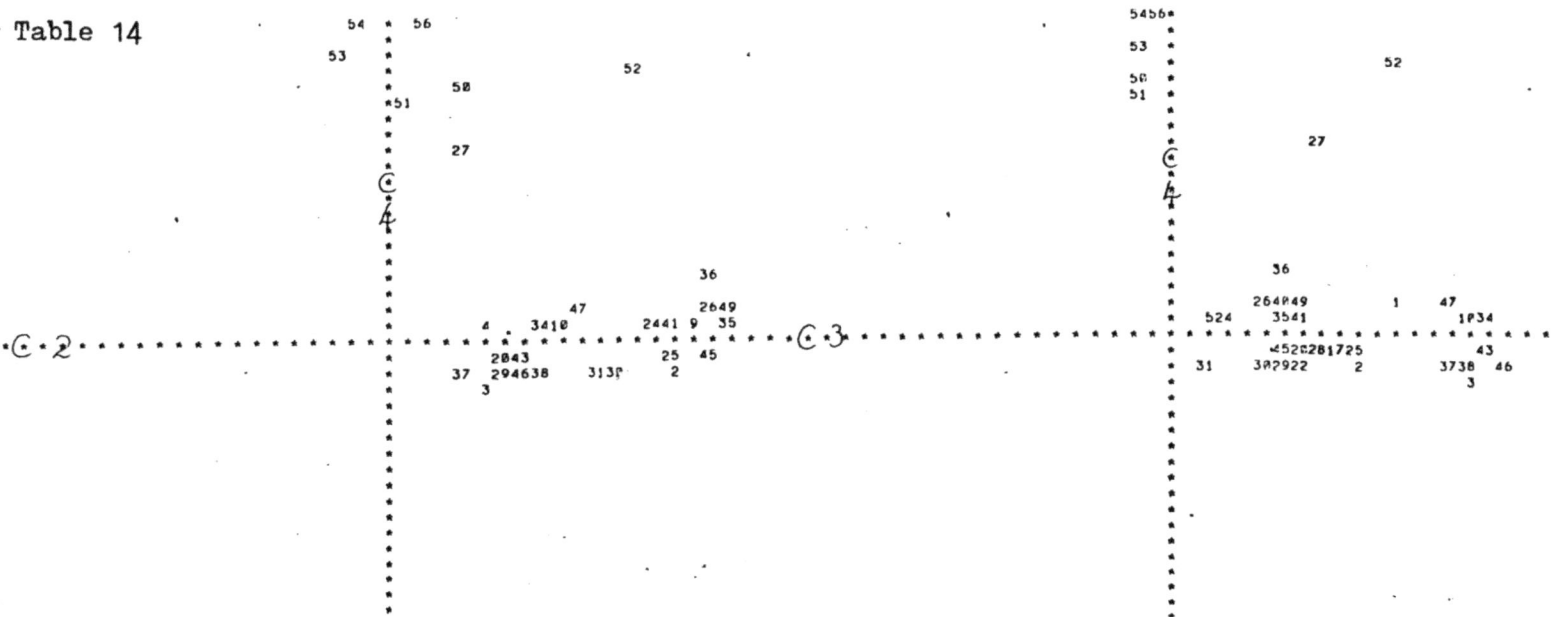

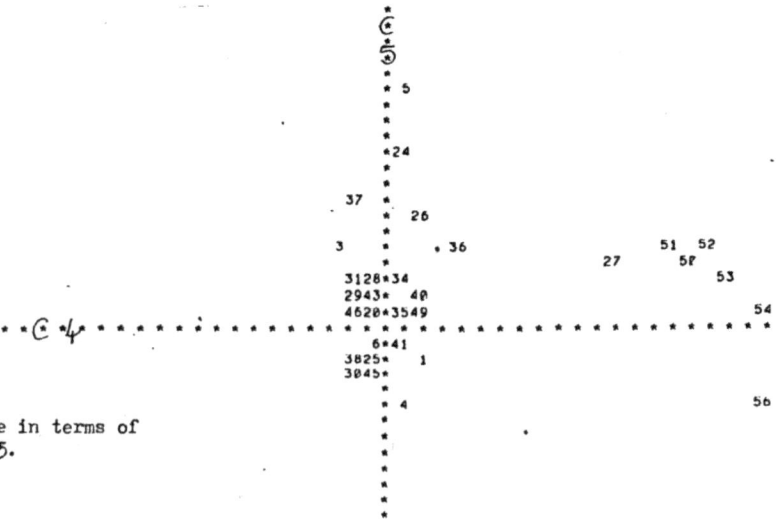

La Bastida skulls

Plot of variables for the Bastida assemblage in terms of their loadings on principal components 1 - 5.

Table 15

		Comp. 1	Comp.2	Comp.3	Comp.4	Comp.5	Comp.6	Comp.7
		57.6%	15.0%	5.8%	3.9%	3.7%	2.8%	2.0%
1	g-op	0,35117	0,76789	0,19136	0,26658	-0,07153	0,19768	-0,00680
2	eu-eu	0,36062	0,80188	0,20808	0,22224	-0,04091	0,05218	0,09217
3	ft-ft	0,49011	0,59901	0,13123	0,10985	-0,23043	0,38441	0,10325
4	co-co	0,40450	0,58677	0,16371	0,15382	-0,23511	0,18222	0,14148
5	zy-zy	0,19328	0,11535	0,60980	0,36486	0,27528	0,05991	0,54245
6	ast-ast	0,27962	0,73978	0,26120	0,38663	0,00512	0,15608	-0,10609
7	ms-ms	0,16080	0,68230	0,37074	0,46248	0,03555	0,17787	-0,13065
8	au-au	0,15778	0,67903	0,36506	0,47068	0,02295	0,17589	-0,12918
9	ba-b	0,24697	0,37880	0,69651	0,48202	-0,01971	0,01853	-0,12802
10	po-b H	0,12669	0,82553	0,18013	0,33396	-0,09644	0,09068	0,04965
11	n-pr	0,75433	0,52124	0,27427	0,20438	-0,07696	0,13219	-0,02389
12	ba-pr	0,11720	0,29666	0,87120	0,10704	0.16422	0,07166	0,26495
13	n-ns	0,75803	0,51419	0,27468	0,21505	-0,07819	0,13204	-0,03317
14	NB	0,82420	0,29921	0,09323	0,37881	-0,01787	0,14560	0,04517
15	mf-ek	0,76180	0,51980	0,27584	0,16932	-0,06912	0,14212	-0,00380
16	OH	0,77016	0,52438	0,23521	0,18402	-0,06426	0,13801	0,01483
17	mf-mf	0,81923	0,15557	0,11288	0,38965	0,00557	0,19302	0,06831
18	n-ba	0,11589	0,29539	0,87183	0,10632	0,16877	0,07636	0,26553
19	pr-alv	0,70793	0,48089	0,26640	0,06499	0,01156	0,15597	0,26265
20	ekm-ekm	0,81877	0,32467	0,04693	0,38033	0,00258	0,14589	0,08176
21	ol-sta	0,62124	0,37121	0,02841	0,36301	-0,19534	-0,06692	-0,14375
22	enm-enm	0.80080	0,30433	0,09185	0,43694	-0,00878	0,14637	0,03018
23	ba-o	0,19494	0,11557	0,60816	0,36706	0,27198	0,05571	0,54369
24	FMB	0,32956	0,34106	0,22633	0,81973	0,16320	0,07061	0,04854
25	g-op-g*	0,36212	0,79836	0,22435	0,23348	-0,04106	0,05097	0,07627
26	po-b-po*	0,32170	0,58765	0,40030	0,51032	0,07780	0,05086	-0,09963
27	n-gn	0,21683	0,22984	0,38612	0,49417	0,38760	0,12703	0,52162
28	pr-M3	0,79149	0,37879	-0,02301	0,16069	0,03734	0,14525	0,38383
29	MM	0,60536	0,65571	0,24161	0,20206	-0,05293	0,07006	-0,06536
30	ba-sphba	0,16656	0,34112	0,84314	0,27840	0,03672	0,05763	-0,16642
31	OPBB	0,16934	0,33041	0,85560	0,28287	0,07057	0,06705	-0,08955
32	n-o	0,29046	0,29932	0,18550	0,69518	0,26493	0,08384	0,40815
33	n-b	0,39812	0,53382	0,13787	0,14297	-0,25677	0,63997	0,07488
34	b-l	0,15206	0,89305	0,13918	0,24483	-0,11542	0,08177	0,12401
35	l-i	0,24612	0,82214	0,21464	0,17644	-0,06177	0,07243	0,09053
36	i-o	0,33944	0,33604	0,18904	0,83806	0,09695	0,03717	-0,00393
37	g-n	0,44678	0,44255	0,16971	0,16021	-0,21700	0,63860	-0,00567
38	g-b	0,39689	0,53825	0,12661	0,14321	-0,25477	0,63782	0,07817
39	g-l	0,31302	0,80815	0,24268	0,26734	-0,02380	0,14239	-0,01782
40	g-i	0,35951	0,83850	0,16851	0,19434	-0,09514	0,19467	0,04895
41	g-o	0,29136	0,29927	0,18350	0,69682	0,26150	0,08182	0,40646
42	n-o*	0,33101	0,33860	0,23537	0,81880	0,16163	0,06630	0,05861
43	n-b*	0,23924	0,66259	0,11548	0,16939	-0,22357	0,56920	0,08447
44	b-l*	0,31991	0,83486	0,11265	0,16912	-0,15148	0,11214	0,13969
45	l-o*	0,32990	0,33812	0,24041	0,81571	0,16773	0,06871	0,06638
46	g-b*	0,39192	0.53888	0,11601	0,12647	-0,25848	0,64273	0,08190
47	g-l*	0,38189	0,83946	0,13036	0,16016	-0,09318	0,19296	0,07909
48	g-i*	0,40315	0,83389	0,13998	0,12540	-0,09718	0,18423	0,08438
49	g-o*	0,33098	0,33812	0,23767	0,81829	0,16157	0,06613	0,05873
50	kdl-kdl	-0,01555	0,01088	-0,01934	0,05787	0,83909	0,19990	-0,06576
51	go-go	-0,02213	-0,07007	0,07242	0,10330	0,87480	-0,01170	0,03177
52	ML	0,04534	0,02833	0,13694	0,16661	0,86529	0,14252	0,09904
53	gn-id	-0,08410	-0,19956	0,08937	0,07919	0,77268	-0,32974	0,06463
54	MRH	-0,03320	-0,10638	0,10989	0,09698	0,85304	-0,12071	0,06418
55	MRB	-0,11974	-0,23497	0,05753	0,09496	0,77897	-0,36127	0,06085
56	MA	-0,10490	-0,20526	0,03781	0.06602	0.84393	-0,31514	0,02354

Rotated principal component matrix (varimax rotation) for Cova de Beni Sid skulls.

Loadings on the first 7 components (i.e. those which severally account for at least 2% of the variance) are given and the percentage of the variance accounted for by each component is shown at the head of each column. The numbers 1-56 beside the variables is their key for the graphical representations of the components (Beni Sid principal components graphs 1-10).

Component 1 receives heavy loadings from measurements on the upper face.

Component 2 receives heavy loadings from the parietal, squamous occipital and temporal bones in both sagittal and coronal planes and also from the height of the zygomatic process of the maxilla.

Component 3 receives heavy loadings from the bizygomatic breadth and from the pars basilaris of the occiput and the projections from it in the sagittal plane of the bregma, nasion, prosthion and opisthion.

Component 4 receives heavy loadings from the squamous occiput mainly in the sagittal plane (although the breadth of the foramen magnum loads on this factor also) and sagittal projections on the occiput of the frontal bone.

Component 5 reflects mandibular morphology.

Component 6 appears to reflect the frontal bone in the sagittal plane.

Component 7 receives weak loadings from the bizygomatic breadth, the length of the foramen magnum and total facial height.

Plots for Table 15

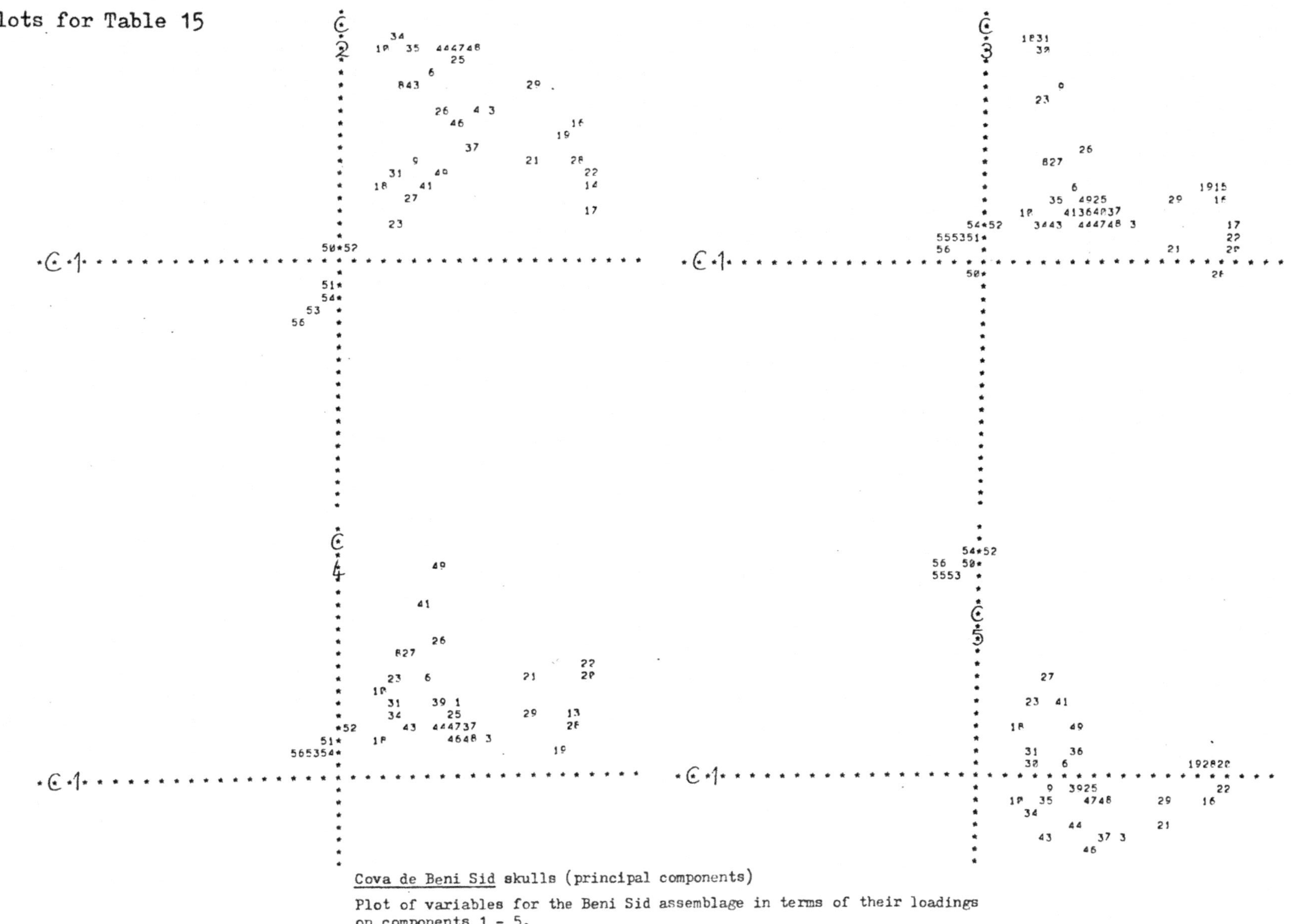

Cova de Beni Sid skulls (principal components)

Plot of variables for the Beni Sid assemblage in terms of their loadings on components 1 - 5.

Plots for Table 15

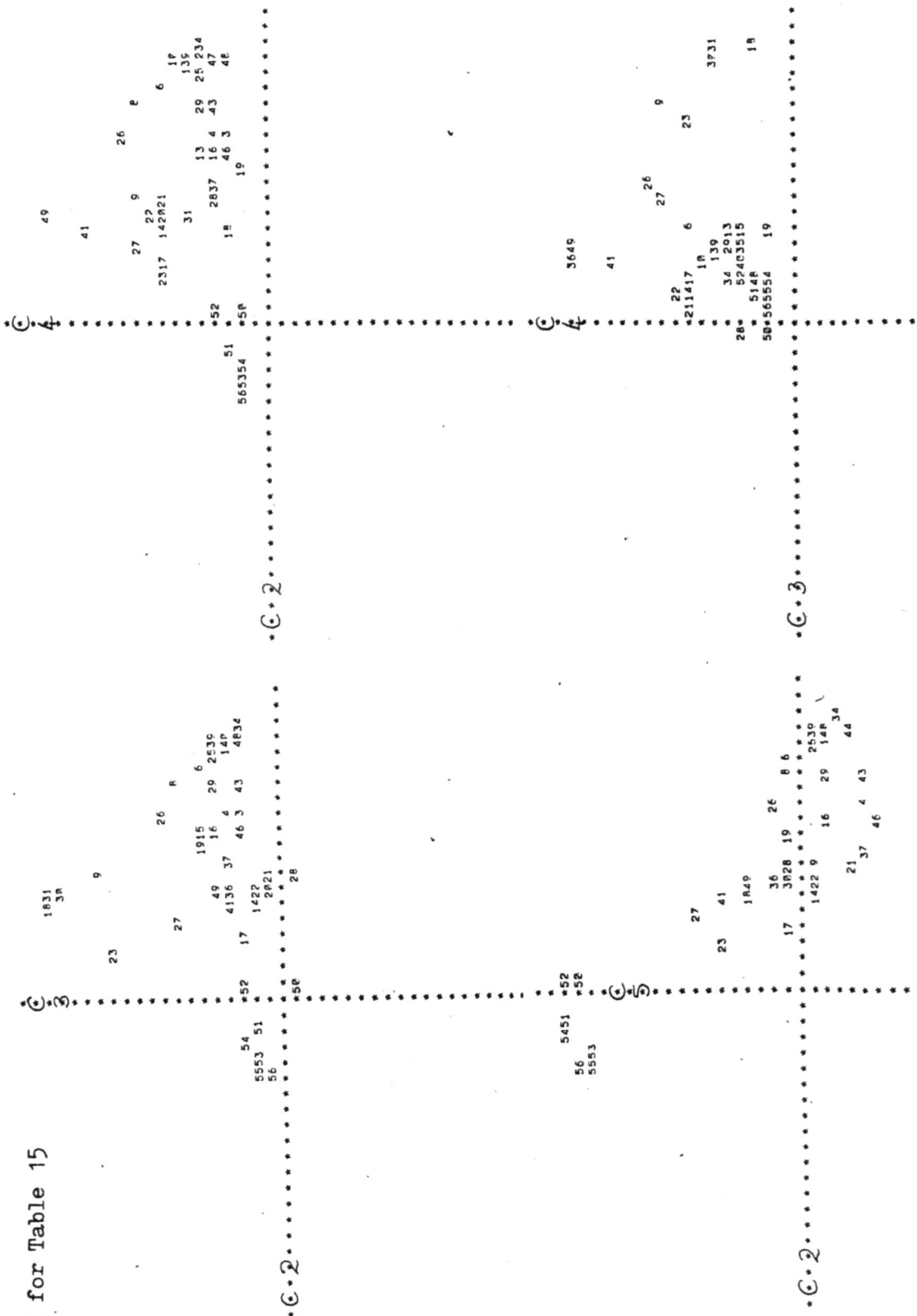

<u>Cova de Beni Sid</u> skulls (principal components)

Plot of variables for the Beni Sid assemblage in terms of their loadings on components 1 - 5.

Table 16

		Comp.1 40.3%	Comp.2 19.8%	Comp.3 11.1%	Comp.4 9.1%	Comp.5 7.6%	Comp.6 6.3%	Comp.7 4.7%	Comp.8 3.7%	Comp.9 2.9%
1	g-op	0.10064	0.82195	0.18141	0.14044	-0.15927	-0.04675	-0.06675	0.26221	0.09794
2	eu-eu	0.22173	0.75532	-0.02277	-0.21075	0.12725	0.19237	0.38685	-0.16669	0.11243
3	ft-ft	0.20217	0.87339	0.21660	-0.17525	0.14106	0.06914	0.19938	0.07339	0.00467
4	co-co	0.33693	0.70031	0.15952	-0.28494	0.50425	-0.03662	0.06326	0.10527	0.03490
5	zy-zy	0.08475	0.01741	-0.18594	0.15758	0.24122	0.00284	0.28537	0.11979	0.14052
6	ast-ast	0.21220	0.75322	0.07941	0.49868	-0.08650	0.04361	-0.02966	-0.23823	0.17681
7	ms-ms	0.10712	0.19310	0.13095	0.05087	0.95634	0.08902	0.06403	0.11045	-0.06556
8	au-au	0.21896	0.42375	0.18335	-0.06171	0.73115	0.05279	-0.01124	0.32732	-0.01465
9	ba-b	0.78062	0.38835	-0.05443	0.29648	0.02725	-0.32297	0.07598	0.06829	0.11122
10	po-b H	0.33340	-0.10913	0.08258	0.37539	0.70317	0.02557	-0.07991	0.25925	0.03566
11	n-pr	0.79137	0.17202	-0.03903	0.00976	0.20603	-0.34169	0.16710	0.22997	-0.01932
12	ba-pr	0.55299	0.47853	-0.05233	0.42478	0.10369	-0.23758	0.24082	0.34300	0.00802
13	n-ns	0.78182	0.08281	-0.02417	-0.04628	0.23994	-0.29507	0.17886	0.26285	-0.00832
14	NB	0.85374	0.12071	0.01268	0.17206	0.13280	-0.19383	0.08847	0.14830	0.03188
15	mf-ek	0.75946	0.05649	-0.06697	-0.00320	0.22925	-0.11865	-0.27774	0.35365	-0.03574
16	OH	0.47897	0.12293	-0.17210	0.06479	0.31507	0.09343	-0.08631	0.78674	0.04298
17	mf-mf	0.54446	0.26926	-0.13863	0.07220	0.32636	-0.06004	-0.04620	0.70381	0.04639
18	n-ba	0.75266	0.39906	-0.00301	0.33329	0.06637	-0.34036	0.07256	0.06662	-0.07630
19	pr-alv	0.91137	-0.06490	0.12245	-0.20575	0.10039	-0.11615	0.12773	0.23508	-0.14060
20	ekm-ekm	0.98174	-0.00649	0.11699	-0.00609	0.02218	-0.02705	0.04589	0.11407	0.02392
21	ol-sta	0.93551	0.10391	-0.20949	-0.00165	0.08686	0.19667	0.08488	-0.09985	-0.09036
22	enm-enm	0.95036	-0.01036	-0.20832	-0.01565	0.02951	0.25204	0.08787	-0.05577	-0.00990
23	ba-o	0.60235	0.10131	0.06562	0.59151	-0.13769	-0.31718	0.09005	0.16202	0.03330
24	FMB	0.68821	-0.24295	0.16379	0.59451	-0.20009	-0.15657	0.13489	-0.07159	-0.08541
25	g-op-g*	0.05810	0.84232	-0.02773	0.11753	0.40516	0.08213	0.15606	0.08343	0.03499
26	po-b-po*	0.10455	0.04610	0.12146	0.11414	0.97693	0.14416	0.00589	0.02508	-0.09122
27	n-gn	0.38957	0.13750	0.56093	0.23239	-0.01552	-0.16951	0.02006	0.19823	-0.56842
28	pr-M^3	0.91640	-0.07290	0.11882	-0.20734	0.10494	-0.11485	0.12844	0.23301	-0.10197
29	MM	0.59467	0.20402	-0.03190	0.14018	0.29985	-0.06198	-0.11469	0.68829	-0.08853
30	ba-sphba	0.86711	0.34614	0.03521	0.05383	0.06040	-0.16252	0.04687	-0.00342	0.12232
31	OPBB	0.76526	0.38738	-0.01349	0.31043	0.06470	-0.35355	0.07573	0.07471	0.07519
32	n-o	0.73557	0.64573	0.61281	0.52760	0.42013	0.43192	0.38562	0.28965	0.11987
33	n-b	0.43910	-0.18700	-0.33270	0.33452	0.47510	0.11297	-0.03130	0.52598	-0.09446
34	b-l	0.22034	0.55901	0.29473	-0.22216	-0.15510	0.23807	-0.13529	0.48642	0.11023
35	l-i	0.10692	0.55038	0.04730	0.35488	-0.16656	0.15832	-0.13923	0.11194	0.68680
36	i-o	0.30959	0.07683	0.40334	0.67762	0.06229	0.16222	0.12511	0.27115	0.38291
37	g-n	0.24844	0.33141	0.50975	0.01417	-0.41401	0.67273	0.01906	-0.43979	-0.15584
38	g-b	0.25213	0.02212	0.13632	-0.04602	0.05392	-0.00909	0.98462	-0.09730	-0.00286
39	g-l	0.29663	0.12419	0.17617	-0.05358	-0.04126	-0.07693	0.94713	-0.01732	-0.01702
40	g-i	0.14292	0.57730	0.17802	0.15296	-0.18926	0.00232	0.38199	0.02868	0.64333
41	g-o	0.73557	0.64573	0.61281	0.52760	0.42013	0.43192	0.38562	0.28965	0.11987
42	n-o*	0.03086	0.04606	0.22799	0.97310	0.11297	0.04663	-0.10628	-0.00215	0.01851
43	n-b*	-0.41609	0.25035	0.09269	-0.02044	0.15370	1.01217	-0.07780	-0.03194	0.05577
44	b-l*	-0.02867	0.77481	0.29345	0.07892	0.07723	0.08677	-0.18046	0.02438	-0.13937
45	l-o*	0.06475	0.04921	0.14743	0.98413	0.15459	0.01166	-0.07226	0.00312	0.02883
46	g-b*	-0.30971	0.11384	-0.12970	0.00332	0.40560	0.94652	-0.06038	0.20096	0.14995
47	g-l*	-0.20748	0.68538	0.13730	0.04759	0.23300	0.44192	-0.22081	0.13497	-0.02548
48	g-i*	-0.08226	0.21415	0.05668	0.20415	-0.06251	-0.11556	0.67806	-0.10999	0.55962
49	g-o*	0.05181	-0.09414	0.25002	0.64482	0.14164	-0.25133	0.50436	0.10103	-0.08663
50	kdl-kdl	-0.07209	0.05862	0.99320	0.07553	0.08258	0.01529	0.05396	-0.16490	0.17533
51	go-go	0.13095	0.18480	0.86534	0.15757	0.06673	-0.01345	0.02818	-0.17407	-0.41013
52	ML	0.73557	0.64573	0.61281	0.52760	0.42013	0.43192	0.38562	0.28965	0.11987
53	gn-id	0.19146	0.17776	0.84596	0.17821	0.05004	-0.08196	0.02075	-0.08081	-0.44865
54	MRH	-0.29405	0.15754	0.77918	0.21350	0.12942	0.16255	0.27919	0.27035	0.16405
55	MRB	-0.04206	0.05025	0.99800	0.08600	0.07333	-0.03309	0.04902	-0.10471	0.17357
56	MA	-0.33072	0.17060	0.73833	0.21696	0.13840	0.21954	0.30248	0.26186	0.16051

<u>Rotated principal components matrix (varimax rotation) for Cueva de las Lechuzas skulls.</u>

Loadings on the first 9 principal components (i.e. those which in each case account for at least 2% of the variance) are given and the percentage of the variance accounted for by each component is shown at the head of each column. The numbers 1-56 beside the variables is their key for the graphical presentations of the components (<u>Lechuzas</u> principal components graphs 1-10).

Component 1 receives heavy loadings from upper splanchnocranial (including maxillary and palatal), basi-occipital and foramen magnum dimensions as well as mandibular length and __ projections on the basion and opisthion.

Component 2 receives heavy loadings from the parietal and squamous occipital bones in the sagittal and coronal planes.

Component 3 principally reflects mandibular morphology.

Component 4 appears to reflect squamous occipital dimensions in the sagittal plane, especially the arcs.

Component 5 appears to reflect temporal bone dimensions in the coronal plane.

Component 6 appears to reflect frontal bone dimensions in the sagittal plane, especially the arcs.

Component 7 appears to reflect calvarial sagittal dimensions above the inion.

Component 8 receives loadings from orbital height, interorbital breadth and the height of the zygomatic process of the maxilla, as well as from the nasion-bregma distance somewhat below the 0.6 level.

Component 9 receives loadings from the squamous occiput in the sagittal plane.

Component 10 receives no loadings above the cut-off of 0.6 used for interpreting loading patterns (2.2% of total variance).

Component 11 receives no loadings above the cut-off of 0.6 used for interpreting loading patterns (2.1% of total variance).

Consequently Components 10 and 11 are not shown in the above table.

Using the fundamentally different technique of principal factoring on a reduced variable list of 13 variables chosen so as to reduce as far as possible missing value entries 4 of the maximum possible of 16 invoked factors were found to account for the totality of the variance. The variables chosen were g-op, zy-zy, ast-ast, n-b, l-i, i-o, g-o*, ba-b, ba-o, NB, CH, gn-id, kdl-kdl. The first factor seems very similar to Component 1, the second to Components 2 + 9, the third to Component 3 and the fourth to Component 4. Both OH and n-b loaded on the first factor between 0.5 and 0.6. No variables were used among the group which loaded heavily on Component 5. Perhaps Components 1 and 8 are not really independent groupings. It is unclear what significance to assign to the other calvarial Components 6 and 7 given that variables loading on them were not included in this reduced analysis.

Plots for Table 15

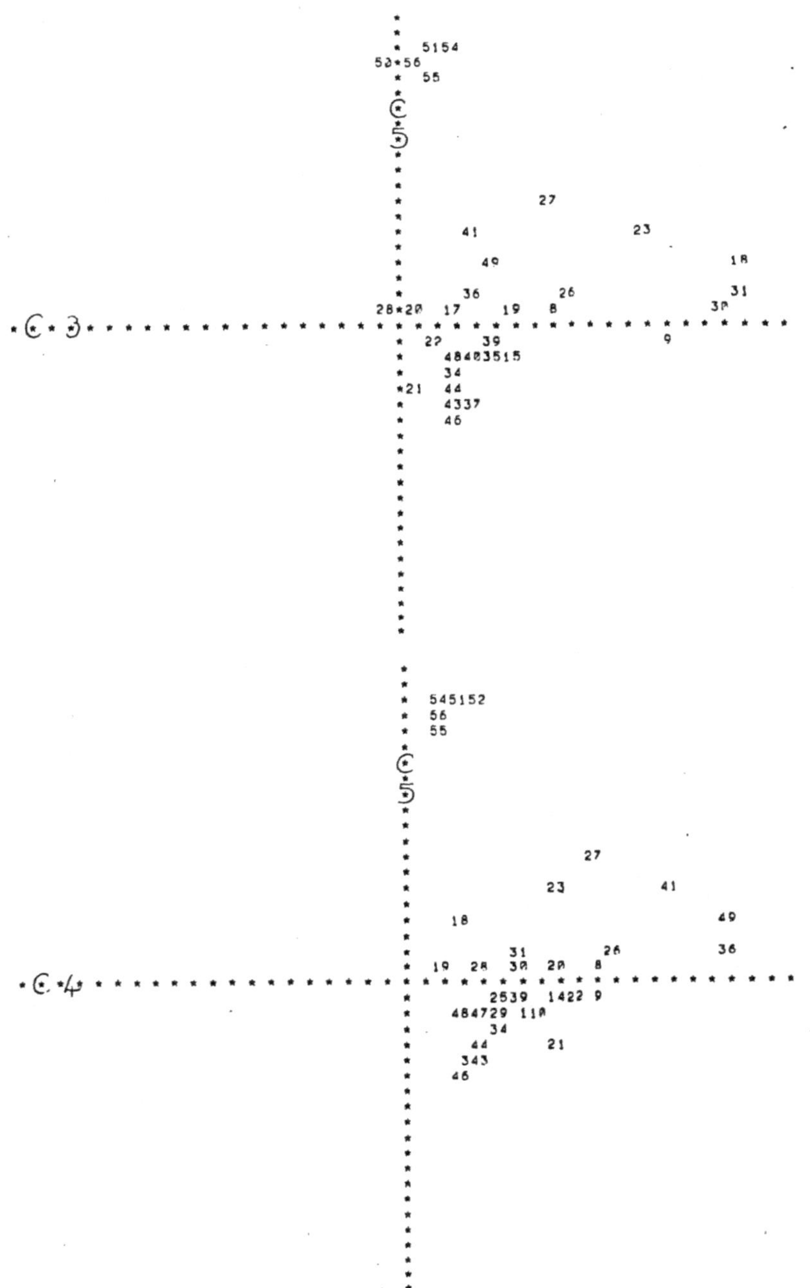

<u>Cova de Beni Sid</u> skulls (principal components)

Plot of variables for the Beni Sid assemblage in terms of their loadings on components 1 - 5.

Plots for Table 16

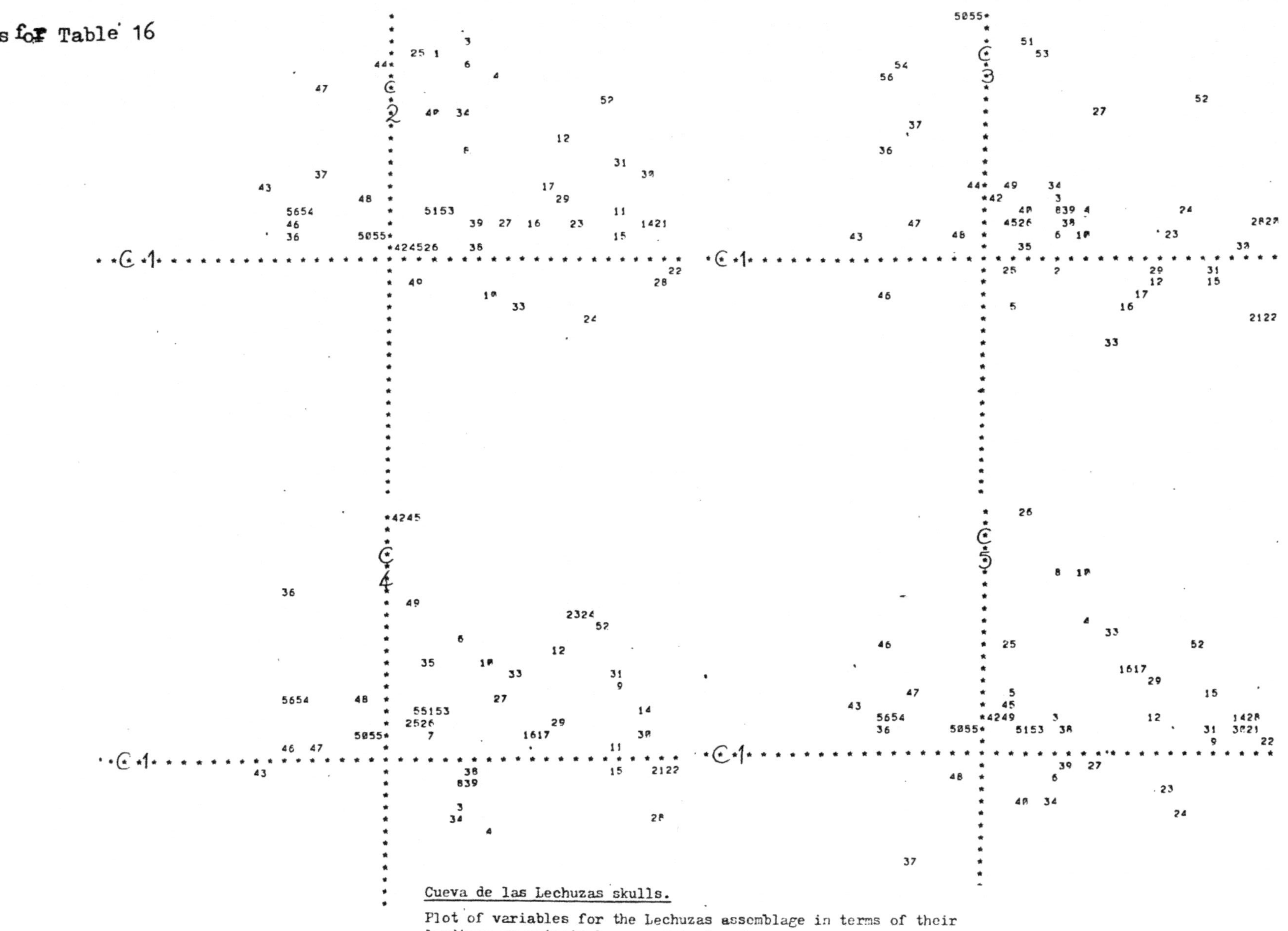

Cueva de las Lechuzas skulls.

Plot of variables for the Lechuzas assemblage in terms of their loadings on principal components 1 - 4.

Plots for Table 16

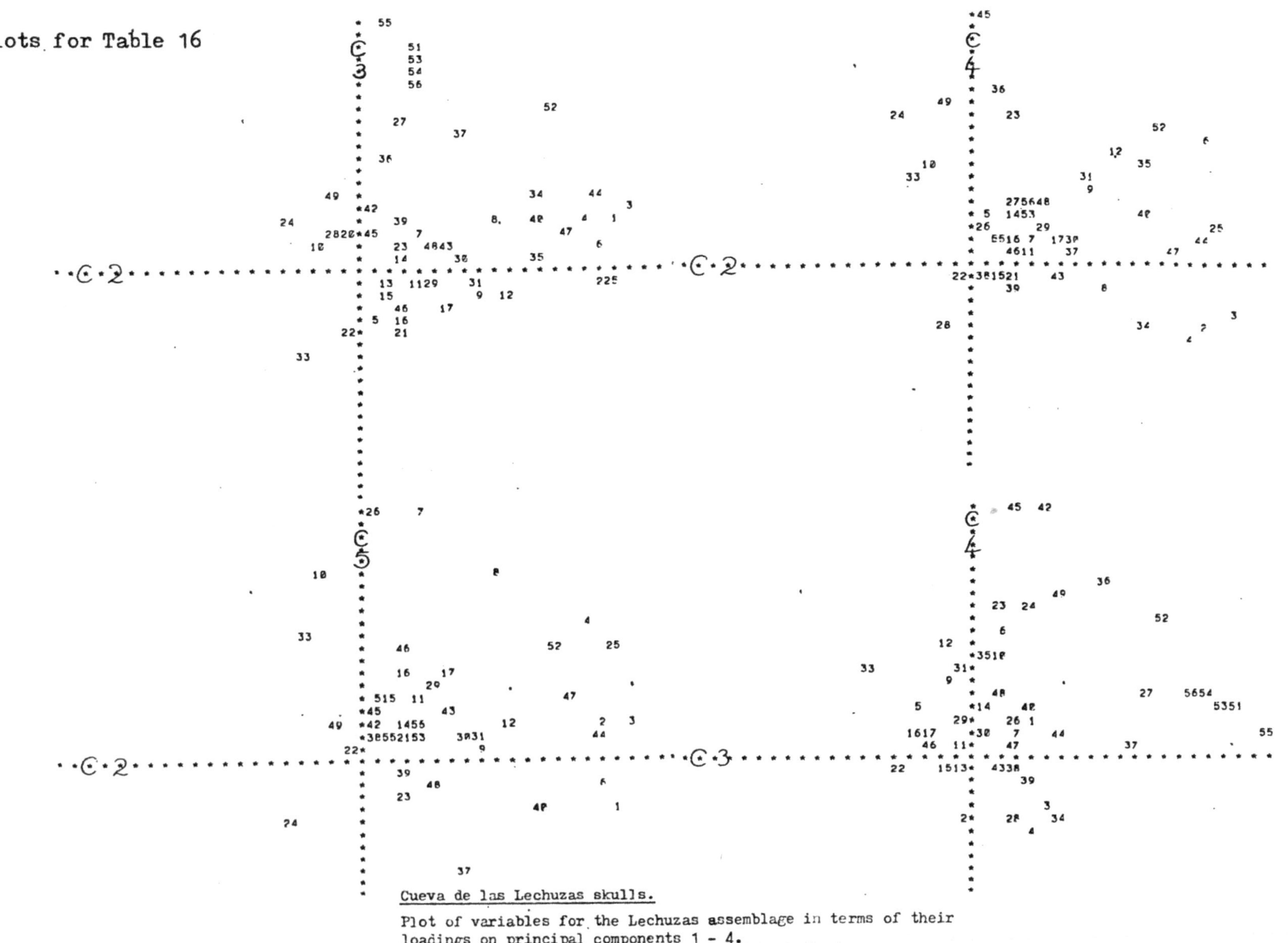

Cueva de las Lechuzas skulls.

Plot of variables for the Lechuzas assemblage in terms of their loadings on principal components 1 - 4.

Plots for Table 16

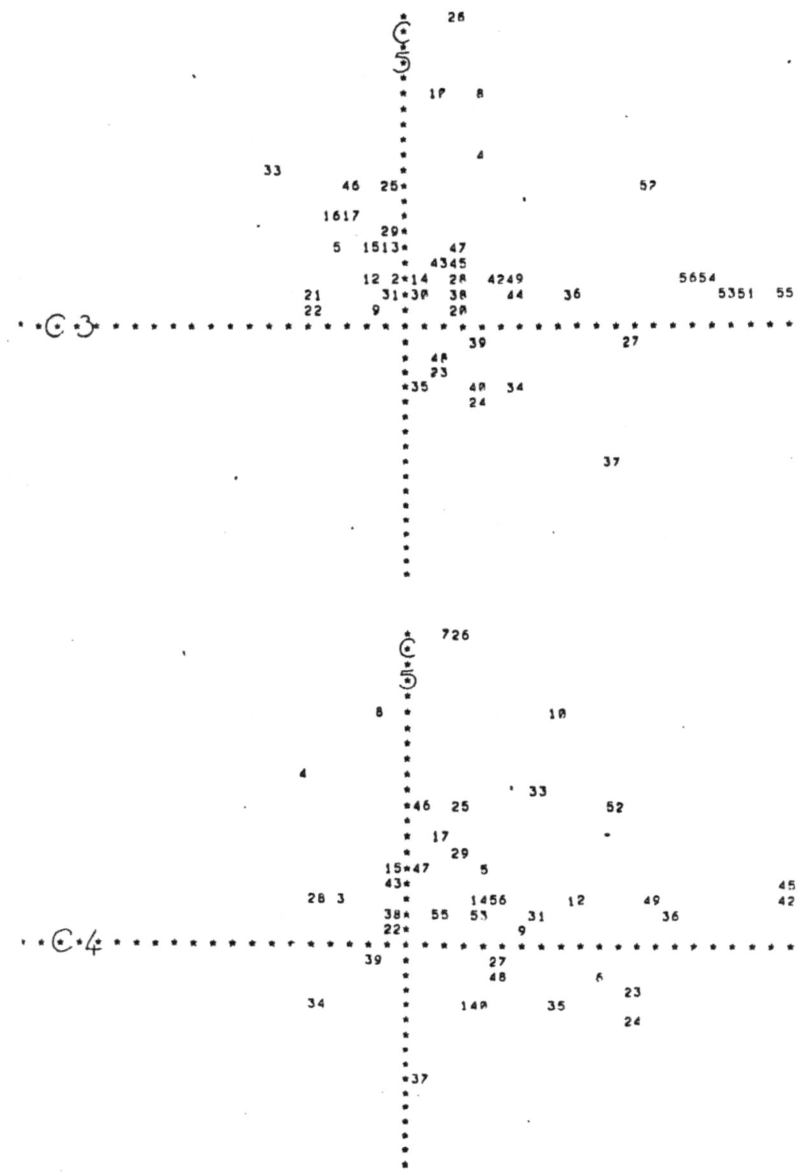

Cueva de las Lechuzas skulls.

Plot of variables for the Lechuzas assemblage in terms of their loadings on principal components 1 - 4.

Table 17

		Comp.1 58.7%	Comp.2 14.0%	Comp.3 11.1%	Comp.4 6.6%	Comp.5 3.8%	Comp.6 2.9%	Comp.7 2.4%	Comp.8 2.2%
1	g-op	0.88295	0.22545	-0.09529	0.07750	0.24329	0.19528	0.02619	-0.14505
2	eu-eu	0.96122	0.16829	-0.04851	0.07816	0.16675	0.02406	0.03969	0.05516
3	ft-ft	0.88382	0.21682	-0.03063	0.10476	0.04593	0.18941	0.03296	0.23528
4	co-co	0.83574	0.10073	0.01001	0.09351	0.16364	0.09578	0.11122	0.25328
5	zy-zy	0.16818	0.08242	0.18444	0.08412	-0.02976	0.04570	0.98748	-0.03381
6	ast-ast	0.57343	0.19918	-0.02130	0.16747	0.30542	0.58876	0.09880	0.03370
7	ms-ms	0.49076	0.14478	0.00756	0.34369	0.28569	0.70032	0.10019	0.06435
8	au-au	0.49285	0.15446	0.01014	0.32384	0.27625	0.70715	0.09352	0.05761
9	ba-b	0.20862	0.39924	-0.03336	0.82147	0.14527	0.20498	-0.04782	0.05718
10	po-b H	0.71689	0.29219	-0.05642	0.09520	0.18047	0.47196	0.03444	0.02200
11	n-pr	0.18972	0.82813	-0.01945	0.40649	0.06801	-0.02020	-0.01691	0.06627
12	ba-pr	0.14947	0.61747	0.00047	0.67068	0.03146	0.17214	0.03276	-0.02315
13	n-ns	0.19114	0.90760	-0.05417	0.27794	0.14028	0.07875	0.00218	0.07561
14	NB	0.16963	0.96023	-0.00390	0.08292	0.06570	0.06735	0.04019	0.05470
15	mf-ek	0.19730	0.36196	0.10658	0.26621	0.14152	0.34273	0.54028	0.11226
16	OH	0.18361	0.61839	0.05193	0.45868	0.18197	0.34325	0.03947	0.04023
17	mf-mf	0.14137	0.76781	0.02825	0.28326	0.13317	-0.05447	0.13212	0.30843
18	n-ba	0.19227	0.39791	-0.01063	0.80328	0.07822	0.19028	0.01209	0.07507
19	pr-alv	0.19406	0.90527	-0.05261	0.27721	0.12449	0.07933	0.01008	0.07766
20	ekm-ekm	0.17770	0.96034	-0.00762	0.09684	0.04177	0.05823	0.06421	0.03231
21	ol-sta	0.19180	0.93925	-0.03192	0.15298	0.10821	0.08742	0.00377	0.02038
22	enm-enm	0.17780	0.96215	-0.00146	0.07996	0.05546	0.04336	0.04535	0.04119
23	ba-o	0.13529	0.31441	-0.00181	0.77610	0.38719	0.00598	0.12884	0.02344
24	FMB	0.13469	0.31734	-0.00131	0.77758	0.38606	0.00744	0.12473	0.02551
25	g-op-g*	0.88816	0.21552	-0.03004	0.10091	0.05069	0.19811	0.01289	0.23581
26	po-b-po*	0.52023	0.25205	0.01974	0.30912	0.13649	0.62680	0.05965	0.14853
27	n-gn	0.69580	0.61790	0.59890	0.47143	0.39915	0.23978	0.28294	0.14108
28	pr-M3	0.19281	0.90648	-0.05438	0.26501	0.12994	0.08182	0.02117	0.07186
29	MM	0.24796	0.77482	-0.03737	0.30720	0.10657	0.18801	0.03810	-0.19398
30	ba-sphba	0.17396	0.30126	0.00099	0.81747	0.20193	0.11562	0.05096	0.09498
31	OPBB	0.17449	0.38815	-0.03473	0.67157	0.28425	0.20090	0.08125	0.10544
32	n-o	0.69580	0.61790	0.59890	0.47143	0.39915	0.23978	0.28294	0.14108
33	n-b	0.55510	0.28217	-0.02021	0.10411	0.20347	0.12887	0.04826	0.53113
34	b-l	0.87964	0.19981	-0.01894	0.15936	0.08539	0.00193	0.03715	0.18551
35	l-i	0.85729	0.09070	-0.03242	0.19934	0.16264	0.29408	-0.00453	-0.20950
36	i-o	0.33620	0.02975	0.05511	0.39283	0.79946	0.10265	0.02964	-0.12012
37	g-n	0.61235	0.19131	0.04778	0.22347	0.21187	0.10649	-0.00028	0.63298
38	g-b	0.85860	0.17685	-0.11221	0.03059	0.18564	0.00952	0.02834	0.07543
39	g-l	0.96059	0.18761	-0.05896	0.07492	0.16973	0.02649	0.02353	0.04782
40	g-i	0.93177	0.03488	-0.01957	0.24206	0.08215	0.16857	0.06652	-0.13655
41	g-o	0.33697	0.18268	-0.01103	0.21210	0.90574	0.11477	0.01744	0.04450
42	n-o*	0.28468	0.21992	0.01887	0.27675	0.74678	0.24678	-0.01902	0.33598
43	n-b*	0.63602	0.28992	0.01525	0.24890	0.15622	0.12900	0.03090	0.57753
44	b-l*	0.76452	0.25303	-0.00271	0.06214	0.28845	0.00092	0.04549	0.25656
45	l-o*	0.33943	0.16611	-0.00282	0.20368	0.90738	0.10933	-0.01045	0.08381
46	g-b*	0.92800	0.16592	-0.06988	0.15028	0.21187	0.05217	0.02907	0.06977
47	g-l*	0.95991	0.17367	-0.06152	0.08381	0.18443	0.04325	0.02707	0.04580
48	g-i*	0.87071	0.07668	-0.04103	0.22640	0.15895	0.28013	0.03401	-0.24177
49	g-o*	0.34523	0.15874	0.00200	0.19744	0.90952	0.12324	0.00132	0.05968
50	kdl-kdl	0.69580	0.61790	0.59890	0.47143	0.39915	0.23978	0.28294	0.14108
51	go-go	0.69580	0.61790	0.59890	0.47143	0.39915	0.23978	0.28294	0.14108
52	ML	0.69580	0.61789	0.59890	0.47143	0.39915	0.23978	0.28294	0.14108
53	gn-id	-0.29317	-0.20976	0.91286	0.02792	-0.10357	-0.04455	0.53950	0.17908
54	MRH	-0.31773	0.05518	1.03426	0.03359	0.01522	-0.12914	0.02036	-0.23966
55	MRB	-0.09081	-0.09719	1.08329	-0.11343	0.03664	0.14652	-0.01694	-0.06841
56	MA	-0.05329	-0.12092	1.10318	-0.08791	-0.06885	-0.08239	0.00562	0.14907

Rotated principal component matrix (varimax rotation) for Cova de les Llometes skulls.

Loadings on the first 8 components (each of which accounts for at least 2% of the total variance) are given and the percentage of the variance accounted for by each component is shown at the head of each column. The numbers 1-56 beside the variables is the key for the graphical presentations of the components (Llometes graphs 1-8).

Component 1 receives heavy loadings from the frontal, parietal and squamous occipital above the inion in both sagittal and coronal planes and also from mandibular length and breadths, as well as total facial height (but not symphysial height).

Component 2 receives heavy loadings from splanchnocranial dimensions from the bridge of the nose to the mandible.

Component 3 receives heavy loadings from all mandibular dimensions but in contrast to the preceding two components the heaviest loadings are from the symphysial height and the height and minimum breadth of the ramus. Total facial height loads fairly heavily on this component.

Component 4 receives heavy loadings from the basi-occiput and foramen magnum as well as from sagittal projections on the basion from the prosthion, nasion and bregma.

Component 5 receives loadings from i-o, g-o, l-o* and g-o* and seems to imply characteristics of the shape in the sagittal profile of the lower part of the squamous occipital bone between inion and opisthion.

Component 6 reflects coronal plane dimensions of the lower part of the temporal bone.

Component 7 receives loadings from the bizygomatic and orbital breadths and symphysial height.

Component 8 reflects sagittal plane dimensions of the frontal bone.

The fundamentally different method of principal factor analysis was undertaken using a reduced variable list of 16 variables in order to minimise missing value entries (g-op, zy-zy, ast-ast, n-b, b-l*, l-i, i-o, g-o*, ba-pr, pr-alv, ba-b, ba-o, NB, OH, gn-id, n-gn). Factor 1 in this analysis corresponds to Components 2 + 4, the second factor to Components 1 + 6, the third to Component 5 and the fourth has no loadings of 0.6 or greater.

Plots for Table 17

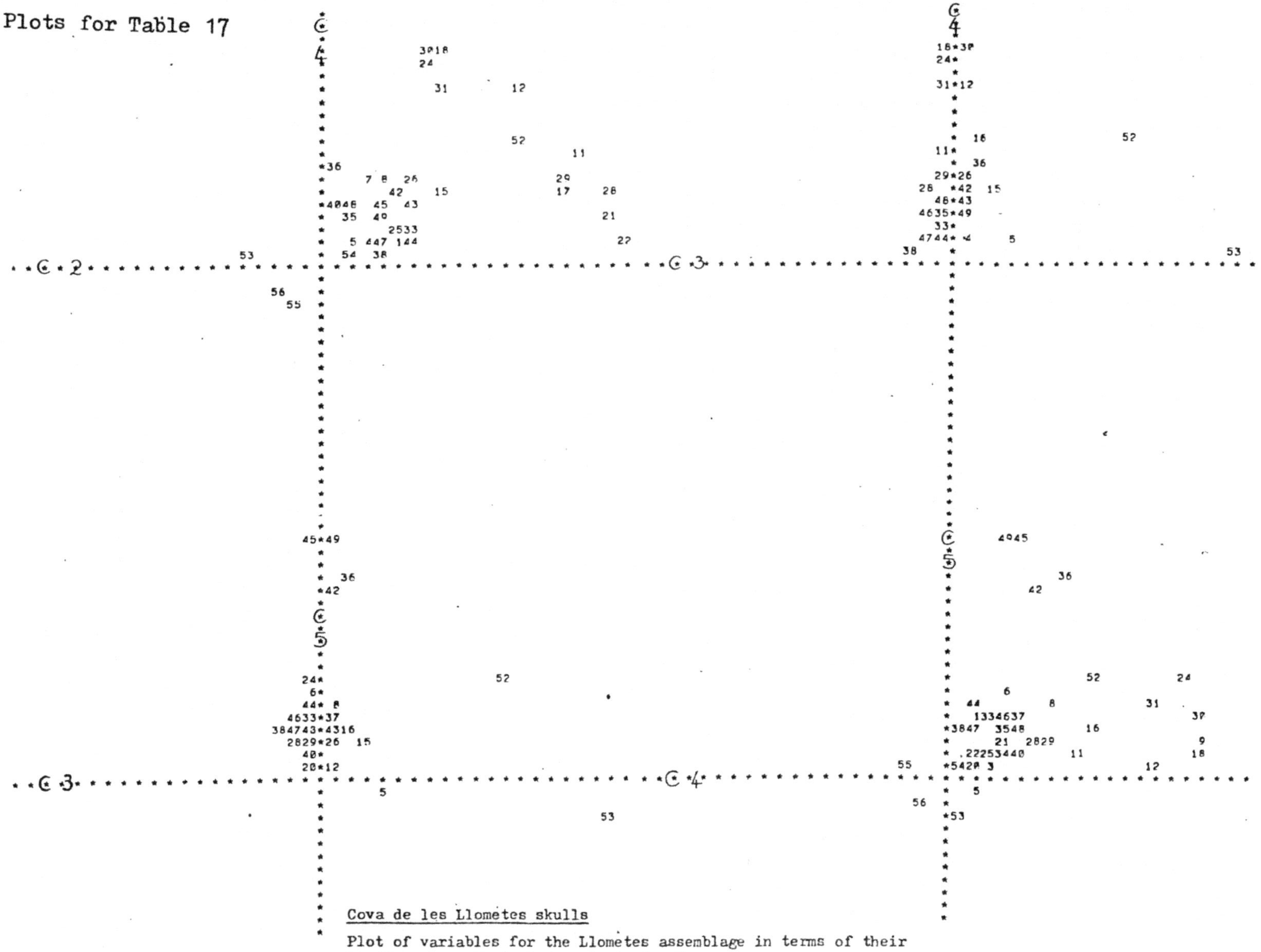

Cova de les Llometes skulls

Plot of variables for the Llometes assemblage in terms of their loadings on principal components 1 - 8.

Plots for Table 17

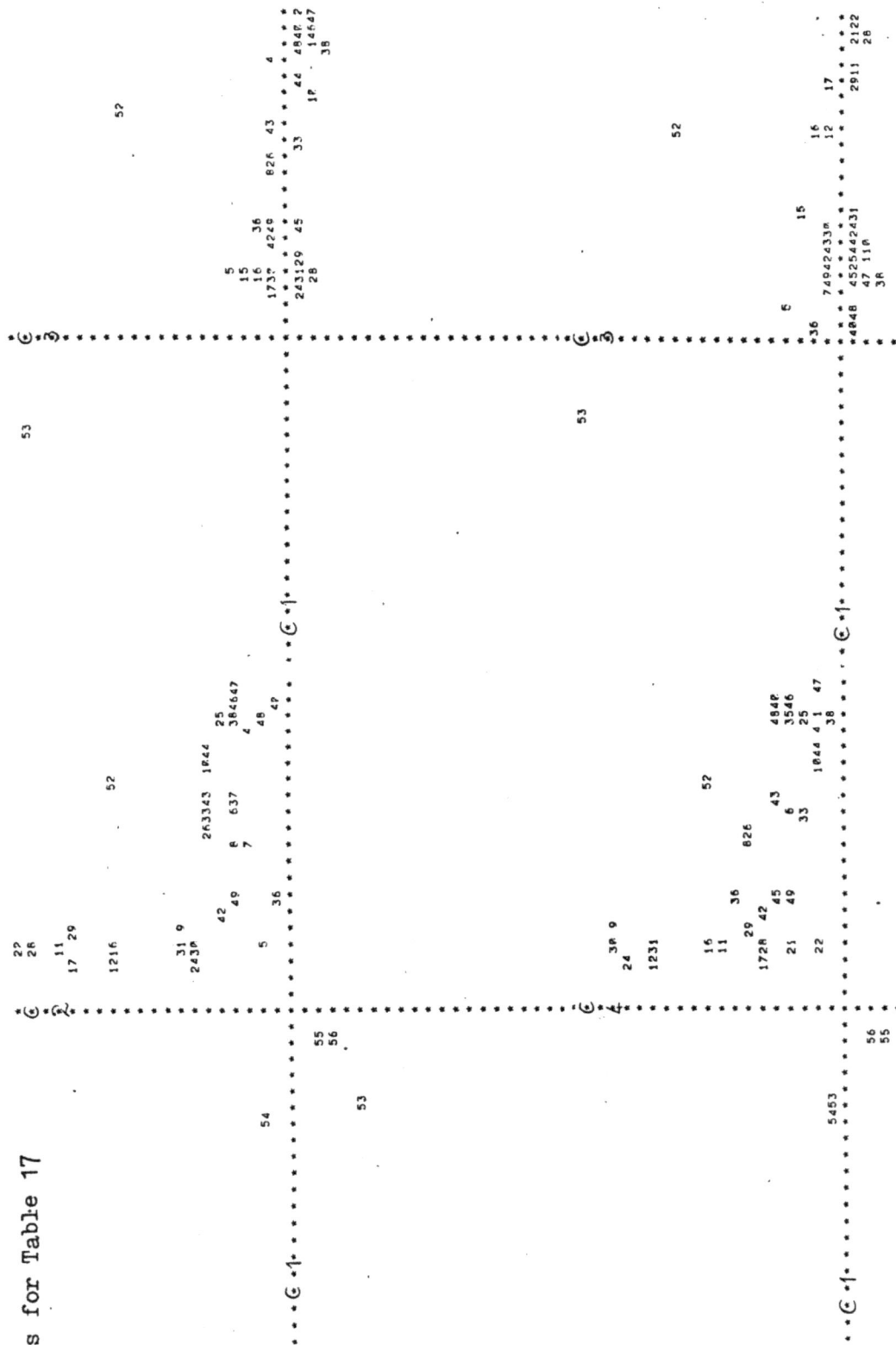

<u>Cova de les Llometes skulls</u>

Plot of variables for the Llometes assemblage in terms of their loadings on principal components 1 - 8.

Table 18

		Comp.1 70.0%	Comp.2 12.5%	Comp.3 9.4%	Comp.4 7.5%	Comp.5 3.5%	Comp.6 2.9%	Comp.7 2.3%
1	g-op	0.78501	0.22327	0.10101	0.02757	0.26109	0.03638	0.51460
2	eu-eu	0.44016	0.16092	0.61641	-0.00520	0.37082	0.06155	0.47825
3	ft-ft	0.47524	0.08361	0.60292	-0.04129	0.36909	0.50294	0.01389
4	co-co	0.42420	0.07233	0.48456	-0.04015	0.51037	0.42984	0.33373
5	zy-zy	0.28695	0.95797	0.07297	0.04493	0.06307	0.15468	0.05934
6	ast-ast	0.26621	0.34861	0.84948	0.01185	0.10256	0.22595	0.08109
7	ms-ms	0.13749	-0.12697	0.96275	0.21991	0.12068	0.20083	0.09459
8	au-au	0.55952	0.17530	0.75509	-0.02542	0.14805	0.19386	0.10044
9	ba-b	-0.01979	0.36276	0.28943	0.07445	0.10361	0.91762	0.08582
10	po-b H	0.45594	0.07493	0.61002	-0.03642	0.37591	0.51551	0.00983
11	n-pr	0.94616	0.21152	0.18652	0.02319	0.15510	0.07880	0.07082
12	ba-pr	0.28695	0.95797	0.07297	0.04493	0.06307	0.15468	0.05934
13	n-ns	0.94003	0.23570	0.18680	0.01659	0.15382	0.08009	0.06923
14	NB	0.93113	0.27218	0.17609	0.00734	0.15017	0.08566	0.07135
15	mf-ek	0.93945	0.24154	0.18043	0.01509	0.15257	0.08251	0.07148
16	OH	0.94091	0.23290	0.18616	0.01733	0.15388	0.08014	0.06967
17	mf-mf	0.95910	0.14384	0.18301	0.04383	0.15796	0.07606	0.07627
18	n-ba	0.28695	0.95797	0.07297	0.04493	0.06307	0.15468	0.05934
19	pr-alv	0.92769	0.28259	0.17902	0.00465	0.15000	0.08529	0.06951
20	ekm-ekm	0.91205	0.32971	0.16508	-0.00538	0.14498	0.09249	0.07218
21	ol-sta	0.93137	0.27119	0.17191	0.00795	0.14957	0.08697	0.07310
22	enm-enm	0.92954	0.26271	0.19401	0.01035	0.15321	0.07924	0.06457
23	ba-o	0.02159	0.45868	0.30919	0.04193	0.05114	0.85784	0.10252
24	FMB	0.47984	0.39013	0.06695	0.03099	0.45303	0.46962	-0.09428
25	g-op-g*	0.46038	0.09456	0.60614	-0.04322	0.36820	0.51465	0.01217
26	po-b-po*	0.47445	0.07843	0.59650	-0.03900	0.38769	0.50268	0.00486
27	n-gn	0.65726	0.54235	0.42597	0.49801	0.30726	0.43322	0.22477
28	pr-M³	0.92964	0.27865	0.18096	0.00559	0.15052	0.08443	0.06896
29	MM	0.92823	0.26315	0.19631	0.01060	0.15346	0.07851	0.06358
30	ba-sphba	0.65726	0.54235	0.42597	0.49801	0.30726	0.43322	0.22477
31	OPBB	0.65726	0.54235	0.42597	0.49801	0.30726	0.43322	0.22477
32	n-o	0.28695	0.95797	0.07297	0.04493	0.06307	0.15468	0.05934
33	n-b	0.77393	0.19130	0.10253	0.03952	0.26784	0.03089	0.53378
34	b-l	0.44030	0.10987	0.27124	0.02312	0.79734	0.18518	0.27730
35	l-i	0.44104	0.24835	0.37842	0.00847	0.72245	0.17492	-0.08834
36	i-o	-0.05169	0.28139	0.28469	0.10605	0.12754	0.95247	0.08003
37	g-n	0.74354	0.11624	0.06136	0.07830	0.27972	0.03001	0.61063
38	g-b	0.62096	0.11344	0.38652	-0.00372	-0.00060	0.33686	0.59230
39	g-l	0.78453	0.20942	0.10235	0.03215	0.26346	0.03423	0.52011
40	g-i	0.72203	0.11973	0.48451	-0.00875	-0.12850	0.41142	0.20058
41	g-o	0.28695	0.95797	0.07297	0.04493	0.06307	0.15468	0.05934
42	n-o*	0.28695	0.95797	0.07297	0.04493	0.06307	0.15468	0.05934
43	n-b*	0.78239	0.17689	0.10073	0.04351	0.26863	0.03050	0.53631
44	b-l*	0.45126	0.10689	0.26295	0.02184	0.79171	0.18977	0.28332
45	l-o*	0.12542	0.63574	-0.10940	0.07669	0.47781	0.62265	-0.09190
46	g-b*	0.62193	0.10416	0.38559	-0.00089	0.00021	0.33639	0.59516
47	g-l*	0.94434	0.21698	0.18897	0.02172	0.15515	0.07831	0.06949
48	g-i*	0.71517	0.16648	0.48232	-0.02169	-0.12694	0.40918	0.19550
49	g-o*	0.28695	0.95797	0.07297	0.04493	0.06307	0.15468	0.05934
50	kdl-kdl	0.65726	0.54235	0.42597	0.49801	0.30726	0.43322	0.22477
51	go-go	0.65726	0.54235	0.42597	0.49801	0.30726	0.43322	0.22477
52	ML	0.65727	0.54235	0.42597	0.49801	0.30726	0.43322	0.22477
53	gn-id	-0.05304	0.05040	-0.00497	1.09607	-0.03332	0.01419	-0.01784
54	MRH	-0.03057	0.05121	0.02629	1.04229	0.00946	0.03322	0.00989
55	MRB	0.65726	0.54235	0.42598	0.49801	0.30726	0.43322	0.22478
56	MA	-0.05302	0.05029	-0.00499	1.09676	-0.03330	0.01414	-0.01789

Rotated principal component matrix (varimax rotation) for Cova del Palanqués skulls

Loadings on the first 7 components are given and the percentage of the variance accounted for by each component is shown at the head of each column. The numbers 1-56 beside the variables is their key for the graphical presentations of the components (Palanqués graphs 1-5).

Component 1 receives heavy loadings from splanchnocranial elements together with mandibular breadth, the pars basilaris of the occiput and the sagittal dimensions of the frontal.

Component 2 receives heavy loadings from the bizygomatic breadth and the sagittal relations of the upper face vis-à-vis the foramen magnum.

Component 3 reflects calvarial breadth.

Component 4 reflects mandibular development in the sagittal plane.

Component 5 reflects the sagittal development of the parietal and squamous occiput.

Component 6 receives heavy loadings from basibregmatic distance and the lower part of the squamous occiput in the sagittal plane.

Component 7 reflects weakly the development of the frontal bone.

A principal factor analysis with iteration and varimax rotation was also performed on a reduced variable list of 16 variables for which there were few missing value entries. The method differs fundamentally from principal components analysis (see under Cova de Beni Sid for details). Of the possible 16 factors invoked only three were required to account for the totality of the variance. The first factor was similar to Component 1 above as regards the variables loading heavily on it, the second to Component 6 above, and the third to Component 3 above. Discrimination of loading patterns similar to those of the other four components of the principal components analysis seems to have been lost with the drastic reduction in the number of variables used.

Plots for Table 18

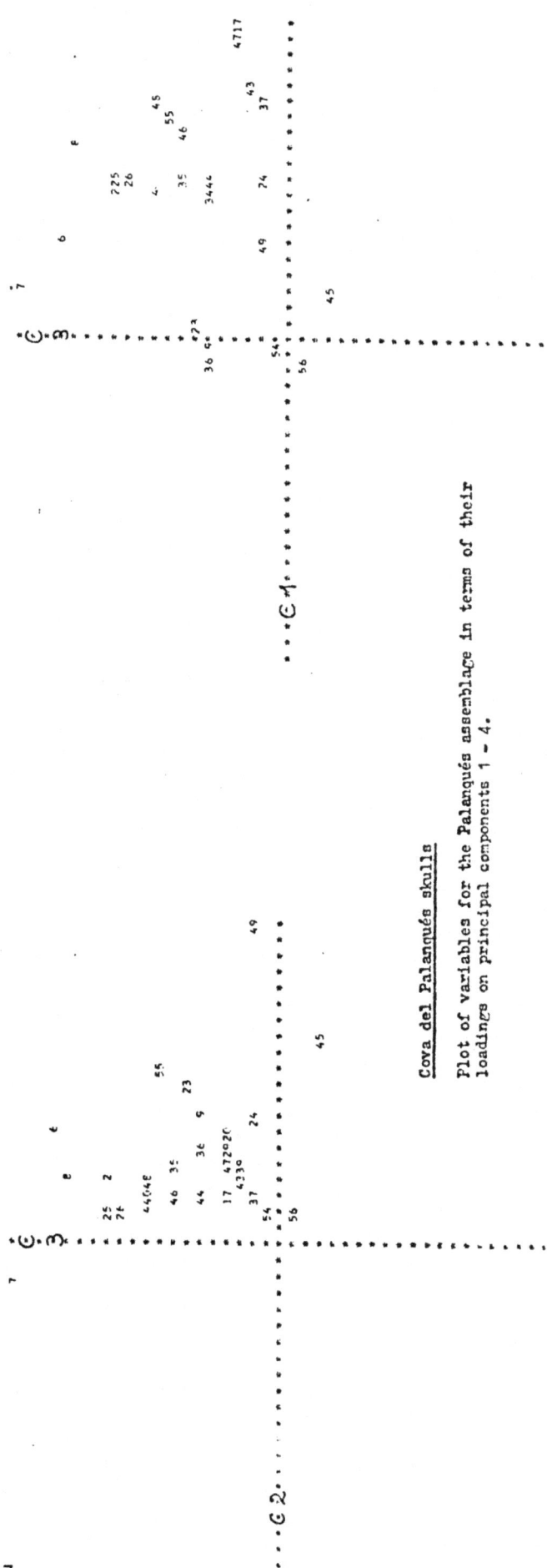

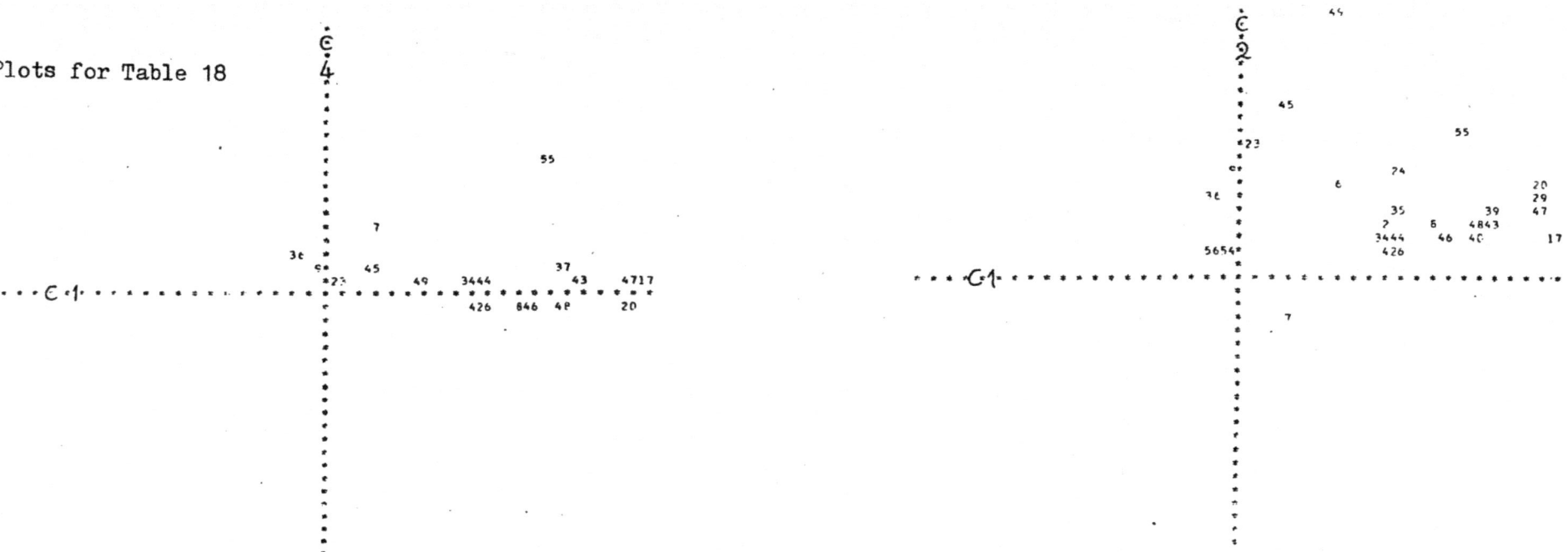

Cova del Palanqués skulls

Plot of variables for the Palanqués assemblage in terms of their loadings on principal components 1 - 4.

Plots for Table 18

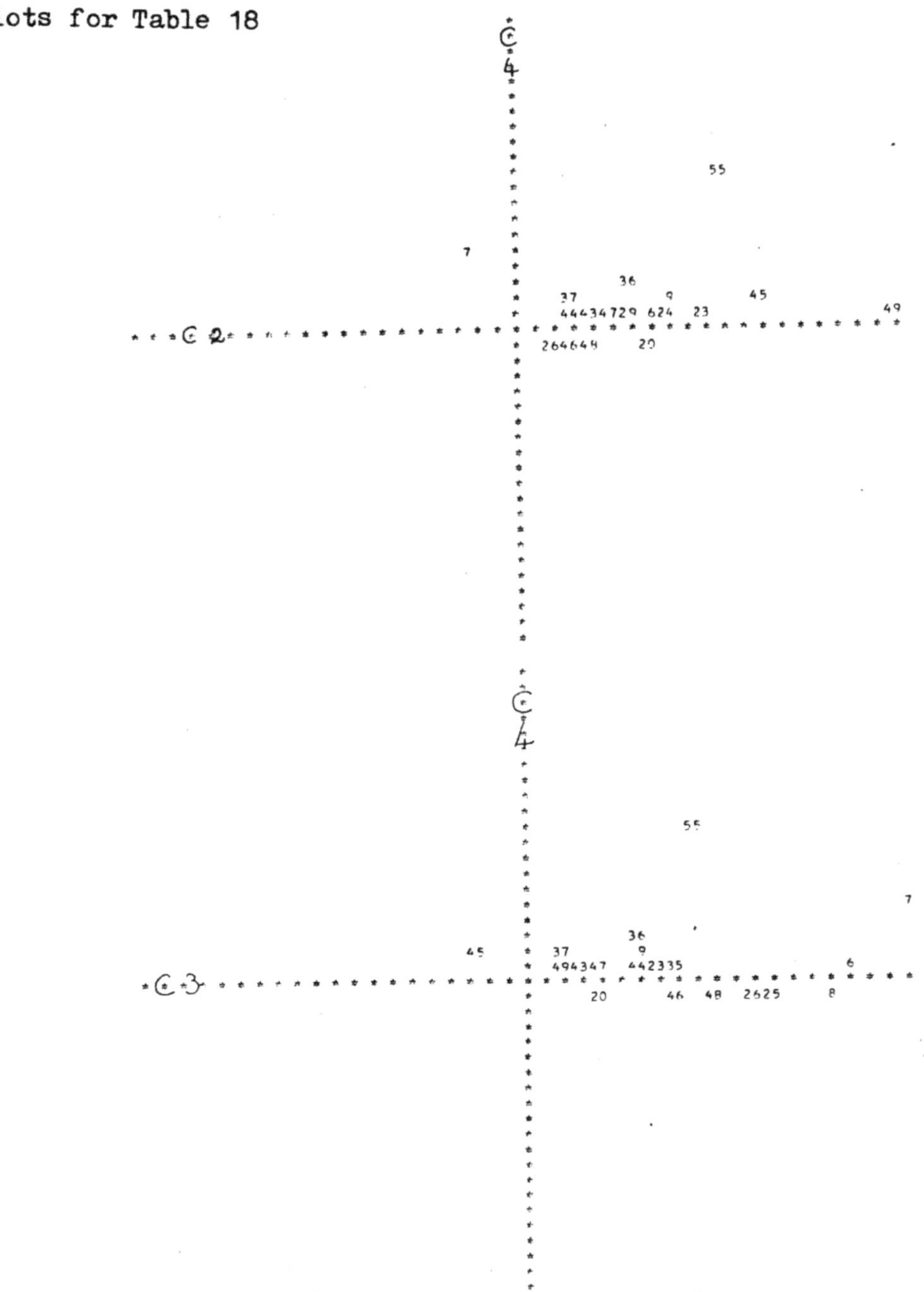

Cova del Palanqués skulls

Plot of variables for the **Palanqués** assemblage in terms of their loadings on principal components 1 - 4.

Table 19

		Comp.1 40.8%	Comp.2 13.5%	Comp.3 11.0%	Comp.4 5.8%	Comp.5 4.1%	Comp.6 3.0%	Comp.7 2.7%
1	g-op	0.87500	0.10019	0.21437	-0.01307	0.12591	0.00282	0.01230
2	eu-eu	0.66510	-0.03357	0.28917	-0.12116	0.23625	-0.00398	0.15184
3	ft-ft	0.17727	0.26570	0.18158	-0.04788	0.11088	-0.04277	0.84035
4	co-co	0.34892	0.14256	0.20556	-0.29218	0.06534	-0.02151	0.68679
5	zy-zy	0.14861	0.50277	0.31794	0.06610	0.13464	-0.28765	0.04238
6	ast-ast	0.49060	0.17784	0.40137	-0.09792	0.45816	0.06620	-0.16082
7	ms-ms	0.30779	0.33872	0.21214	-0.05745	0.73704	-0.05412	0.03695
8	au-au	0.46799	0.22794	0.39007	-0.09348	0.52947	0.06874	-0.03574
9	ba-b	0.31672	0.15999	0.66975	0.05119	0.52836	0.13511	0.13931
10	po-b H	0.81180	0.21994	0.21722	-0.06492	0.12035	0.02136	-0.05889
11	n-pr	0.07006	0.79346	0.17414	0.14083	0.12230	0.00354	0.32075
12	ba-pr	0.11497	0.49662	0.44321	0.05633	0.56249	-0.04812	0.14749
13	n-ns	0.18652	0.89429	0.09725	0.08569	0.08995	0.01932	0.14420
14	NB	0.09831	0.92099	0.02450	0.03537	0.04979	0.07017	0.00626
15	mf-ek	0.13146	0.84925	0.14704	0.04646	0.19519	0.01297	0.01231
16	OH	0.16358	0.93478	0.11254	0.05188	0.09987	0.05141	0.04760
17	mf-mf	0.21602	0.83169	0.18205	-0.00332	0.27616	-0.02260	-0.03826
18	n-ba	0.29441	0.08079	0.75159	0.08265	0.40476	0.14383	0.12884
19	pr-alv	0.17732	0.86089	0.15110	-0.04659	0.10565	0.02704	0.04841
20	ekm-ekm	0.09154	0.63509	-0.04109	0.00978	-0.05847	-0.03154	0.09967
21	ol-sta	0.04234	0.78516	0.26353	-0.01648	-0.02656	-0.15592	0.05136
22	enm-enm	0.11935	0.84623	0.13279	-0.08931	0.19790	-0.14183	-0.00386
23	ba-o	0.22692	0.17557	0.87013	0.08837	0.21944	0.08774	0.11289
24	FMB	0.17519	0.25133	0.83333	0.01694	0.20247	-0.11417	0.17857
25	g-op-g*	0.83728	0.14617	0.24468	0.04162	0.19977	-0.04104	0.00159
26	po-b-po*	0.52531	0.31534	0.37719	-0.08658	0.43527	0.09617	-0.01115
27	n-gn	0.09384	0.53220	0.19452	0.21073	-0.00651	0.12010	-0.05149
28	pr-M3	0.21152	0.89415	0.11673	-0.07095	0.13289	0.01672	-0.01513
29	MM	0.09392	0.87289	0.09772	0.06419	0.09029	0.23120	-0.03467
30	ba-sphba	0.24495	0.27641	0.41263	0.12452	0.71651	0.22252	0.09057
31	OPBB	0.24493	0.27918	0.40733	0.12040	0.72266	0.22313	0.09719
32	n-o	0.24026	0.19288	0.88839	-0.01440	0.06052	-0.11681	0.13625
33	n-b	0.61493	0.24625	0.20918	-0.13695	0.07275	-0.12973	0.19038
34	b-l	0.77037	0.05517	0.18121	-0.14583	0.05566	0.02938	-0.02603
35	l-i	0.71965	0.13221	0.30924	-0.16314	0.20014	0.05027	-0.16068
36	i-o	0.23984	0.07721	0.81159	-0.00632	0.12566	0.13699	-0.11305
37	g-n	0.63552	0.24905	0.23521	-0.11246	0.09542	-0.11463	0.13667
38	g-b	0.74979	0.03620	0.11617	-0.12821	-0.03832	0.03138	0.45857
39	g-l	0.84991	0.18038	0.17920	-0.00794	-0.00845	0.01659	0.08932
40	g-i	0.76028	0.17571	0.28390	-0.06263	0.18894	0.04514	0.05792
41	g-o	0.29064	0.11856	0.91752	0.07555	0.09335	0.11378	0.06693
42	n-o*	0.29668	0.11191	0.91618	0.07463	0.07560	0.10366	0.06100
43	n-b*	0.56506	0.30134	0.42759	-0.05935	0.09274	0.08088	0.01251
44	b-l*	0.47478	0.19830	0.41086	-0.22360	0.11154	0.11579	-0.26146
45	l-o*	0.21828	0.09901	0.89230	0.01693	0.05873	0.10538	-0.05165
46	g-b*	0.83885	0.10346	0.10531	-0.13503	0.01825	0.02784	0.30035
47	g-l*	0.90911	0.13860	0.15039	-0.05571	0.05237	0.01609	0.11785
48	g-i*	0.81709	0.16358	0.30677	-0.08131	0.21422	0.03073	-0.06433
49	g-o*	0.29589	0.11321	0.91645	0.07425	0.07769	0.10362	0.06151
50	kdl-kdl	0.06280	-0.00795	0.22700	0.31224	0.12353	0.87704	-0.03402
51	go-go	-0.21368	0.14073	0.06287	0.64775	-0.03453	0.47508	0.00699
52	ML	0.06244	-0.00165	0.23058	0.31115	0.12904	0.87300	-0.02637
53	gn-id	-0.13771	0.12227	-0.01034	0.87308	-0.06640	0.06875	-0.10145
54	MRH	-0.15804	-0.01362	0.11068	0.90146	0.07346	0.15068	-0.03724
55	MRB	-0.05070	-0.03349	0.09136	0.93114	0.07348	0.09512	-0.07794
56	MA	-0.13230	0.06310	0.02747	0.93017	-0.01407	0.07585	-0.00132

Rotated principal component matrix (varimax rotation) for Cova de la Pastora skulls.

Loadings on the first seven components (each of which accounts for at least 2% of the total variance) are given and the percentage of the variance accounted for by each component is shown at the head of each column. The numbers 1-56 beside the variables is their key for the graphical representations of the components (Pastora graphs 1-21).

Component 1 receives heavy loadings from the frontal, parietal and squamous occipital above the inion in both sagittal and coronal planes.

Component 2 receives heavy splanchnocranial loadings from from the orbits to the palate.

Component 3 receives heavy loadings from the foramen magnum and projections on it in the sagittal plane of landmarks from the glabella to the lambda.

Component 4 reflects several mandibular dimensions other than overall length and breadth

Component 5 receives heavy loadings from the basi-occiput and bimastoid breadth.

Component 6 receives heavy loadings from bicondylar breadth and mandibular length.

Component 7 receives heavy loadings from the maximum and minimum frontal breadths.

Component 8 (not illustrated in table) shows no loadings above the cut-off arbitrarily taken as 0.6 for interpreting osteometrical dimensions even though this component accounted for 2.2% of total variance.

The fundamentally different method of principal factoring was also undertaken on a reduced variable list of 22 variables chosen to minimise missing value entries (g-op, eu-eu, ft-ft, zy-zy, ast-ast, n-pr, n-b, n-b*, l-i, i-o, g-i, n-gn, g-o*, ba-pr, n-ba, ba-b, ba-o, NB, OH, gn-id, kdl-kdl, pr-alv). Of the 22 possible invoked factors only 5 were required to account for the totality of the variance. The first factor corresponds to Component 2, the second to Component 3, the third to Component 1, the fourth reflects mandibular dimensions but n-gn and kdl-kdl gave loadings of below 0.5, and the fifth seems to reflect Component 7. The Pastora skulls included several complete specimens and it seems probable that the seven Components identified represent independently assorting groups of elements in the cranial assemblage.

Plots for Table 19

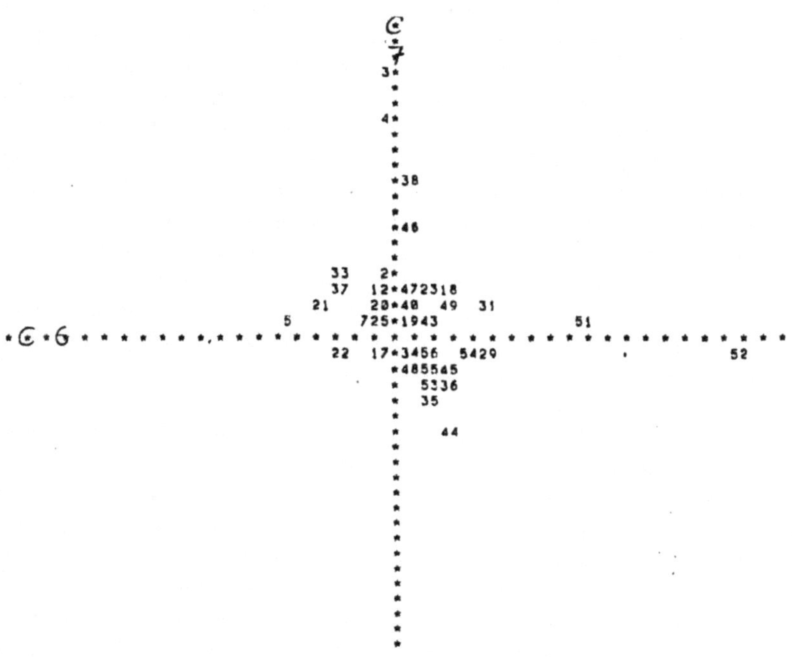

Cova de la Pastora skulls

Plot of variables for the Pastora assemblage in terms of their loadings on principal components 1 - 7.

Plots for Table 19

Cova de la Pastora skulls

Plot of variables for the Pastora assemblage in terms of their loadings on principal components 1 - 7.

Plots for Table 19

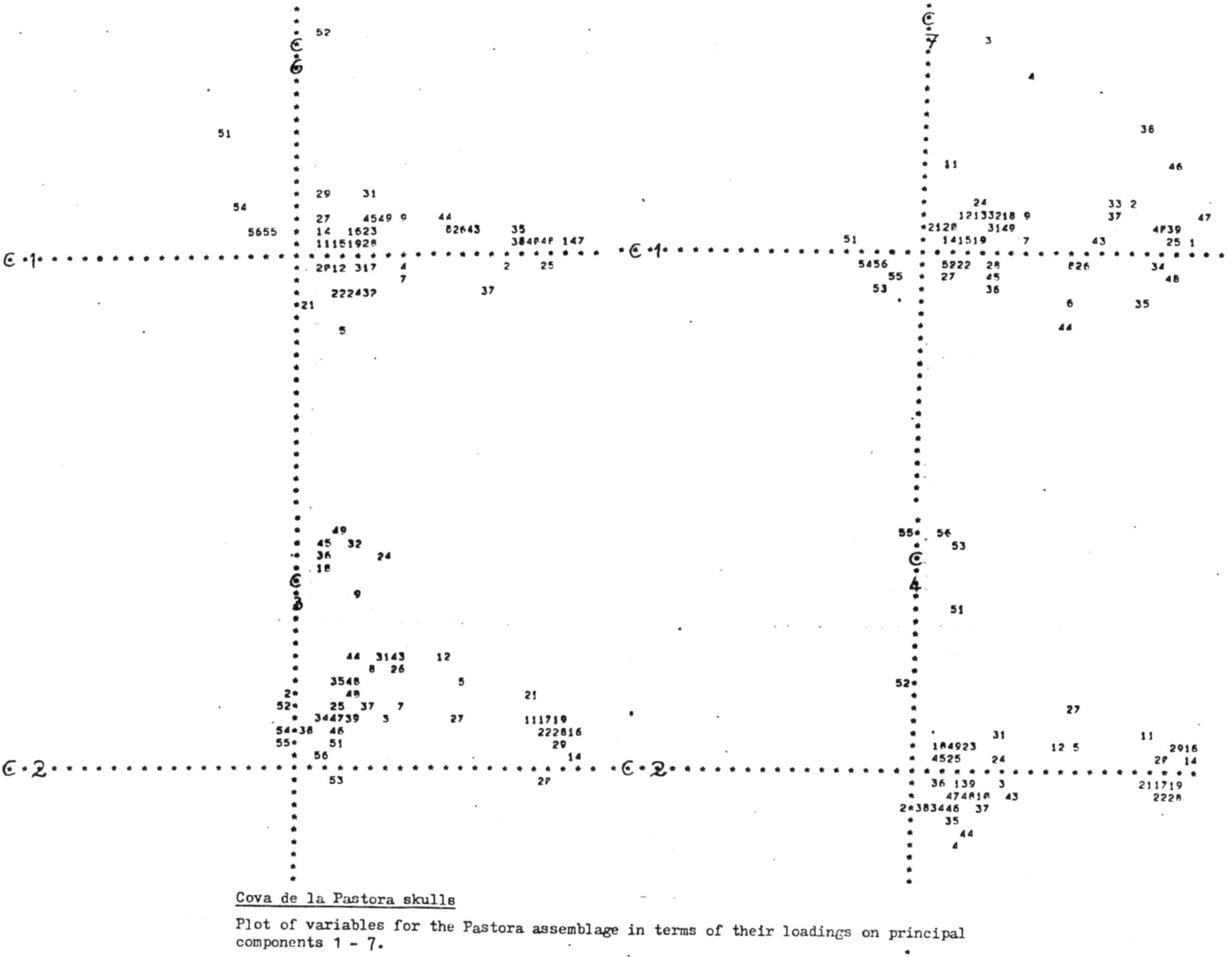

Cova de la Pastora skulls

Plot of variables for the Pastora assemblage in terms of their loadings on principal components 1 - 7.

Plots for Table 19

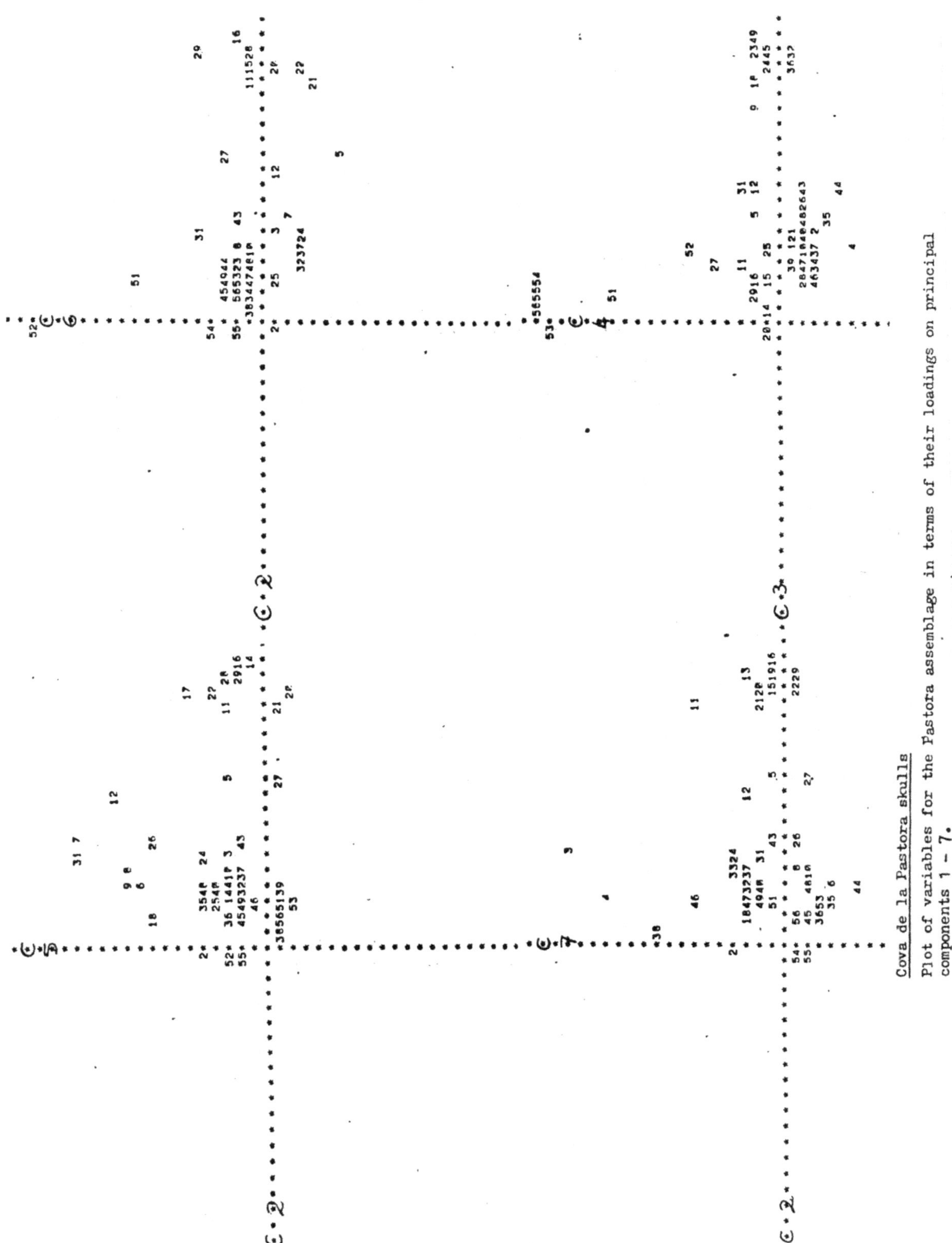

Cova de la Pastora skulls

Plot of variables for the Pastora assemblage in terms of their loadings on principal components 1 - 7.

Plots for Table 19

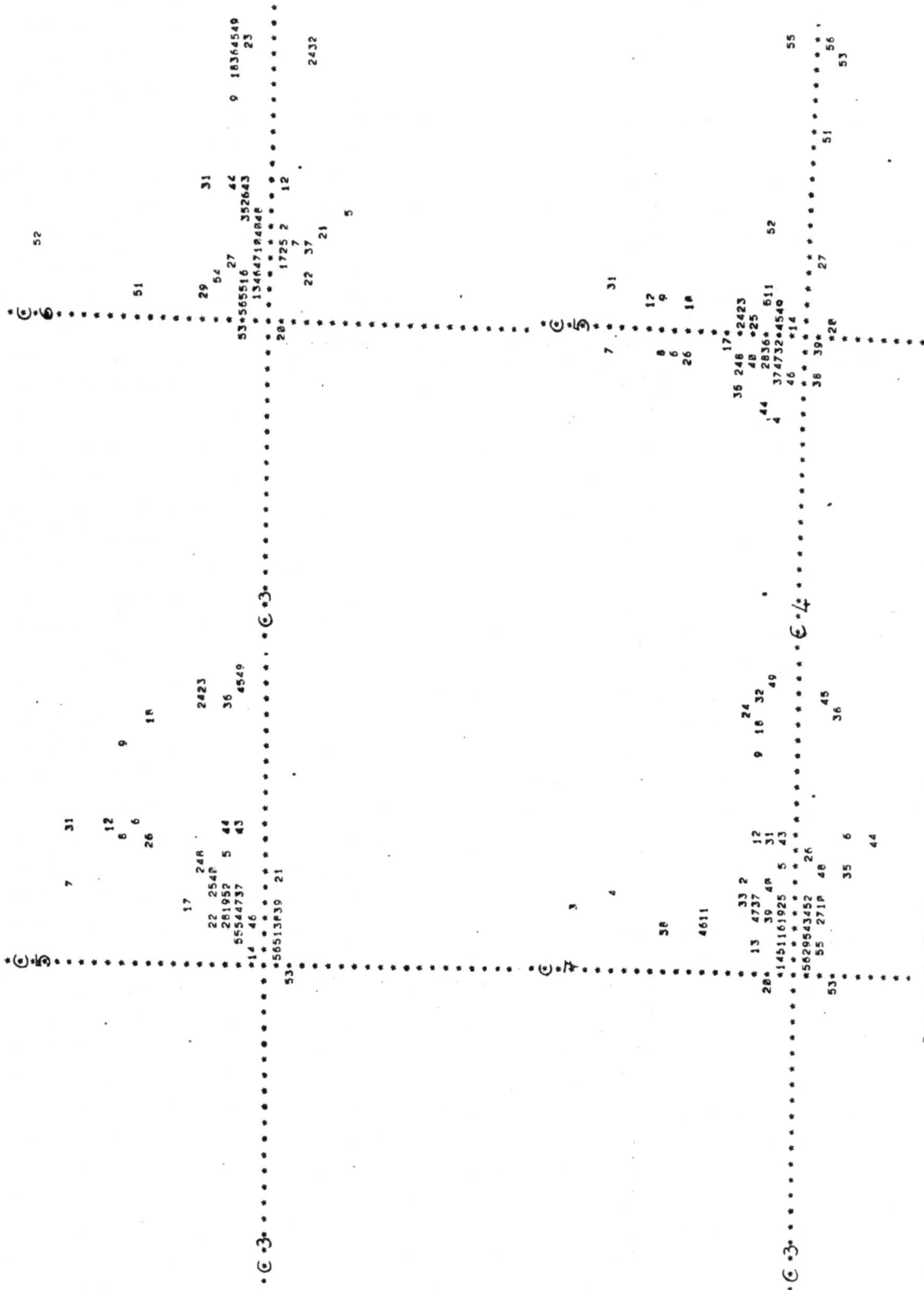

Cova de la Pastora skulls

Plot of variables for the Pastora assemblage in terms of their loadings on principal components 1 - 7.

Plots for Table 19

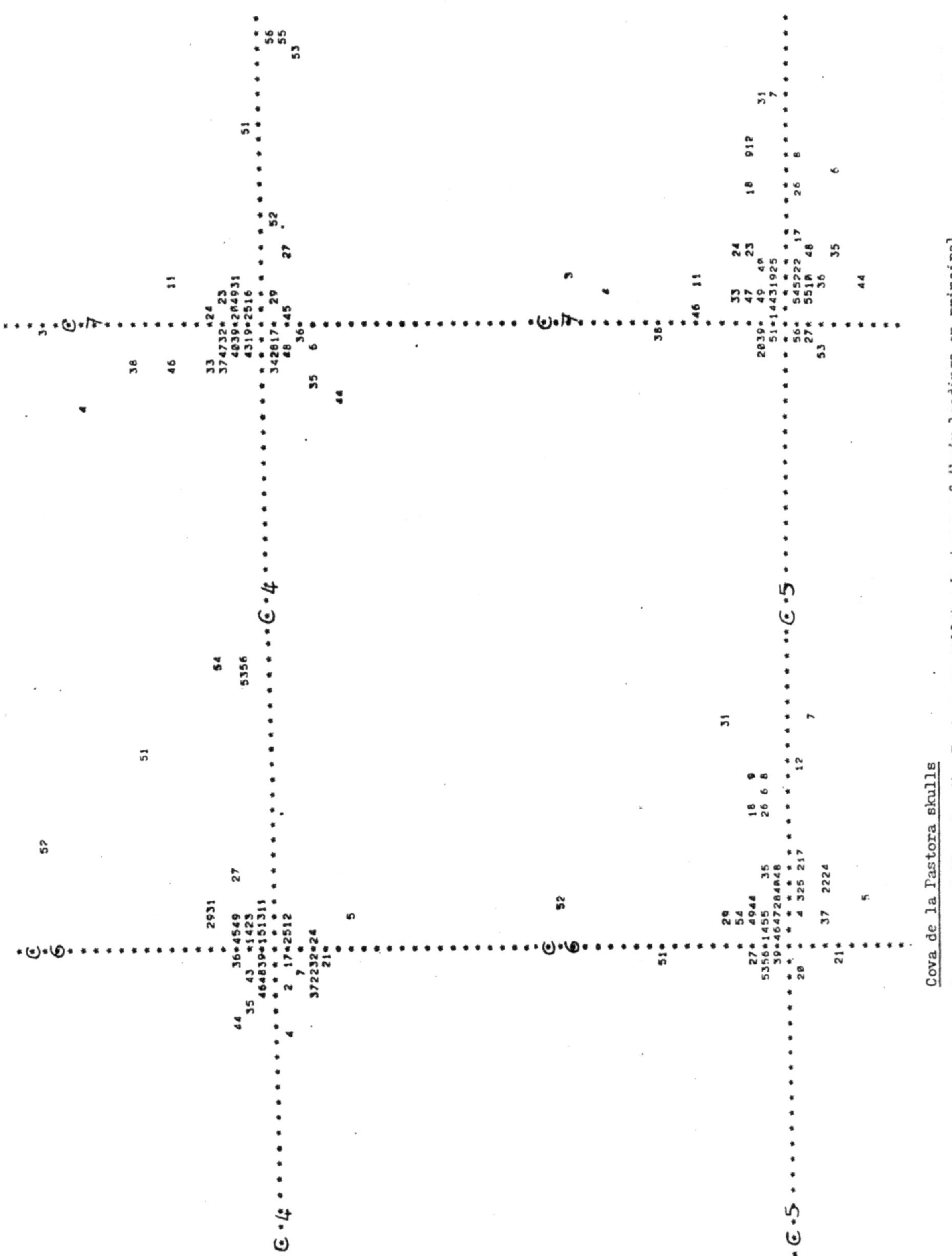

Cova de la Pastora skulls

Plot of variables for the Pastora assemblage in terms of their loadings on principal components 1 - 7.

Table 20

		Comp.1 51.1%	Comp.2 13.1%	Comp.3 10.0%	Comp.4 9.6%	Comp.5 4.2%	Comp.6 4.1%	Comp.7 2.6%	Comp.8 2.3%
1	g-op	0,67452	0,19237	0,02210	0,46205	0,36848	-0,13684	0,14431	0,05865
2	eu-eu	0,55352	0,21833	0,01543	0,50280	0,40197	-0,13662	0,18433	0,06205
3	ft-ft	0,69805	-0,02672	0,24331	0,27885	0,14026	0,05305	0,01522	-0,09469
4	oo-oo	0,64189	0,20302	0,04270	0,45556	0,37397	0,02231	0,14165	-0,12614
5	zy-zy	0,09401	0,15380	0,94156	0,16112	0,18796	0,01001	0,08147	0,01845
6	ast-ast	0,72095	0,17192	0,03797	0,50556	0,31684	-0,00602	0,06911	-0,09616
7	ms-ms	0,54104	0,29229	-0,30811	0,47174	0,40736	0,09649	-0,07922	-0,09775
8	au-au	0,53504	0,28034	0,01508	0,55755	0,44521	0,02228	0,16939	-0,13268
9	ba-b	0,17523	0,00056	0,64427	0,09081	0,47208	0,02327	0,49639	-0,03056
10	po-b H	0,69530	0,07943	0,03953	0,50919	0,28546	-0,02838	0,01176	-0,06173
11	n-pr	0,27110	0,94136	-0,20784	0,12492	0,00164	0,05735	0,05682	0,01301
12	ba-pr	0,09401	0,15380	0,94156	0,16112	0,18796	0,01001	0,08147	0,01845
13	n-ns	0,26854	0,92825	-0,21237	0,14844	-0,02840	0,05806	0,09850	0,01649
14	NB	0,25265	0,83416	0,36429	0,20992	0,10286	-0,03290	0,10517	-0,02434
15	mf-ek	0,09401	0,15380	0,94156	0,16112	0,18796	0,01001	0,08147	0,01845
16	OH	0,20155	0,63285	0,54149	0,03180	0,30214	-0,00184	-0,16425	-0,01956
17	mf-mf	0,25894	0,86300	0,28850	0,21234	0,07916	-0,02559	0,11695	-0,02100
18	n-ba	0,33641	-0,07577	0,48491	0,14632	0,27875	0,00593	0,67227	-0,00295
19	pr-alv	0,10089	0,67475	0,29886	0,53664	0,07459	-0,05013	-0,06590	0,01973
20	ekm-ekm	0,09109	0,35939	0,39666	0.77725	-0,05131	-0,01804	0,15235	0,03789
21	ol-sta	0,74358	0,54062	0,52011	0,43461	0,48428	0,72680	0,26508	0,40715
22	enm-enm	0,08252	0,33919	0,37620	0,80235	-0,05366	-0,01385	0,13665	0,04201
23	ba-o	0,17526	0,00048	0,64399	0,09075	0,47216	0,02331	0,49656	-0,03057
24	FMB	0,17382	0,00447	0,65767	0,09362	0,46773	0,02139	0,48831	-0,03032
25	g-op-g*	0,47778	0,29921	0,01216	0,51928	0,53044	-0,10465	0,25358	0,00903
26	po-b-po*	0,46155	0,32210	0,03904	0,52905	0,49633	-0,10518	0,29161	0,00241
27	n-gn	0,74358	0,54062	0,52011	0,43461	0,48427	0,72688	0,26508	0,40715
28	pr-M3	0,18179	0.70259	0,30889	0,58286	0,08465	-0,04771	-0,00210	-0,00653
29	MM	0,10507	0,65735	0,33471	0,57885	0,07274	-0,05633	-0,04831	0,01597
30	ba-sphba	0,37526	0,21814	0,35150	0,26943	0,12041	-0,02882	0,74611	-0,01146
31	[illegible]	0,29447	0,23663	0,16774	0,64949	0,05024	-0,03375	0,63507	0,00580
32	n-o	0,35850	-0,11348	0,31682	0,10316	0,02020	-0,02193	0,14393	0,03819
33	n-b	0,91087	0,13911	0,09754	0,06540	0,21272	0,00184	0,07977	-0,08481
34	b-l	0,83933	0,04489	0,09776	0,35620	0,12276	-0,05551	-0,01911	-0,02844
35	l-i	0,64289	0,18625	0,02131	0,48337	0,34762	-0,14972	0,09960	0,07559
36	i-o	0,39211	-0,15954	0,25150	0,11716	0,79160	0,07743	0.12410	-0,05796
37	g-n	0.87102	0,13694	0,07626	-0,12182	0,07336	-0,10853	0,06990	0,12728
38	g-b	0,88961	0,19161	0,11796	-0,04751	0,19708	-0,14758	0,15187	0,08955
39	g-l	0,87014	0,20029	0,10755	0,00516	0,22843	-0,14572	0,16351	0,09213
40	g-i	0,74020	0,23541	0,05304	0,15340	0,40492	-0,12055	0,20486	0,05378
41	g-o	0,35766	-0,11283	0,31767	0,10314	0,02053	-0,02220	0,14373	0,03842
42	n-o*	0,40652	0,21182	0,20938	0,04318	0,05749	-0,04514	0,00896	0,00066
43	n-b*	0.90753	0,13575	0,08333	0,05626	0,22368	0,00262	0,08314	-0,08242
44	b-l*	0,84307	0,10384	0,09650	0,15365	0,20166	-0,01020	0,02845	-0,06786
45	l-o*	0,40396	0,20734	0,22172	0,04658	0,05837	-0,04722	0,00592	0,00226
46	g-b*	0,93515	0,13763	0,10694	-0,01403	0,16516	-0,03176	0,08391	-0,03746
47	g-l*	0,91558	0,15312	0,09717	0,04980	0,20692	-0,02013	0,09009	-0,05112
48	g-i*	0,64434	0,21206	0,00547	0,49182	0,42170	0,01087	0,11612	-0,11725
49	g-o*	0,40594	0,21134	0,21245	0,04347	0,05677	-0,04524	0,01228	0,00001
50	kdl-kdl	-0,03931	-0,00727	0,01121	0,00985	-0,00458	0,45197	-0,02121	0,88685
51	go-go	-0,08951	0,01644	-0,00437	-0,03679	-0,00516	0.70900	0,02573	0,55144
52	ML	-0,03931	-0,00728	0,01121	0,00985	-0,00458	0,45197	-0,02122	0,88686
53	gn-id	-0,24833	0,05418	-0,00431	-0,13484	-0,01637	0,83876	0,07979	0,15830
54	MRH	-0,12345	0,01581	-0,00782	-0,05335	-0,01090	0.82751	0,02954	0,44738
55	MRB	-0,03210	-0,06018	0,00066	-0,00225	-0,05940	1,01789	-0,07706	0,03826
56	MA	-0,02441	-0,06436	0,00166	0,00222	-0.06147	1,01506	-0,08355	0,03000

Rotated principal component matrix (varimax rotation) for Camí Real d'Alacant skulls.

Loadings on the first 8 components (those which in each case account for at least 2% of the variance) are given and the percentage of the variance accounted for by each component is shown at the head of each column. The numbers 1-56 beside the variables is their key for the graphical presentations of the components (Camí Real graphs 1-10).

Component 1 receives heavy loadings from frontal, parietal and squamous occipital bones in the sagittal and coronal planes, as well as from the total facial height and palatal length.

Component 2 receives heavy loadings from upper facial dimensions, viz. n-pr, n-ns, NB, OH, mf-mf, pr-alv, pr-M3.

Component 3 receives heavy loadings from the bizygomatic breadth, orbital breadth, and projections on the basion of the bregma and prosthion as well as the length and breadth of the foramen magnum.

Component 4 reflects the breadth of the basi-occiput, maxilla and to a lesser degree perhaps the temporal, parietal and frontal bones.

Component 5 reflects the occipital bone between inion and opisthion in the sagittal plane.

Component 6 reflects mandibular dimensions of length and height, total facial height and palatal length.

Component 7 receives heavy loadings from the length of the basi-occiput and the projection on the basion of the nasion.

Component 8 receives heavy loadings from dimensions of mandibular breadth.

Using the fundamentally different method of principal factor analysis on a reduced variable list of 13 variables chosen to avoid as many missing value entries as possible for the Camí Real assemblage (g-op, zy-zy, ast-ast, n-b, l-i, i-o, g-o*, ba-b, ba-o, NB, OH, gn-id, kdl-kdl). Four factors could be extracted, the first received heavy loadings from g-op, ast-ast, n-b, l-i recalling Component 1. The second received heavy loadings from ba-b and ba-o and also i-o, while only very just below the cut-off point used arbitrarily to define 'heavy' of 0.6 were zy-zy and g-o*; the factor seems similar to Components 3 + 7. Factor 3 received heavy loadings from NB and OH, reflecting Component 2. Factor 4 received a heavy loading from gn-id followed below the cut-off point by kdl-kdl, reflecting Components 6 + 8. In order to try to improve definition the variable list was then expanded by adding ML, ba-pr, n-ba, pr-alv. However only four factors were found to account for all of the variance. They may be regarded as the same as previously found, where the first is joined by ML, the second by ba-pr and n-ba, the third by pr-alv and the fourth was unchanged. A minimal conclusion might be the acceptance of the independence of the elements represented respectively by Component 1, Component 2, Component 8 and perhaps Components 3 + 7. Possibly Component 5 should also be regarded as comprising independently assorting elements.

Plots for Table 20

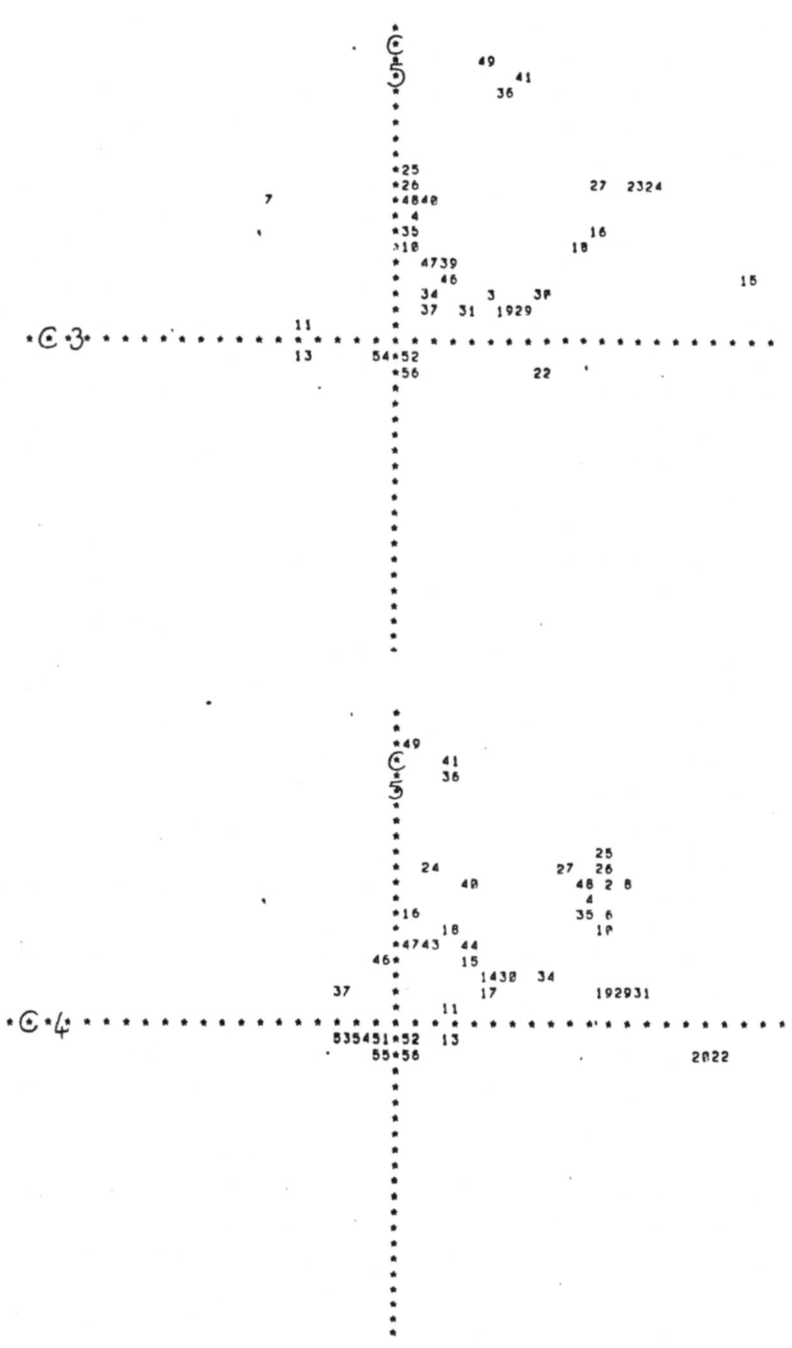

Camí Real d'Alacant skulls

Plot of variables for the Camí Real d'Alacant assemblage in terms of their loadings on principal components 1 - 5.

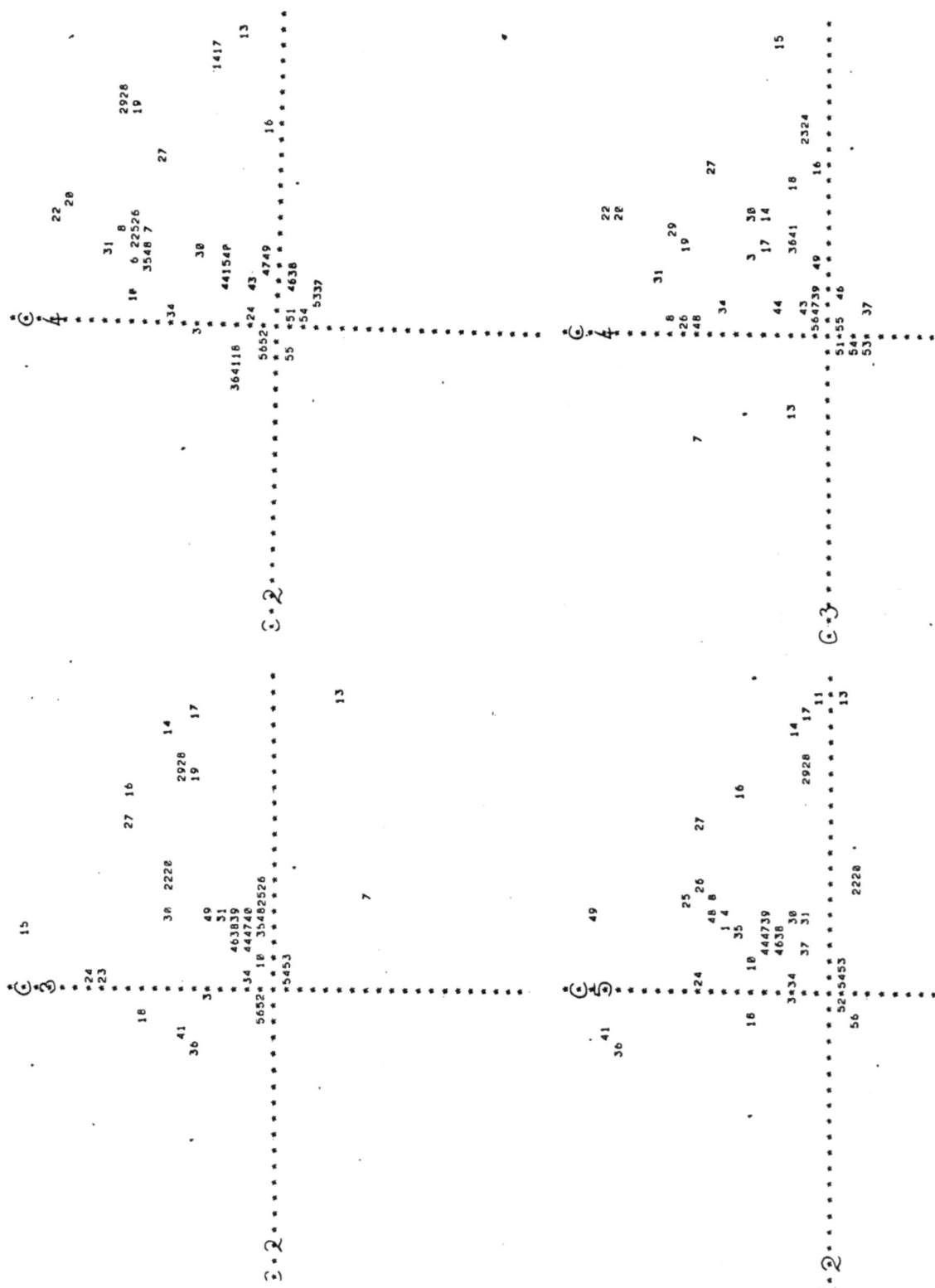

Camf Real d'Alacant skulls

Plot of variables for the Camf Real d'Alacant assemblage in terms of their loadings on principal components 1 - 5.

Plots for Table 20

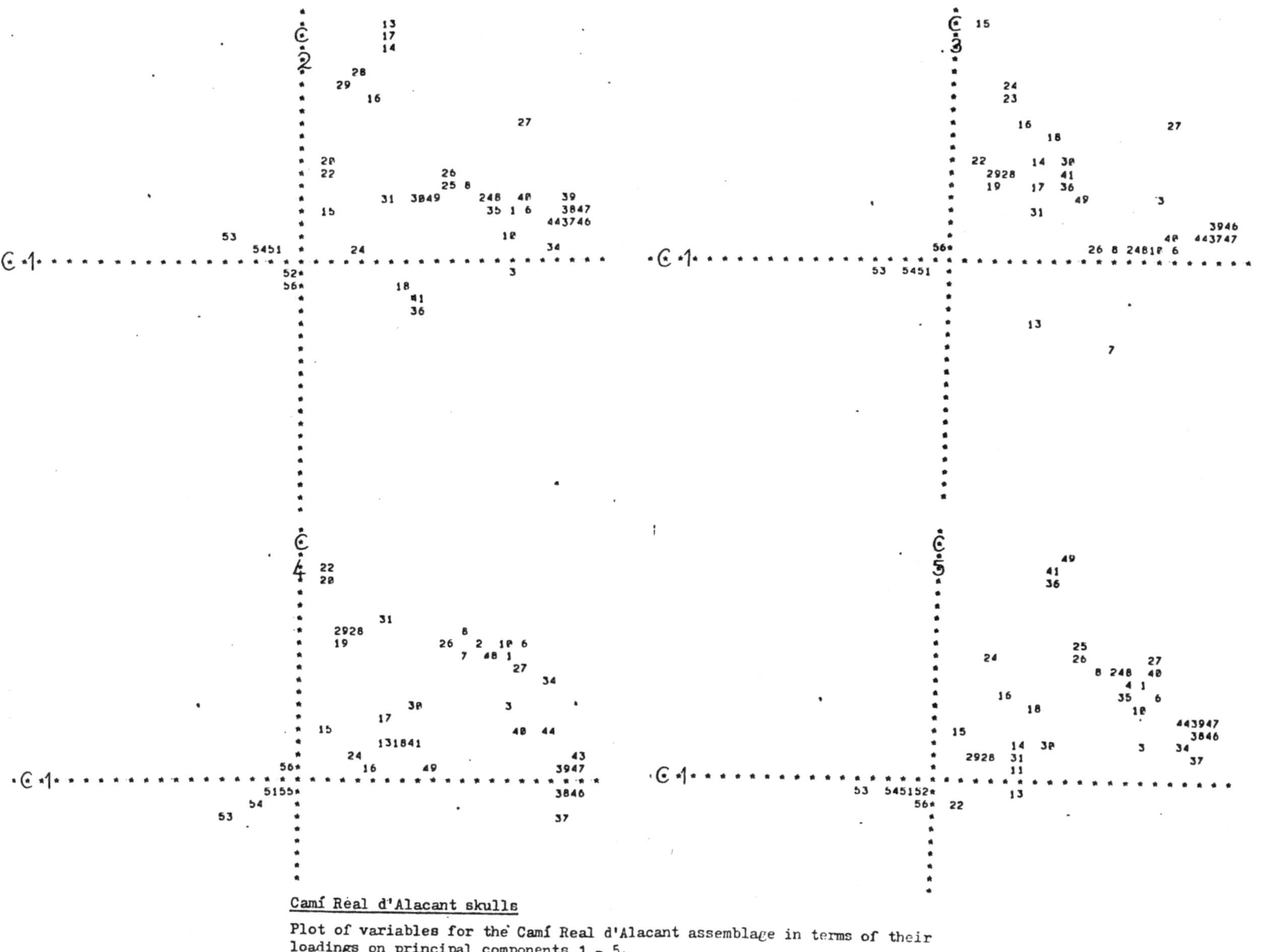

Camí Real d'Alacant skulls

Plot of variables for the Camí Real d'Alacant assemblage in terms of their loadings on principal components 1 - 5.

Table 21		Comp.1	Comp.2	Comp.3	Comp.4	Comp.5	Comp.6
		69.7%	15.7%	8.6%	5.8%	2.7%	2.7%
1	g-op	0,83386	0,25328	-0,01781	0,17671	0,05969	0,45052
2	eu-eu	0,63371	0,18854	0,01484	0,43904	0,10627	0,55376
3	ft-ft	0,15673	0,27416	0,12544	0,89065	0,33233	0,17903
4	co-co	0,66863	0,32670	-0,06869	0,61496	-0,01165	0,18111
5	zy-zy	0,25029	0,40942	0,48146	0,07126	0,35910	0,12730
6	ast-ast	0,96066	0,22327	0,01098	0,18410	0,08836	-0,01103
7	ms-ms	0,40283	0,40004	0,19864	0,26724	0,75099	0,01345
8	au-au	0,59701	0,38141	0,11761	0,14531	0,58433	0,03920
9	ba-b	0,74037	0,52889	0,05486	0,05202	0,24569	-0,06409
10	po-b H	0,86423	0,39040	0,06935	0,06243	-0,03461	-0,01088
11	n-pr	0,15466	0,87054	0,06262	0,32862	0,01570	0,12311
12	ba-pr	0,49533	0,82712	0,11051	0,00389	0,15432	-0,14464
13	n-ns	0,66609	0,60366	0,67348	0,38833	0,17800	0,13059
14	NB	0,11305	0,80106	0,12252	0,35654	0,19425	0,30451
15	mf-ek	0,23482	0,91026	0,05979	0,30125	-0,00322	0,18155
16	OH	0,20396	0,89466	0,09358	0,30669	-0,03306	0,22481
17	mf-mf	0,30224	0,73321	0,03422	0,30609	0,17498	0,39094
18	n-ba	0,49398	0,82528	0,11251	0,00802	0,15612	-0,14499
19	pr-alv	0,23728	0,90392	0,05521	0,30564	0,00956	0,19313
20	ekm-ekm	0,11225	0,80355	0,12398	0,36021	0,19274	0,28734
21	ol-sta	0,66609	0,60366	0,67348	0,38833	0,17800	0,13059
22	enm-enm	0,66609	0,60366	0,67348	0,38833	0,17800	0,13059
23	ba-o	0,68619	0,65925	0,10130	-0,07892	-0,00318	-0,07542
24	FMB	0,65029	0,58750	0,18423	-0,11968	-0,10728	-0,03096
25	g-op-g*	0,82608	0,26155	-0,01742	0,18155	0,07083	0,45663
26	po-b-po*	0,72375	0,08450	0,17560	0,15681	0,56204	0,14604
27	n-gn	0,16866	0,26469	0,70326	0,06478	0,20037	0,16209
28	pr-M3	0,34995	0,87754	0,07826	0,19704	0,08132	-0,08533
29	MM	0,66609	0,60366	0,67348	0,38833	0,17800	0,13059
30	ba-sphba	0,49474	0,81566	0,13478	0,00753	0,14525	-0,13914
31	OPBB	0,49827	0,81641	0,13225	0,00393	0,13922	-0,13686
32	n-o	0,66609	0,60366	0,67348	0,38833	0,17800	0,13059
33	n-b	0,32197	0,75943	0,00623	0,41930	0,17947	0,17236
34	b-l	0,8022[illegible]	0,27170	-0,00417	0,17973	0,08727	0,47776
35	l-i	0,95559	0,21572	-0,00193	0,18888	0,14719	-0,01215
36	i-o	0,94452	0,20699	0,05904	0,18377	0,11733	0,01369
37	g-n	0,14699	0,31327	0,03059	0,93757	0,18223	-0,03481
38	g-b	0,66609	0,60366	0,67348	0,38833	0,17800	0,13059
39	g-l	0,85512	0,31036	-0,01882	0,27206	0,05491	0,22147
40	g-i	0,95222	0,24599	0,01901	0,17272	0,12831	-0,00558
41	g-o	0,66609	0,60366	0,67348	0,38833	0,17800	0,13059
42	n-o*	0,57424	0,64394	0,05702	0,14285	0,36692	-0,13119
43	n-b*	0,30618	0,42504	0,06362	0,79632	-0,12231	0,02883
44	b-l*	0,67689	0,32183	0,02183	0,45749	-0,12468	0,30849
45	l-o*	0,88072	0,19819	0,11556	0,06102	0,12273	0,03604
46	g-b*	0,63968	0,33412	-0,07853	0,66996	-0,04577	0,12171
47	g-l*	0,68051	0,38486	-0,06954	0,37596	0,00382	0,50017
48	g-i*	0,94013	0,25178	0,01098	0,18990	0,15760	-0,01131
49	g-o*	0,86779	0,37938	0,03081	0,04031	0,26535	-0,00375
50	kdl-kdl	0,04637	0,11179	0,89619	0,01741	0,06643	0,09433
51	go-go	-0,07953	-0,00500	0,99781	-0,03004	-0,00302	-0,02683
52	ML	0,66609	0,60366	0,67348	0,38833	0,17800	0,13059
53	gn-id	-0,32069	-0,18105	1,11084	-0,13357	-0,05308	-0,28170
54	MRH	-0,12856	-0,05379	1,08599	-0,05059	-0,05668	-0,09690
55	MRB	-0,12101	-0,04113	1,08768	-0,05380	-0,04486	-0,08388
56	MA	0,66609	0,60366	0,67348	0,38833	0,17800	0,13059

Rotated principal component matrix (varimax rotation) for Cova del Morro de la Barsella skulls.

Loadings on the first 6 principal components (i.e. those which each account for at least 2% of the variance) are given and the percentage of the variance accounted for by each component is shown at the head of each column. The numbers 1-56 beside the variables is their key for the graphical presentations of the components (Barsella graphs 1-10).

Component 1 receives heavy loadings from both sagittal and coronal measurements of the calvarium and of the base of the skull as far forward as the palate. The frontal bone does not fully participate.

Component 2 receives heavy loadings from the upper face and the basi-occiput as well as the projection on the latter of the face. The sagittal dimensions of the frontal bone load on this component.

Component 3 receives heavy loadings from all mandibular dimensions and some possibly related upper splanchnocranial dimensions.

Component 4 reflects the frontal bone in both sagittal and coronal planes.

Component 5 receives heavy loadings from the temporal bone in the coronal plane.

Component 6 weakly reflects the parietal bone in sagittal and coronal planes.

A principal factor analysis was also performed with iteration (see example from Cova de Beni Sid for explanation of this method) on a reduced variable list of 17 variables chosen to reduce the number of missing value entries. The loadings were printed out for the first 3 factors (which in this truncated data set accounted for the totality of the variance) which correspond closely to Components 1, 2 and 3 as described above. The variables used were g-op, zy-zy, ast-ast, n-b, b-l*, l-i, i-o, g-o*, ba-pr, n-ba, ba-b, ba-o, NB, OH, pr-alv, gn-id, kdl-kdl. The method is less robust than is principal components analysis though the drawback is perhaps in part compensated by the elimination of very many missing data entries. Perhaps it may be inferred that the first three principal components reflect important orthogonal aspects of Barsella cranial morphology on which greater reliance can be placed than can on the other three.

Plots for Table 21

Cova del Morro de la Barsella skulls

Plot of variables for the Morro de la Barsella assemblage in terms of their loadings on principal components 1 - 5.

Plots for Table 21

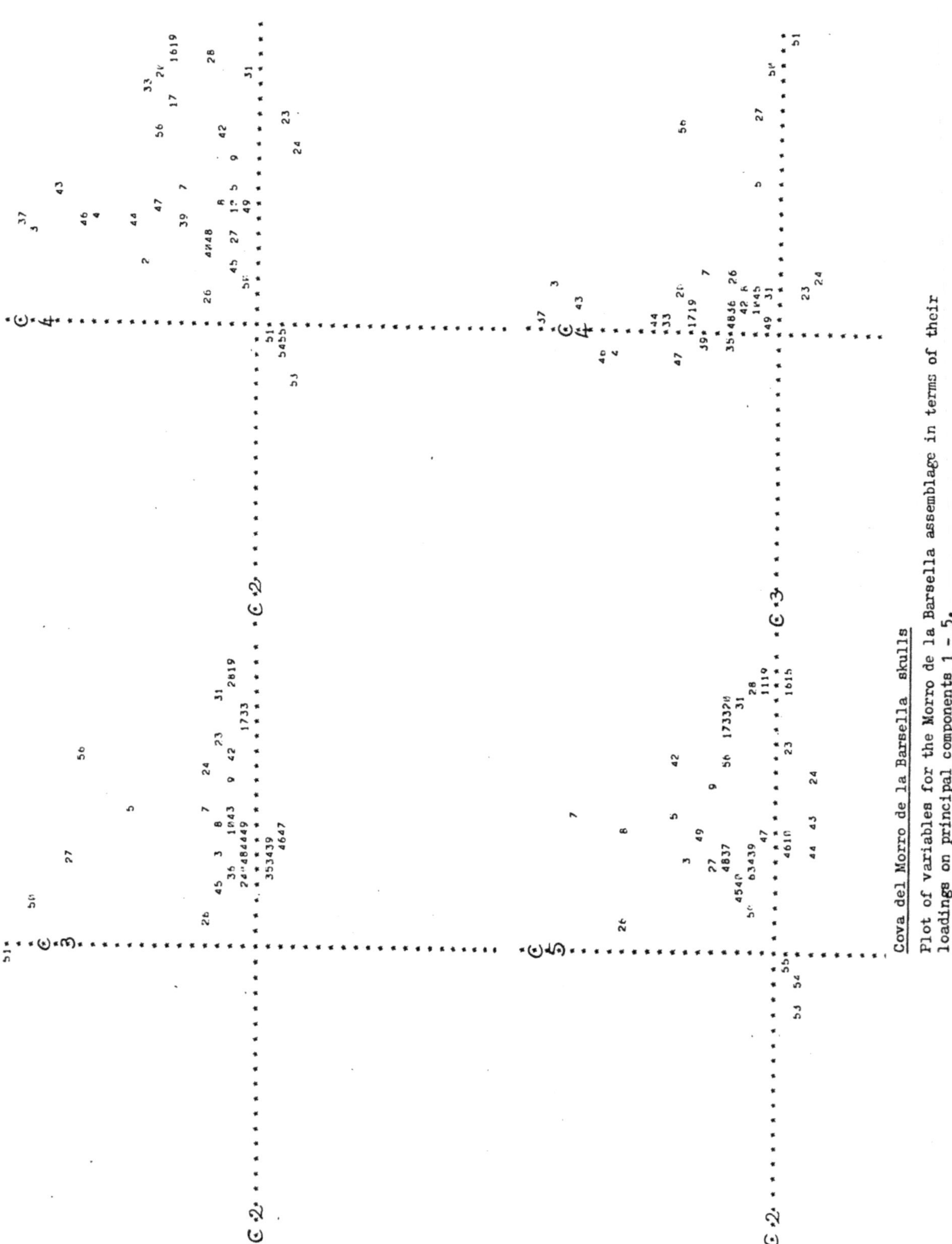

Cova del Morro de la Barsella skulls

Plot of variables for the Morro de la Barsella assemblage in terms of their loadings on principal components 1 - 5.

Plots for Table 21

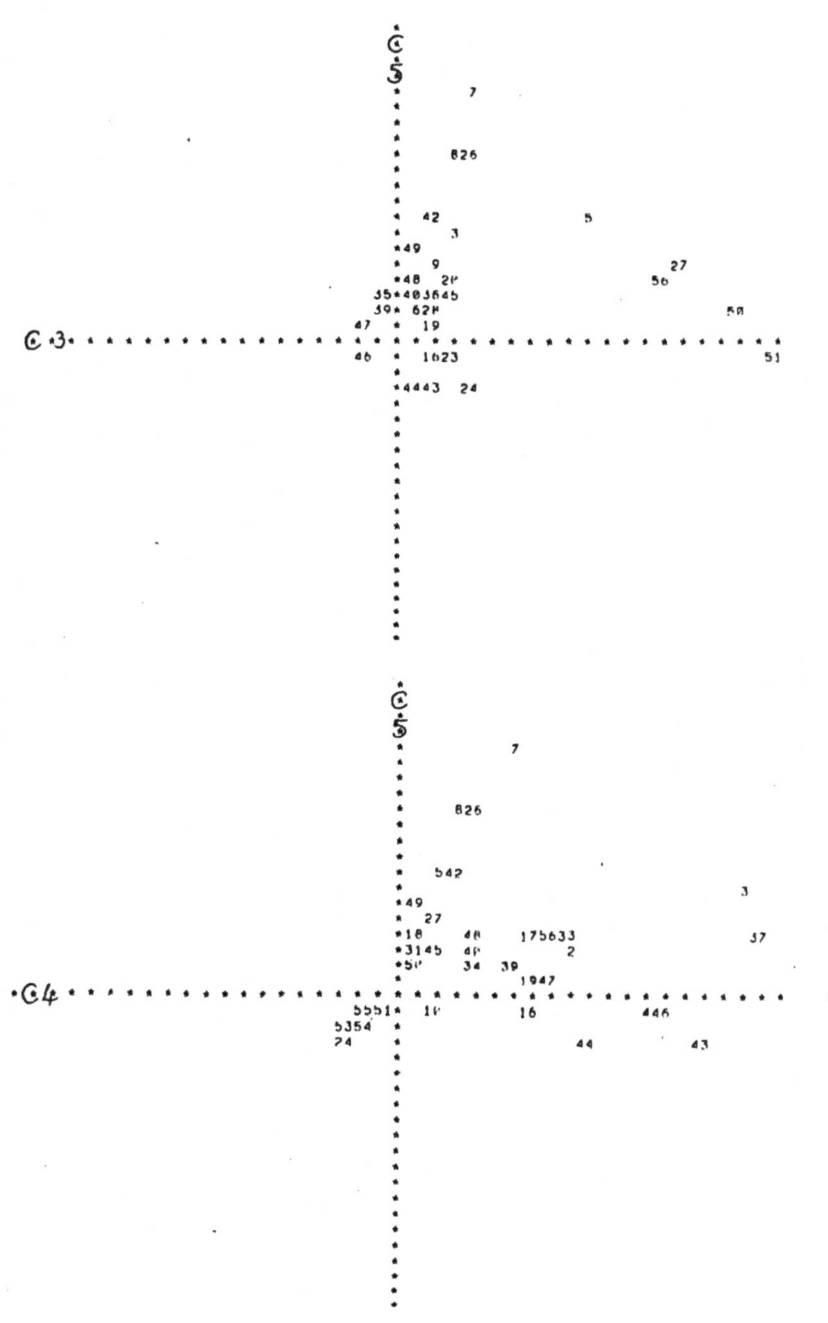

Cova del Morro de la Barsella skulls

Plot of variables for the Morro de la Barsella assemblage in terms of their loadings on principal components 1 - 5.

Table 22

		Factor 1	Factor 2	Factor 3	Factor 4	Factor 5	Factor 6	Factor 7
		64.2%	16.5%	6.3%	4.1%	4.0%	2.9%	2.0%
1	g-op	0,35072	0,76278	0,18858	0,26302	-0,07686	0,20333	-0,00831
2	eu-eu	0,36171	0,79158	0,21115	0,22560	-0,04483	0,06291	0,07799
3	ft-ft	0,48622	0,59535	0,13600	0,11763	-0,24241	0,36566	0,09261
4	co-co	0,39977	0,57273	0,17119	0,16666	-0,23536	0,17846	0,11359
5	zy-zy	0,19859	0,11755	0,63084	0,36230	0,28984	0,07580	0,48796
6	ast-ast	0,28277	0,74013	0,24987	0,37567	0,00188	0,15773	-0,10313
7	ms-ms	0,16739	0,68764	0,35421	0,44770	0,03445	0,17369	-0,13204
8	au-au	0,16482	0,68416	0,34884	0,45525	0,02195	0,17113	-0,12904
9	ba-b	0,24413	0,39024	0,67685	0,48045	-0,01753	0,01626	-0,15712
10	po-b H	0,13910	0,81368	0,18472	0,32473	-0,09982	0,09095	0,05135
11	n-pr	0,75754	0,52381	0,26883	0,20374	-0,08306	0,12535	-0,04280
12	ba-pr	0,12024	0,30056	0,88257	0,10469	0,16851	0,07479	0,21788
13	n-ns	0,76178	0,61669	0,26896	0,21440	-0,08441	0,12480	-0,05285
14	NB	0,81986	0,30244	0,09397	0,37769	-0,01998	0,14708	0,03676
15	mf-ek	0,76541	0,52202	0,27154	0,16852	-0,07551	0,13492	-0,02267
16	OH	0,77379	0,52628	0,23187	0,18315	-0,07012	0,13158	-0,00166
17	mf-mf	0,80545	0,16586	0,11551	0,38802	0,00400	0,19180	0,05541
18	n-ba	0,11918	0,29933	0,88422	0,10344	0,17270	0,07845	0,21901
19	pr-alv	0,70273	0,47990	0,27482	0,07353	0,00606	0,15433	0,23823
20	ekm-ekm	0,81674	0,32666	0,05010	0,37820	0,00107	0,14752	0,07545
21	ol-sta	0,58063	0,37633	0,02811	0,35113	-0,18272	-0,01747	-0,11413
22	enm-enm	0,79915	0,30725	0,09144	0,43516	-0,01030	0,14695	0,02115
23	ba-o	0,20001	0,11769	0,62914	0,36453	0,28698	0,07275	0,48861
24	FMB	0,32914	0,34768	0,22464	0,81835	0,17108	0,07574	0,02903
25	g-op-g*	0,36283	0,78955	0,22570	0,23629	-0,04475	0,06099	0,06262
26	po-b-po*	0,32309	0,59448	0,38510	0,49916	0,07961	0,05284	-0,10834
27	n-gn	0,22578	0,23150	0,41132	0,48413	0,40184	0,14090	0,47669
28	pr-M3	0,79806	0,37421	-0,00304	0,15880	0,03611	0,14428	0,38391
29	MM	0,59797	0,65678	0,23147	0,20647	-0,05945	0,07235	-0,07347
30	ba-sphba	0,16340	0,35089	0,82509	0,28007	0,03676	0,05796	-0,21511
31	OPBB	0,16747	0,33940	0,84287	0,28393	0,07139	0,06736	-0,13956
32	n-o	0,29853	0,30269	0,20901	0,68112	0,27697	0,08865	0,38634
33	n-b	0,39518	0,53014	0,13944	0,14236	-0,26739	0,65614	0,06062
34	b-l	0,15672	0,89051	0,14440	0,24152	-0,12146	0,07411	0,12860
35	l-i	0,25576	0,80512	0,21828	0,17899	-0,06895	0,07484	0,08314
36	i-o	0,33769	0,34286	0,18496	0,83686	0,10389	0,04155	-0,01939
37	g-n	0,44447	0,44728	0,16480	0,15841	-0,22983	0,62101	-0,01401
38	g-b	0,39411	0,53463	0,12839	0,14265	-0,26542	0,65276	0,06450
39	g-l	0,31506	0,80632	0,23614	0,26305	-0,02776	0,14551	-0,02326
40	g-i	0,35773	0,83921	0,16647	0,19208	-0,10023	0,19824	0,04421
41	g-o	0,29941	0,30264	0,20708	0,68250	0,27362	0,08677	0,38447
42	n-o*	0,33036	0,34487	0,23422	0,81804	0,16978	0,07239	0,03855
43	n-b*	0,23882	0,65916	0,11845	0,16758	-0,23285	0,57230	0,07424
44	b-l*	0,32255	0,82541	0,12136	0,17076	-0,15863	0,11150	0,13846
45	l-o*	0,32940	0,34437	0,23973	0,81469	0,17606	0,07501	0,04597
46	g-b*	0,38929	0,53511	0,11806	0,12590	-0,26942	0,65692	0,06898
47	g-l*	0,38021	0,83859	0,13056	0,15854	-0,09819	0,19813	0,07502
48	g-i*	0,40122	0,83224	0,14052	0,12511	-0,10280	0,18935	0,07906
49	g-o*	0,33031	0,34438	0,23655	0,81752	0,16974	0,07230	0,03852
50	kdl-kdl	-0,00722	0,01471	-0,00684	0,06032	0,75899	0,11691	-0,01885
51	go-go	-0,02131	-0,06563	0,07515	0,09869	0,84711	-0,01335	0,02970
52	ML	0,05094	0,03766	0,14183	0,15907	0,83554	0,11529	0,09547
53	gn-id	-0,09191	-0,20501	0,08922	0,07766	0,77401	-0,25555	0,03116
54	MRH	-0,03557	-0,10540	0,11043	0,09419	0,83899	-0,09141	0,04395
55	MRB	-0,12337	-0,23819	0,05846	0,08812	0,79019	-0,29365	0,02742
56	MA	-0,10788	-0,20626	0,03550	0,05745	0,86208	-0,25273	-0,00970

Rotated principal factoring (varimax rotation) for Cova de Beni Sid skulls.

The results of this method bear a striking similarity to those of the principal components analysis of the same skulls. The method is fundamentally different because a number of inferred factors is arbitrarily taken. It was set equal to the number of variables, but only 22 of the 56 factors so invoked were required to account for the entire variance and of those only 7 accounted severally for more than 2% of the variance. The correlation matrix diagonal is replaced by communality estimates but unlike more primitive factoring procedures these are replaced by new communality estimates in terms of the variances accounted for by the factors extracted from the initial reduced correlation matrix. This replacement proceeds iterativelyuntil the differences in the two successive communality estimates are negligible. Loadings on the first 7 factors are given and the percentage of the variance accounted for by each factor is shown at the head of each column. The numbers 1-56 beside the variables is their key for the graphical representations of the factors (Beni Sid factor graphs 1-10).

Factor 1 receives heavy loadings from measurements on the upper face.

Factor 2 receives heavy loadings from the parietal, squamous occipital and temporal bones in both sagittal and coronal planes and also from the height of the zygomatic process of the maxilla.

Factor 3 receives heavy loadings from the bizygomatic breadth and from the pars basilaris of the occiput and the projections from it in the sagittal plane of the bregma, nasion, prosthion and opisthion.

Factor 4 receives heavy loadings from the squamous occiput mainly in the sagittal plane (although the breadth of the foramen magnum loads on this factor also) and sagittal projections on the occiput of the frontal bone.

Factor 5 reflects mandibular morphology.

Factor 6 appears to reflect the frontal bone in the sagittal plane.

Factor 7 receives weak loadings from the bizygomatic breadth, the length of the foramen magnum and the total facial height.

Plots for Table 22

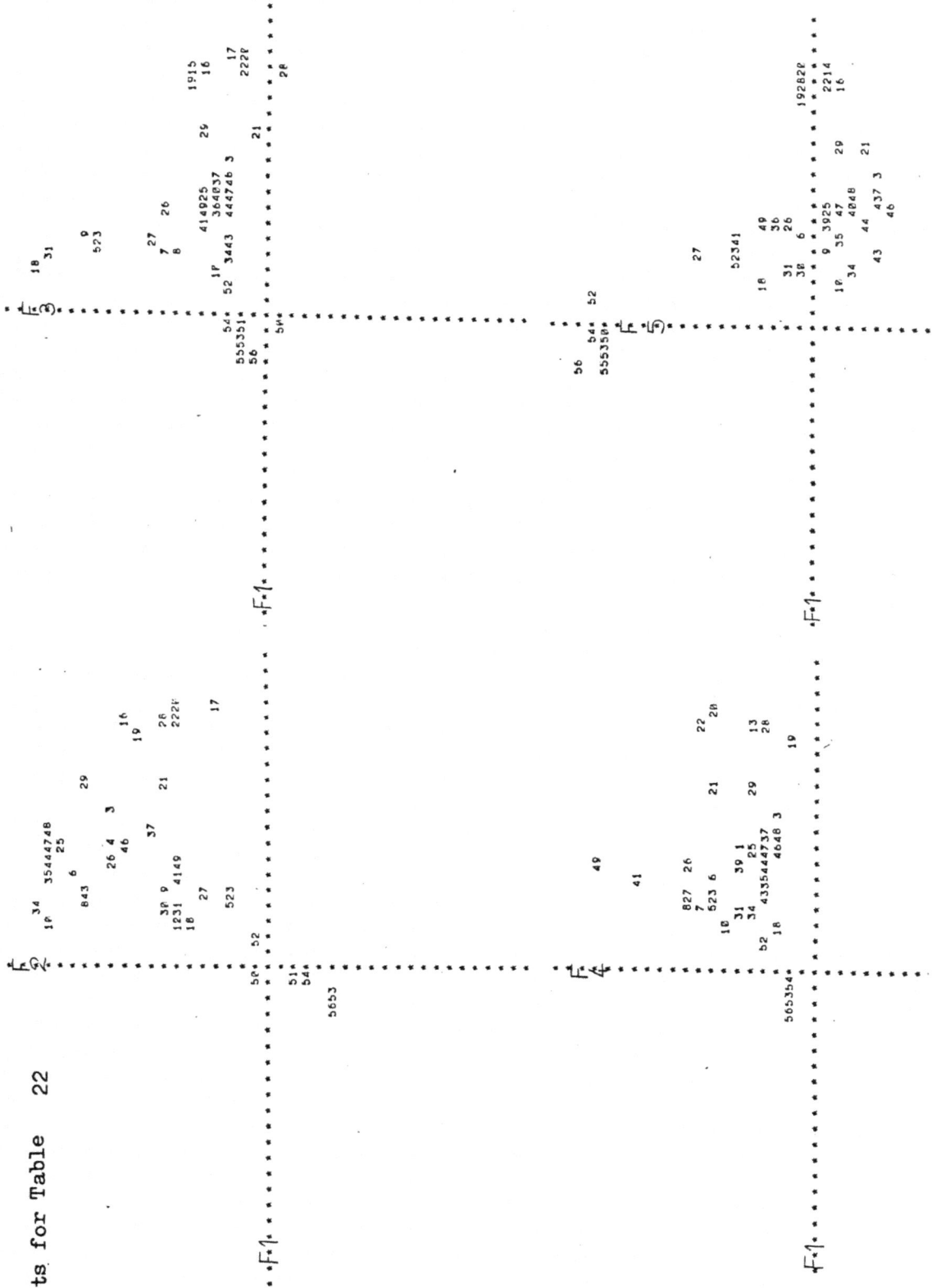

Cova de Beni Sid skulls (factoring)

Plot of variables of the Beni Sid assemblage in terms of their loadings on factors 1 - 5.

Plots for Table 22

F 3

F 2

F 4

F 2

F 5

F 2

F 4

F 3

Cova de Beni Sid skulls (factoring)

Plot of variables of the Beni Sid assemblage in terms of their loadings on factors 1 - 5.

Plots for Table 22

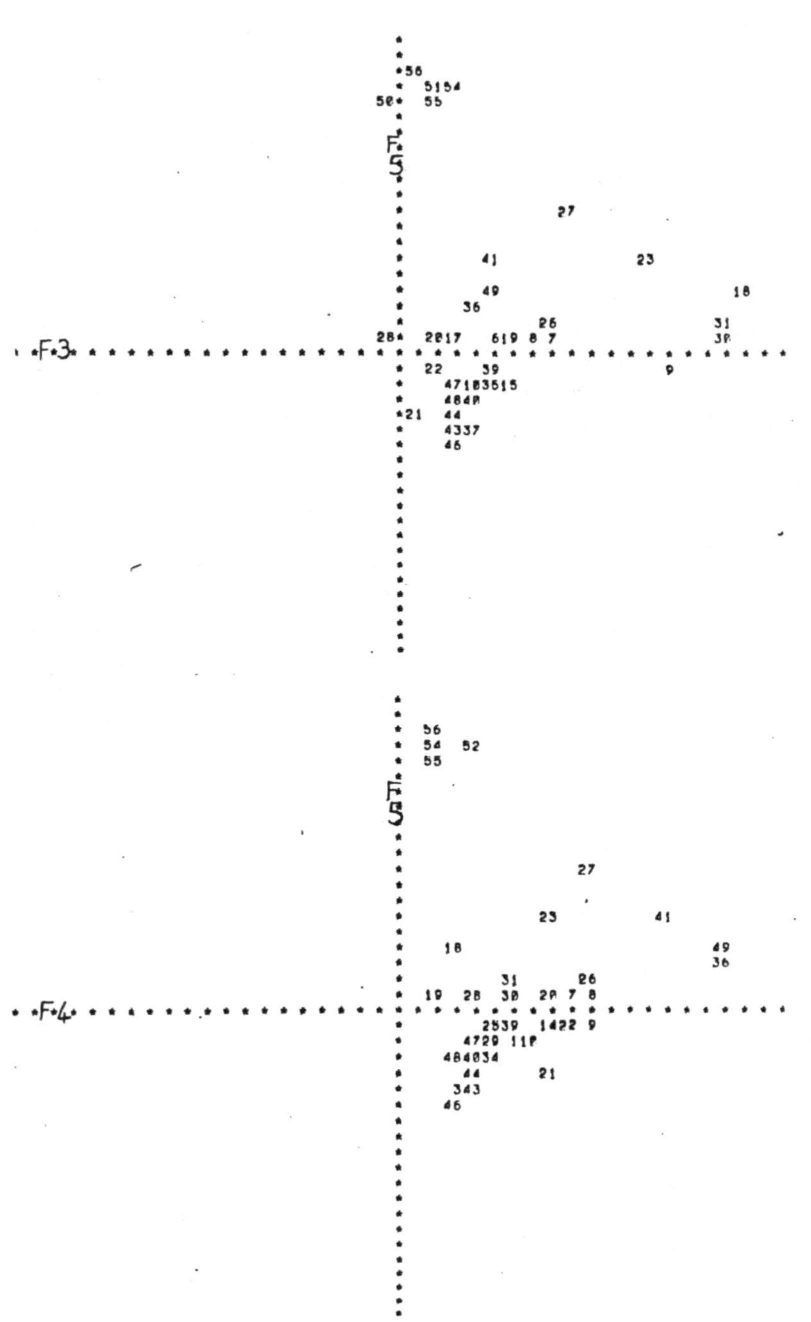

Cova de Beni Sid skulls (factoring)

Plot of variables of the Beni Sid assemblage in terms of their loadings on factors 1 - 5.

Table 23

		Factor 1	Factor 2	Factor 3	Factor 4
		67.2%	17.5%	10.4%	4.9%
1	g-op	0,85390	0,20676	-0,22876	0,23248
2	eu-eu	0,77454	0,17507	-0,08343	0,17873
3	ft-ft	0,72357	0,39501	-0,15327	-0,03913
4	co-co	0,62087	0,28369	-0,13388	-0,05117
5	zy-zy	0,31579	0,48521	0,15521	0,12813
6	ast-ast	0,79745	0,13456	-0,11991	0,21446
7	ms-ms	0,66560	0,28487	-0,02124	0,04261
8	au-au	0,83002	0,28493	-0,08436	-0,00478
9	ba-b	0,81112	0,28970	-0,11186	0,19654
10	n-ns	0,23421	0,91926	0,03273	0,00767
11	NB	0,19507	0,82977	-0,01819	-0,00356
12	mf-ek	0,42621	0,74163	-0,12651	0,07850
13	OH	0,45930	0,74716	-0,13570	0,07472
14	mf-mf	0,34086	0,73913	-0,02065	0,11191
15	n-ba	0,76108	0,35717	-0,13725	0,17413
16	pr-alv	0,19988	0,58786	-0,01830	0,47163
17	enm-enm	0,14889	0,63555	-0,00610	0,41678
18	ba-o	0,59046	0,28074	-0,12869	0,53257
19	FMB	0,49155	0,27535	-0,12826	0,61918
20	g-op-g*	0,86947	0,21183	-0,06712	0,17572
21	po-b-po*	0,85801	0,29094	-0,07731	0,09733
22	n-o*	0,73716	0,16117	-0,14464	0,50414
23	n-b	0,93963	0,22869	-0,16409	0,07888
24	b-l*	0,85640	0,21009	-0,16112	0,13146
25	l-o*	0,68842	0,13230	-0,17676	0,51413
26	kdl-kdl	-0,09931	-0,02962	0,75289	-0,11654
27	go-go	-0,03572	0,07086	0,76289	-0,09231
28	gn-id	-0,13473	-0,00414	0,72100	-0,04129
29	MRH	-0,14563	-0,01746	0,93851	-0,05541
30	MRB	-0,10760	-0,00521	0,90251	-0,02301
31	MA	-0,20706	-0,12433	0,80121	0,12656

Rotated principal factoring (varimax rotation) for El Argar skulls (Jacques' data)

Although this method differs fundamentally from principal components analysis (for further details see legend to factor matrix for Beni Sid) the results are quite similar to the rotated principal components matrix despite omission of the variable g-i. The variance was accounted for by four of the proposed 31 factors after iteration. The principal difference is that maxillary and bizygomatic measurements load together with upper facial dimensions on Factor 2, whereas in the principal components solution they were separated on Components 4 and 2 respectively.

Plots for Table 23

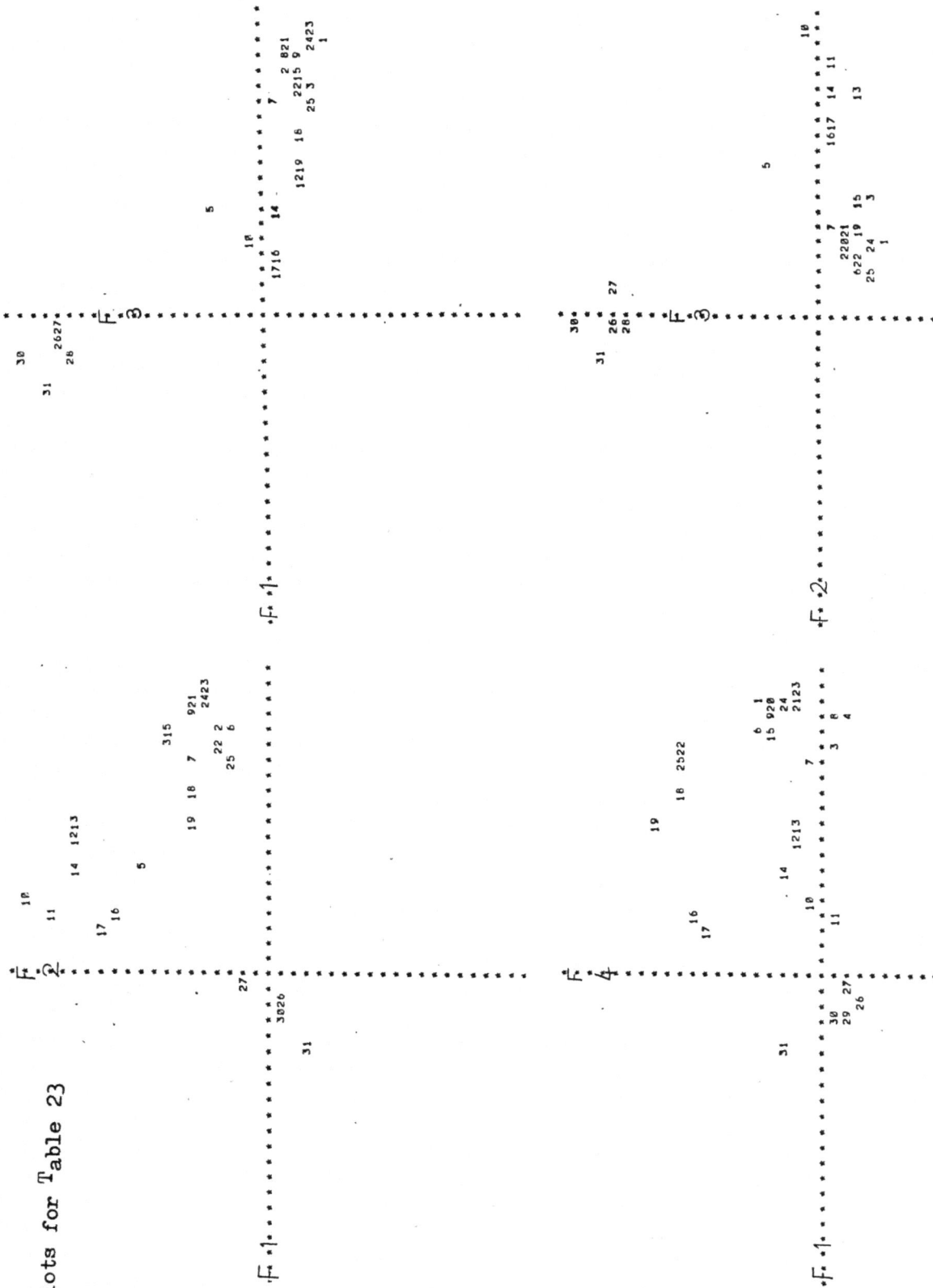

El Argar skulls (principal factoring)

Plot of variables for the El Argar assemblage in terms of their loadings on factors 1 - 4.

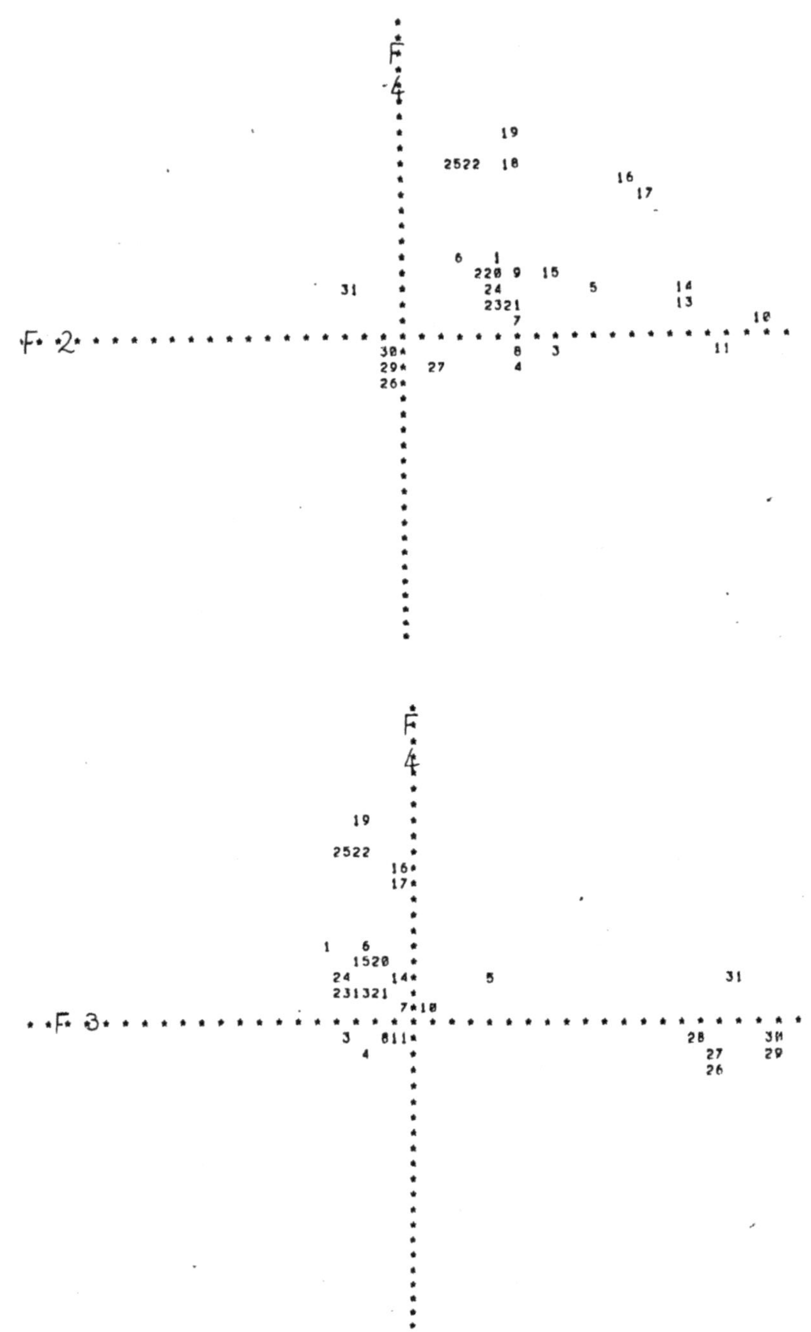

El Argar skulls (principal factoring)

Plot of variables for the El Argar assemblage in terms of their loadings on factors 1 - 4.

Table 24

		Factor 1 66.1%	Factor 2 16.8%	Factor 3 8.3%	Factor 4 5.8%	Factor 5 3.0%
1	g-op	0,40400	0,59953	0,61720	0,04842	0.10899
2	eu-eu	0,63589	0,24980	0,59452	-0,08572	0,07874
3	ft-ft	0,30186	0,43603	0.63045	-0,26175	-0,08224
4	co-co	0,16104	0,36280	0,80970	-0,04305	0,02327
5	zy-zy	0,58813	0,35837	-0,03922	-0,08403	-0,27791
6	ast-ast	0,67227	0,35437	0,54251	-0,01422	0,11599
7	ms-ms	0,90382	0,25041	0,23649	0,05632	-0.10091
8	au-au	0,90949	0,24607	0,23122	0,03231	-0,09679
9	ba-b	0,70261	0,44093	0,36595	0,01422	0,17530
10	n-ns	0,33051	0,85689	0,34024	-0,06952	0,03943
11	NB	0,31745	0,86733	0,29915	-0,12995	-0,01637
12	mf-ek	0,30001	0,89166	0.24206	-0,14656	0,02557
13	OH	0,31597	0,86155	0,31850	-0,11045	0,03005
14	mf-mf	0,33618	0,83800	0,38591	-0,06728	0,03501
15	n-ba	0,56774	0,69974	0,08261	-0,11528	0,08888
16	pr-alv	0,29495	0,88929	0,23022	-0,16181	-0,01477
17	ekm-ekm	0,28037	0,87004	0,29889	-0,12707	-0,01237
18	ba-o	0,69849	0,44289	0,36969	0,02395	0.16010
19	FMB	0,82631	0,40153	0,06673	-0,03304	-0,20107
20	g-op-g*	0,64701	0,27461	0,59709	-0,05251	0,07105
21	po-b-po*	0,90420	0,24861	0,23823	0,04684	-0,10056
22	n-o*	0,83299	0,30374	0,37180	0,07903	0,18219
23	n-b*	0,31251	0,41266	0,72738	-0,11338	0,00504
24	b-l*	0,43389	0,37265	0,71975	0,02546	0,00555
25	l-o*	0,71212	0,24475	0,32467	-0,09151	0,39554
26	kdl-kdl	0,21307	-0,04578	0,00768	0,74487	-0,38416
27	go-go	0,08661	-0,10340	-0,05470	0,68145	-0,46657
28	gn-id	-0,06549	-0,15784	-0,10417	0,69385	-0,13100
29	MRH	-0,05333	-0,10312	-0,09484	0,90342	0,01809
30	MRB	-0,01521	-0,05464	0,02049	0,95520	0,26007
31	MA	-0,04783	-0,05946	0,00938	0.94855	0,24067

Rotated principal factoring (varimax rotation) for La Bastida skulls

The method differs fundamentally from principal components analysis (see under Beni Sid principal factor matrix). 31 variables were selected on the basis of minimisation of missing value entries as far as possible. However, of a possible maximum of 31 factors 5 were sufficient to account for the total variance. The percentage of the total variance accounted for by each is shown at the head of each column. The numbers 1 - 31 beside the variables is their key for the graphical representations (Bastida principal factors graphs 1 - 10).

Factor 1 corresponds to Components 2 + 5 of the principal components analysis.
Factor 2 corresponds to Component 1 of the principal components analysis.
Factor 3 corresponds to Component 3 of the principal components analysis.
Factor 4 corresponds to Component 4 of the principal components analysis.
Factor 5 does not receive heavy loadings from any measurement and perhaps reflects Component 6 of the principal components analysis which was not published in the principal component matrix as it received no significant loadings from any measurement.

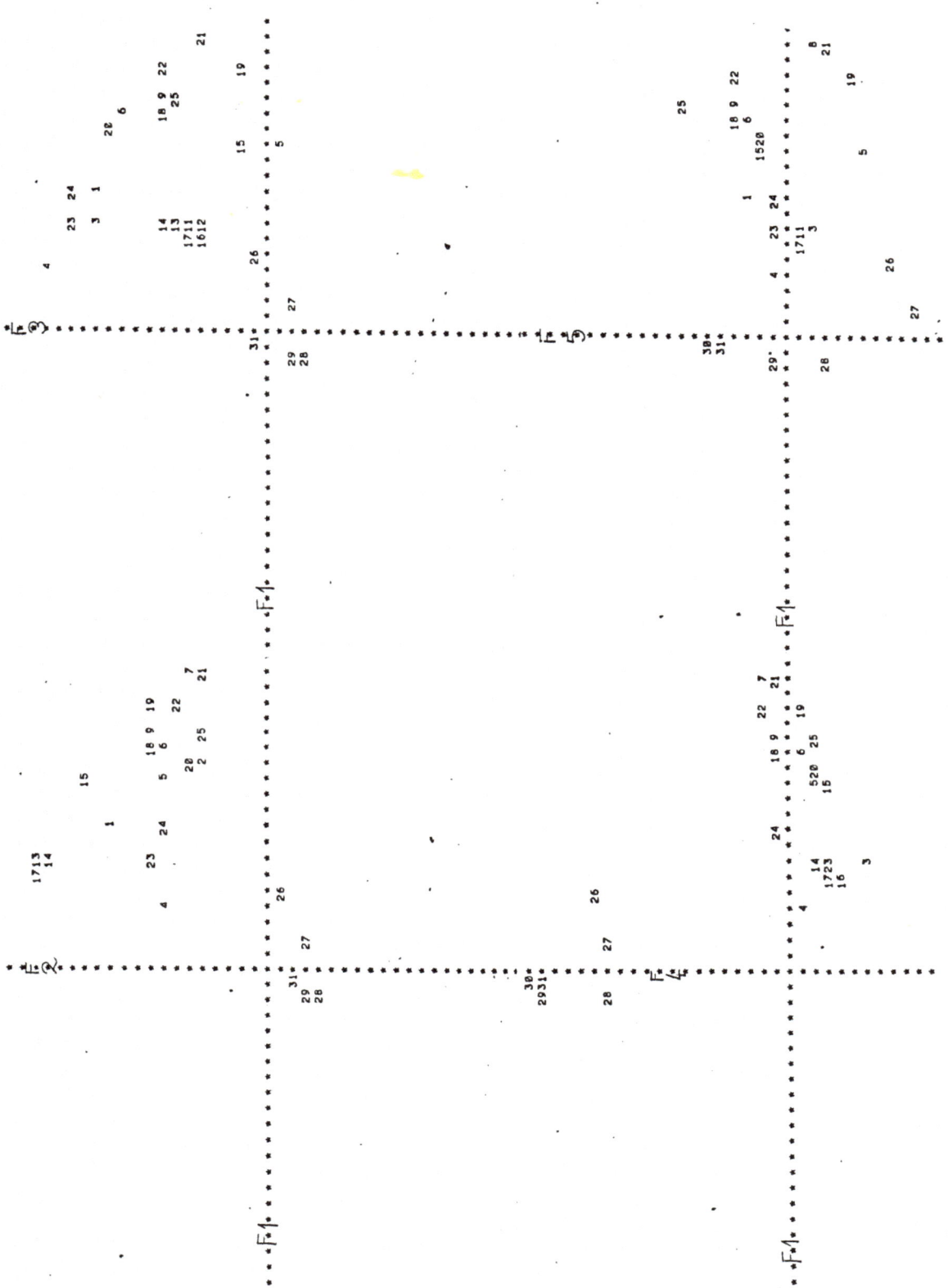

La Bastida skulls

Plot of variables for the La Bastida aseemblage in terms of their loadings on principal factors 1 - 5.

Plots for Table 24

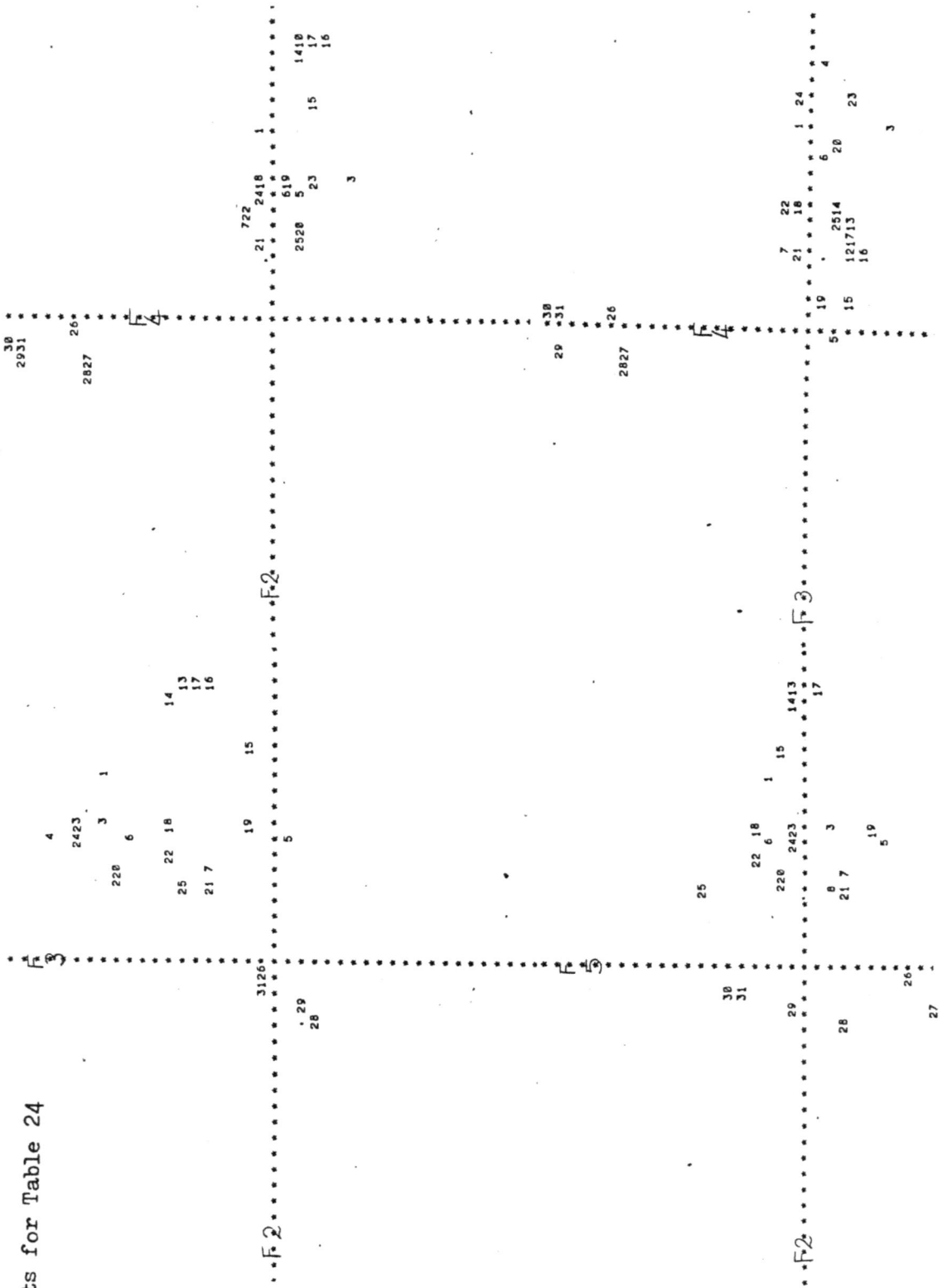

La Bastida skulls
Plot of variables for the La Bastida aseemblage in terms of their loadings on principal factors 1 - 5.

Plots for Table 24

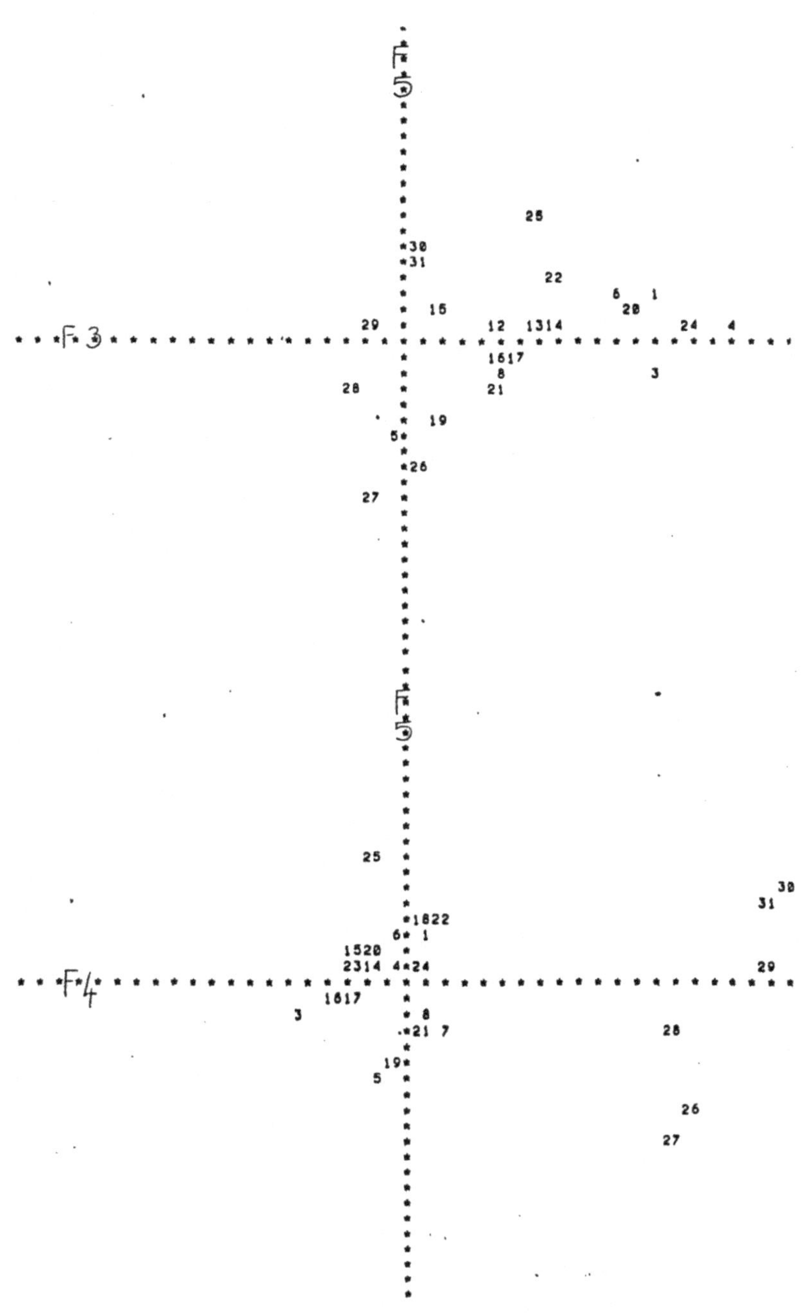

La Bastida skulls
Plot of variables for the La Bastida aseemblage in terms of their loadings on principal factors 1 - 5.

Dendrograms of Southeastern Spanish Prehistoric Crania

Numbering corresponds to enumeration on p.23

Dendrogram 1

0 5 10 25 50 75 90 95 100

W202 Pastora
W208 Pastora
W215 Camí Real
W219 Beni Sid
W228 Beni Sid
W230 Beni Sid
W44 Lechuzas
W43 Lechuzas
W170 Beni Sid
W60 Bastida
J72 Argar
J81 Argar
W78 Llometes
W224 Beni Sid
W97 Llometes
W42 Lechuzas
W62 Bastida
W163 Camí Real
W92 Llometes
W82 Llometes
J8 Argar
J5 Argar
J56 Argar
W14 Barsella
W77 Llometes
J28 Argar
W68 Bastida
W151 Palanqués
J69 Argar
J77 Argar
J20 Argar
J22 Argar
W83 Llometes
J75 Argar
W144 Frontó
W161 Camí Real
J1 Argar
W209 Pastora
W40 Lechuzas
W100 Llometes
W98 Llometes
W157 Camí Real
W64 Bastida
W120 Frontó
J40 Argar
J79 Argar
W80 Llometes
W74 Llometes
J70 Argar
W10 Barsella
W187 Frontó
W191 Palanqués
W153 Palanqués
W127 Pastora
W67 Bastida
W19 Barsella
W85 Llometes
J21 Argar
J30 Argar
J64 Argar
W140 Pastora
W169 Beni Sid
W137 Pastora
W190 Palanqués
W96 Llometes
W84 Llometes
W87 Llometes
J78 Argar
J13 Argar
J26 Argar
J39 Argar
J55 Argar
J71 Argar
J73 Argar
W93 Llometes
W37 Lechuzas
W39 Lechuzas
W155 Camí Real
W167 Beni Sid
W38 Lechuzas
J37 Argar
W119 Frontó
W134 Pastora
W71 Bastida
W223 Beni Sid
W129 Pastora
W46 Lechuzas
W65 Bastida
J82 Argar
W66 Bastida
W88 Llometes
W132 Pastora
W133 Pastora
W172 Beni Sid
W199 Pastora
J48 Argar
W34 Lechuzas
W123 Pastora
J3 Argar
W189 Frontó
W45 Lechuzas
W86 Llometes
J54 Argar
W20 Barsella
J57 Argar
J62 Argar
W8 Barsella
J2 Argar
W16 Barsella
W33 Lechuzas
W168 Beni Sid
W41 Lechuzas
W61 Bastida

W128 Pastora
W213 Camí Real
W216 Camí Real
W222 Beni Sid
J10 Argar
J16 Argar
J29 Argar
J44 Argar
J66 Argar
W94 Llometes
W99 Llometes
W159 Camí Real
W218 Beni Sid
J96 Argar
W73 Bastida
W147 Frontó
J17 Argar
J52 Argar
W139 Pastora
W150 Palanqués
W126 Pastora
W152 Palanqués
W12 Barsella
J36 Argar
W200 Pastora
W204 Pastora
W203 Pastora
W197 Pastora
W214 Camí Real
W198 Pastora
W131 Pastora
W9 Barsella
W81 Llometes
W135 Pastora
J4 Argar
J7 Argar
J15 Argar
J19 Argar
J24 Argar
J25 Argar
W63 Bastida
J74 Argar
J31 Argar
W194 Pastora
W125 Pastora
J32 Argar
J41 Argar
J45 Argar
J63 Argar
J68 Argar
W11 Barsella
W145 Frontó
W121 Pastora
W130 Pastora
W166 Beni Sid
W195 Pastora
J76 Argar
W13 Barsella
W122 Pastora
W165 Beni Sid
W35 Lechuzas
W91 Llometes
W226 Beni Sid
W136 Pastora
W160 Camí Real
W76 Llometes
W79 Llometes
W90 Llometes
W142 Pastora
W146 Frontó
W211 Camí Real
W217 Camí Real
W229 Beni Sid
W21 Barsella
W188 Frontó
W15 Barsella
W18 Barsella
W36 Lechuzas
W69 Bastida
W138 Pastora
W72 Bastida
W75 Llometes
W89 Llometes
W141 Pastora
W143 Pastora
W148 Palanqués
W156 Camí Real
W158 Camí Real
W162 Camí Real
W171 Beni Sid
W173 Beni Sid
W193 Pastora
J12 Argar
W205 Pastora
J9 Argar
J27 Argar
W210 Camí Real
J35 Argar
J38 Argar
W227 Beni Sid
J6 Argar
J42 Argar
J47 Argar
J50 Argar
J51 Argar
J53 Argar
J65 Argar
W212 Camí Real
W220 Beni Sid
W221 Beni Sid
J18 Argar
J33 Argar
J61 Argar
J67 Argar
W225 Beni Sid
J11 Argar
J34 Argar
J43 Argar
J46 Argar
J59 Argar
J83 Argar
J80 Argar
W196 Pastora
J14 Argar
J49 Argar
J58 Argar
W205 Pastora
J60 Argar
W124 Pastora
W201 Pastora
W70 Bastida
W207 Pastora
W149 Palanqués
W192 Pastora
J23 Argar
W7 Barsella

Prehistoric crania from ten southeastern Spanish assemblages (loose mandibles excluded) sorted for metrical data by GENSTAT single-linkage cluster analysis. The discrimination of the first six cases reflects the starting point among some disparate and very incomplete cranial fragments. It is of no significance.

W<u>n</u> = cases measured by Walker (1973)
J<u>n</u> = cases measured by Jacques (1887)

Dendrogram 2

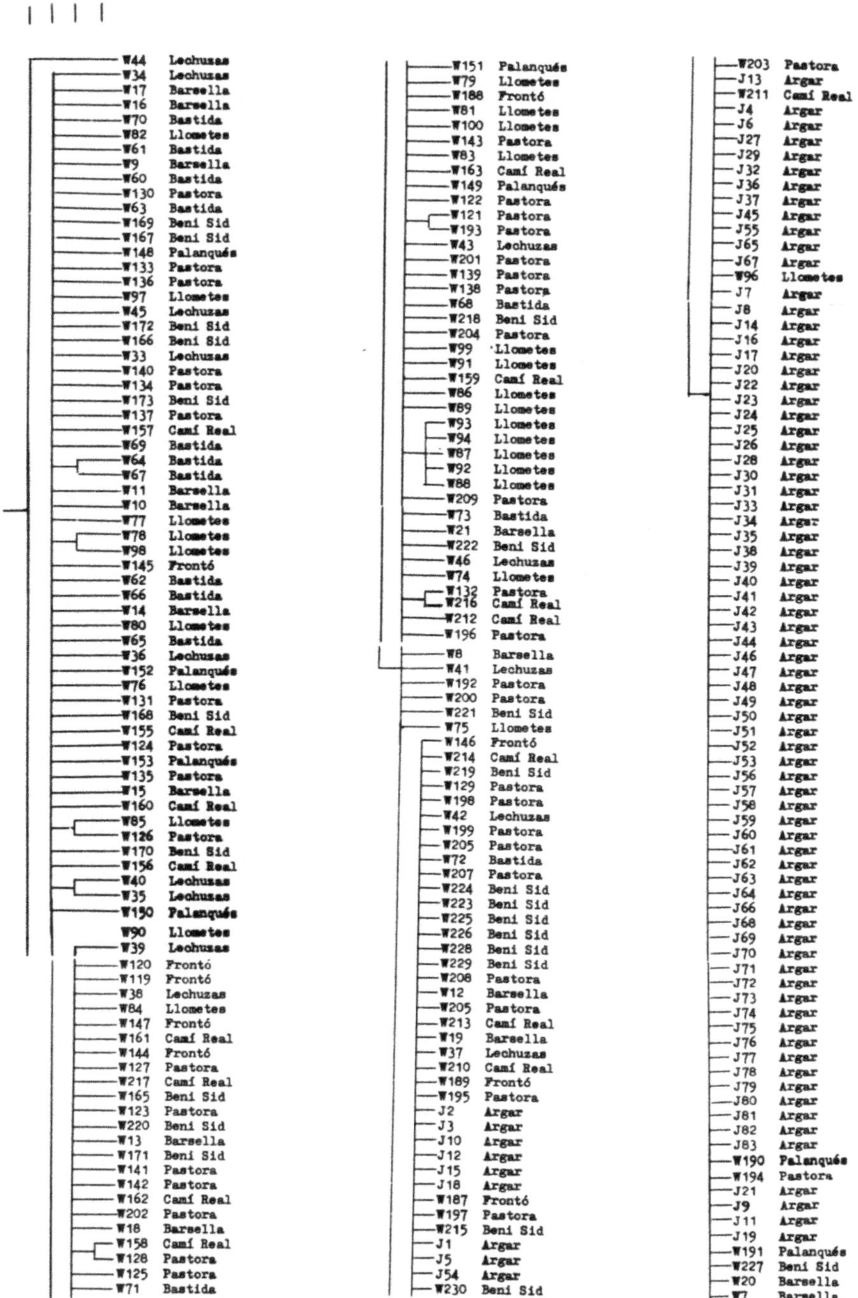

Prehistoric crania from ten southeastern Spanish assemblages (loose mandibles excluded) sorted for metrical and non-metrical data by GENSTAT single-linkage cluster analysis. The largely missing information about non-metrical traits in Jacques (1887) and for the very fragmentary crania W-174 to W-230 perhaps accounts for 100% similarity and the corresponding chain should be ignored.

W<u>n</u> = data from Walker (1973)
J<u>n</u> = data from Jacques (1887)

Dendrogram 3

85 90 95 100

W45 Lechuzas
W44 Lechuzas
W172 Beni Sid
W33 Lechuzas
W43 Lechuzas
J69 Argar
W162 Camí Real
W39 Lechuzas
J59 Argar
W143 Pastora
W170 Beni Sid
J65 Argar
W36 Lechuzas
J5 Argar
J9 Argar
J16 Argar
W9 Barsella
J8 Argar
W140 Pastora
W124 Pastora
W78 Llometes
J62 Argar
W77 Llometes
W14 Barsella
J7 Argar
W11 Barsella
J56 Argar
W171 Beni Sid
J26 Argar
W10 Barsella
W163 Camí Real
W153 Palanqués
W42 Lechuzas
W92 Llometes
W68 Bastida
W133 Pastora
W151 Palanqués
W60 Bastida
J48 Argar
W15 Barsella
W157 Camí Real
J14 Argar
W18 Barsella
W62 Bastida
W128 Pastora
W65 Bastida
J3 Argar
J22 Argar
J29 Argar
J37 Argar
J72 Argar
J28 Argar
W130 Pastora
J76 Argar
W129 Pastora
W10 Barsella
W82 Llometes
J81 Argar
W158 Camí Real
J42 Argar
J63 Argar
W71 Bastida
W150 Palanqués
W89 Llometes
J35 Argar
J36 Argar
W97 Llometes
W98 Llometes
J15 Argar

W74 Llometes
J75 Argar
J55 Argar
W161 Camí Real
J11 Argar
W119 Frontó
J33 Argar
J21 Argar
J82 Argar
W66 Bastida
W145 Frontó
W138 Pastora
W72 Bastida
J2 Argar
W87 Llometes
W38 Lechuzas
W155 Camí Real
W167 Beni Sid
W148 Palanqués
W86 Llometes
J51 Argar
J19 Argar
W93 Llometes
J6 Argar
J61 Argar
W16 Barsella
W135 Pastora
W165 Beni Sid
J12 Argar
J40 Argar
J38 Argar
J4 Argar
W134 Pastora
J70 Argar
J45 Argar
J49 Argar
W83 Llometes
J25 Argar
J24 Argar
W12 Barsella
J46 Argar
J83 Argar
J80 Argar
W75 Llometes
W144 Frontó
J57 Argar
J54 Argar
W13 Barsella
W40 Bastida
J1 Argar
J71 Argar
W69 Bastida
W19 Barsella
J41 Argar
W63 Bastida
J31 Argar
J74 Argar
J58 Argar
J18 Argar
J77 Argar
J20 Argar
J73 Argar
J60 Argar
W35 Lechuzas
W100 Llometes
W127 Pastora
W123 Pastora
W64 Bastida
W70 Bastida

W99 Llometes
W37 Lechuzas
W149 Palanqués
W17 Barsella
W156 Camí Real
J44 Argar
J66 Argar
W146 Frontó
W34 Lechuzas
J79 Argar
W80 Llometes
W61 Bastida
W168 Beni Sid
W41 Lechuzas
W95 Llometes
W169 Beni Sid
W137 Pastora
W96 Llometes
W67 Bastida
J27 Argar
W88 Llometes
W85 Llometes
W46 Lechuzas
J30 Argar
J64 Argar
J34 Argar
W84 Llometes
J10 Argar
J67 Argar
W126 Pastora
W131 Pastora
W121 Pastora
J78 Argar
J13 Argar
J39 Argar
J50 Argar
J53 Argar
J68 Argar
W20 Barsella
W159 Camí Real
W8 Barsella
W152 Palanqués
W81 Llometes
W125 Pastora
J32 Argar
W141 Pastora
J47 Argar
W94 Llometes
W166 Beni Sid
W136 Pastora
W160 Camí Real
W173 Beni Sid
W76 Llometes
W79 Llometes
W90 Llometes
W142 Pastora
W21 Barsella
W73 Bastida
J17 Argar
J52 Argar
W139 Pastora
W147 Frontó
W91 Llometes
W122 Pastora
J43 Argar
W122 Pastora
J43 Argar
W132 Pastora
J23 Argar

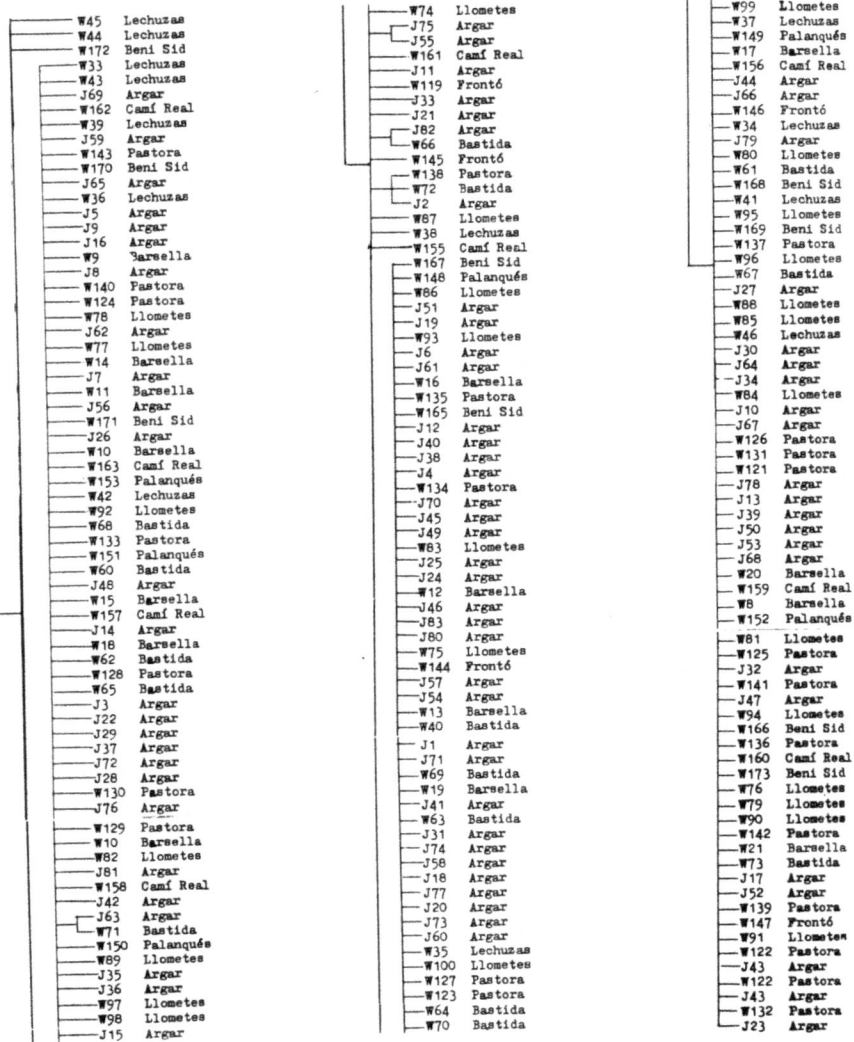

Prehistoric crania from ten southeastern Spanish assemblages (loose mandibles and very incomplete cranial fragments excluded) sorted for metrical data by GENSTAT single-linkage cluster analysis.

W$\underline{n}$ = cases measured by Walker (1973)
J$\underline{n}$ = cases measured by Jacques (1887)

Dendrogram 4

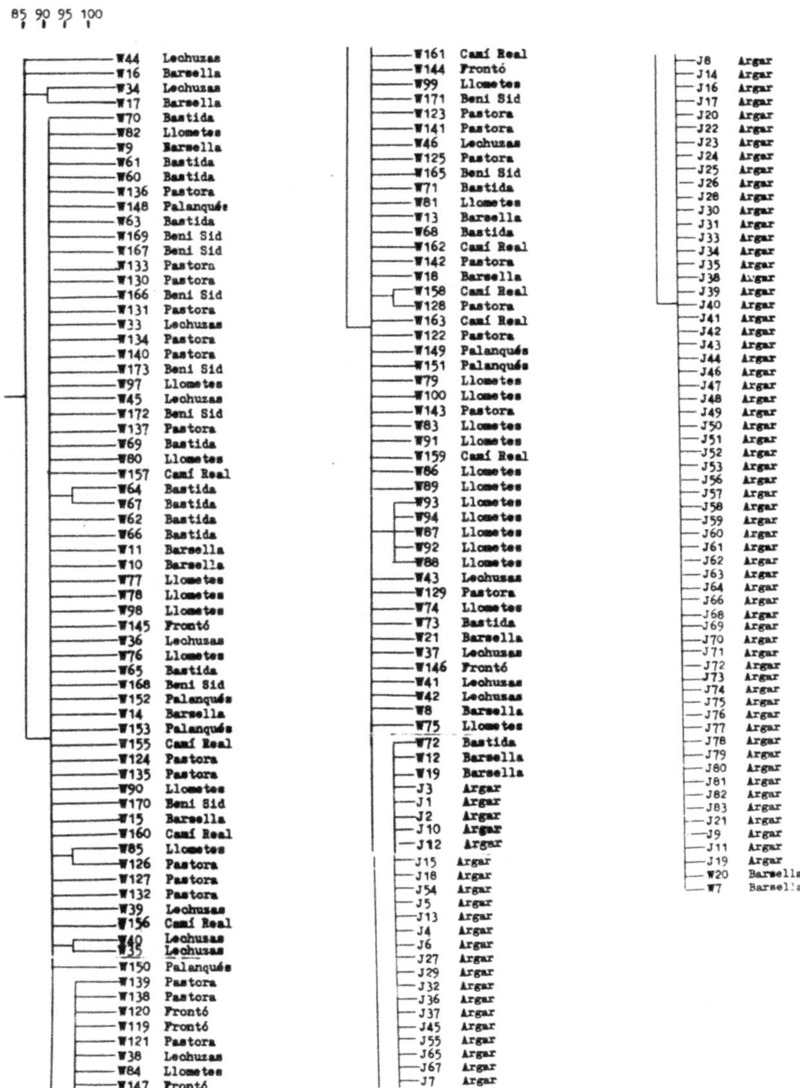

Prehistoric crania from ten southeastern Spanish assemblages (loose mandibles and very fragmentary crania excluded) sorted for metrical and non-metrical data by GENSTAT single-linkage cluster analysis. The 100% similarity of the Argar skulls reflects the lack of published information about epigenetical traits and corresponding preponderance of missing entries, and they should therefore be ignored.

W<u>n</u> = data from Walker (1973)
J<u>n</u> = data from Jacques (1887)

Dendrogram 5

70 75 80 85 90 95 100

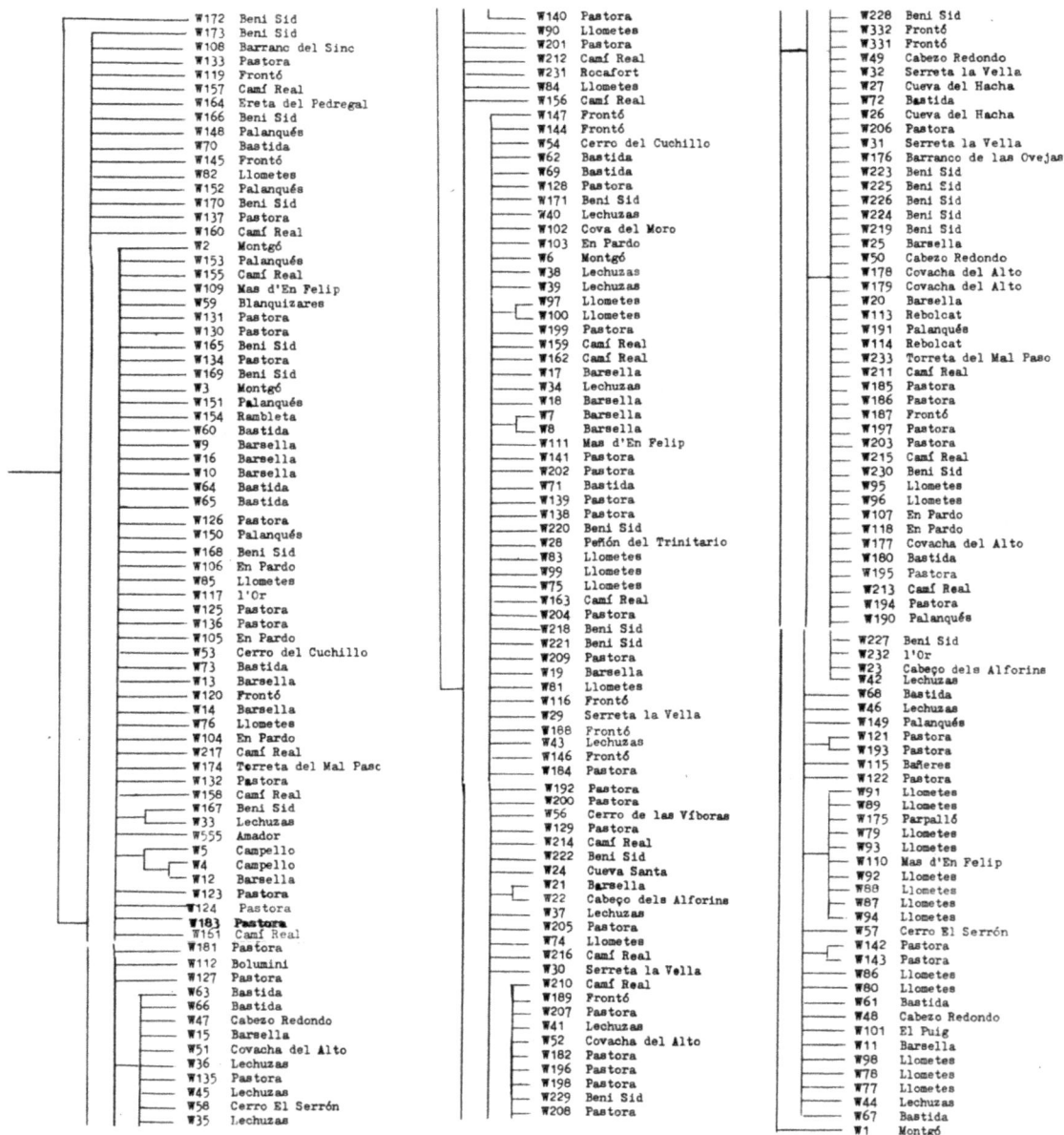

W172 Beni Sid
W173 Beni Sid
W108 Barranc del Sinc
W133 Pastora
W119 Frontó
W157 Camí Real
W164 Ereta del Pedregal
W166 Beni Sid
W148 Palanqués
W70 Bastida
W145 Frontó
W82 Llometes
W152 Palanqués
W170 Beni Sid
W137 Pastora
W160 Camí Real
W2 Montgó
W153 Palanqués
W155 Camí Real
W109 Mas d'En Felip
W59 Blanquizares
W131 Pastora
W130 Pastora
W165 Beni Sid
W134 Pastora
W169 Beni Sid
W3 Montgó
W151 Palanqués
W154 Rambleta
W60 Bastida
W9 Barsella
W16 Barsella
W10 Barsella
W64 Bastida
W65 Bastida
W126 Pastora
W150 Palanqués
W168 Beni Sid
W106 En Pardo
W85 Llometes
W117 l'Or
W125 Pastora
W136 Pastora
W105 En Pardo
W53 Cerro del Cuchillo
W73 Bastida
W13 Barsella
W120 Frontó
W14 Barsella
W76 Llometes
W104 En Pardo
W217 Camí Real
W174 Torreta del Mal Pasc
W132 Pastora
W158 Camí Real
W167 Beni Sid
W33 Lechuzas
W555 Amador
W5 Campello
W4 Campello
W12 Barsella
W123 Pastora
W124 Pastora
W183 Pastora
W161 Camí Real
W181 Pastora
W112 Bolumini
W127 Pastora
W63 Bastida
W66 Bastida
W47 Cabezo Redondo
W15 Barsella
W51 Covacha del Alto
W36 Lechuzas
W135 Pastora
W45 Lechuzas
W58 Cerro El Serrón
W35 Lechuzas

W140 Pastora
W90 Llometes
W201 Pastora
W212 Camí Real
W231 Rocafort
W84 Llometes
W156 Camí Real
W147 Frontó
W144 Frontó
W54 Cerro del Cuchillo
W62 Bastida
W69 Bastida
W128 Pastora
W171 Beni Sid
W40 Lechuzas
W102 Cova del Moro
W103 En Pardo
W6 Montgó
W38 Lechuzas
W39 Lechuzas
W97 Llometes
W100 Llometes
W199 Pastora
W159 Camí Real
W162 Camí Real
W17 Barsella
W34 Lechuzas
W18 Barsella
W7 Barsella
W8 Barsella
W111 Mas d'En Felip
W141 Pastora
W202 Pastora
W71 Bastida
W139 Pastora
W138 Pastora
W220 Beni Sid
W28 Peñón del Trinitario
W83 Llometes
W99 Llometes
W75 Llometes
W163 Camí Real
W204 Pastora
W218 Beni Sid
W221 Beni Sid
W209 Pastora
W19 Barsella
W81 Llometes
W116 Frontó
W29 Serreta la Vella
W188 Frontó
W43 Lechuzas
W146 Frontó
W184 Pastora
W192 Pastora
W200 Pastora
W56 Cerro de las Víboras
W129 Pastora
W214 Camí Real
W222 Beni Sid
W24 Cueva Santa
W21 Barsella
W22 Cabeço dels Alforins
W37 Lechuzas
W205 Pastora
W74 Llometes
W216 Camí Real
W30 Serreta la Vella
W210 Camí Real
W189 Frontó
W207 Pastora
W41 Lechuzas
W52 Covacha del Alto
W182 Pastora
W196 Pastora
W198 Pastora
W229 Beni Sid
W208 Pastora

W228 Beni Sid
W332 Frontó
W331 Frontó
W49 Cabezo Redondo
W32 Serreta la Vella
W27 Cueva del Hacha
W72 Bastida
W26 Cueva del Hacha
W206 Pastora
W31 Serreta la Vella
W176 Barranco de las Ovejas
W223 Beni Sid
W225 Beni Sid
W226 Beni Sid
W224 Beni Sid
W219 Beni Sid
W25 Barsella
W50 Cabezo Redondo
W178 Covacha del Alto
W179 Covacha del Alto
W20 Barsella
W113 Rebolcat
W191 Palanqués
W114 Rebolcat
W233 Torreta del Mal Paso
W211 Camí Real
W185 Pastora
W186 Pastora
W187 Frontó
W197 Pastora
W203 Pastora
W215 Camí Real
W230 Beni Sid
W95 Llometes
W96 Llometes
W107 En Pardo
W118 En Pardo
W177 Covacha del Alto
W180 Bastida
W195 Pastora
W213 Camí Real
W194 Pastora
W190 Palanqués
W227 Beni Sid
W232 l'Or
W23 Cabeço dels Alforins
W42 Lechuzas
W68 Bastida
W46 Lechuzas
W149 Palanqués
W121 Pastora
W193 Pastora
W115 Bañeres
W122 Pastora
W91 Llometes
W89 Llometes
W175 Parpalló
W79 Llometes
W93 Llometes
W110 Mas d'En Felip
W92 Llometes
W88 Llometes
W87 Llometes
W94 Llometes
W57 Cerro El Serrón
W142 Pastora
W143 Pastora
W86 Llometes
W80 Llometes
W61 Bastida
W48 Cabezo Redondo
W101 El Puig
W11 Barsella
W98 Llometes
W78 Llometes
W77 Llometes
W44 Lechuzas
W67 Bastida
W1 Montgó

Prehistoric crania from all southeastern Spanish stations, except El Argar, sorted for non-metrical data by GENSTAT single-linkage cluster analysis. Loose mandibles were excluded from the analysis.
W<u>n</u> = data from Walker (1973)

Dendrogram 6

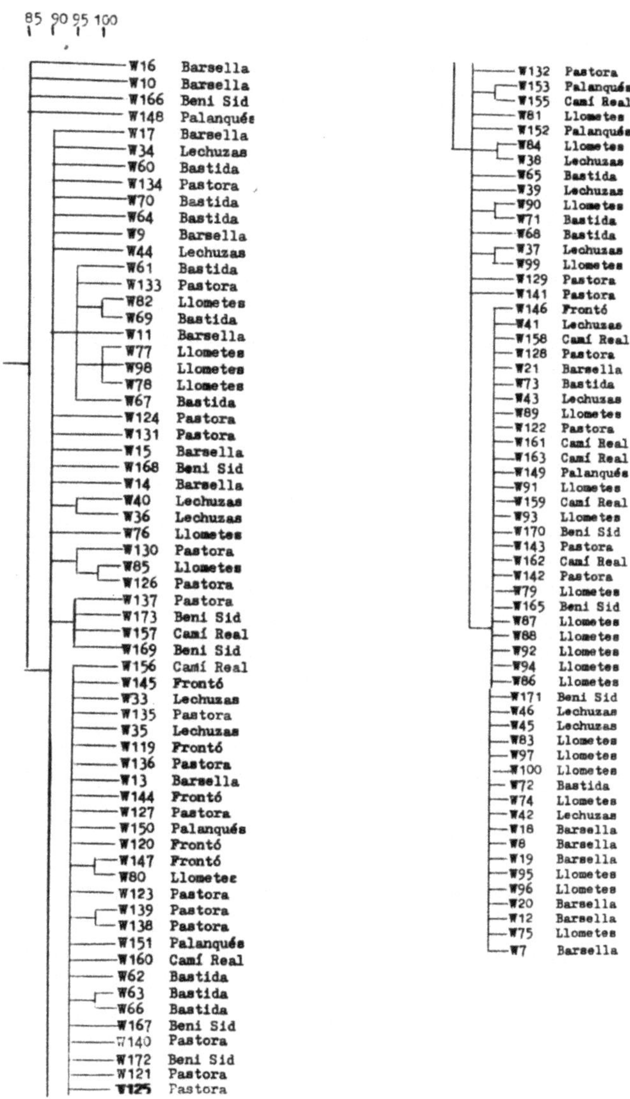

Prehistoric crania from nine southeastern Spanish assemblages (loose mandibles and very incomplete crania excluded) sorted for non-metrical data by GENSTAT single-linkage cluster analysis.

W<u>n</u> = data from Walker (1973)

Dendrogram 7

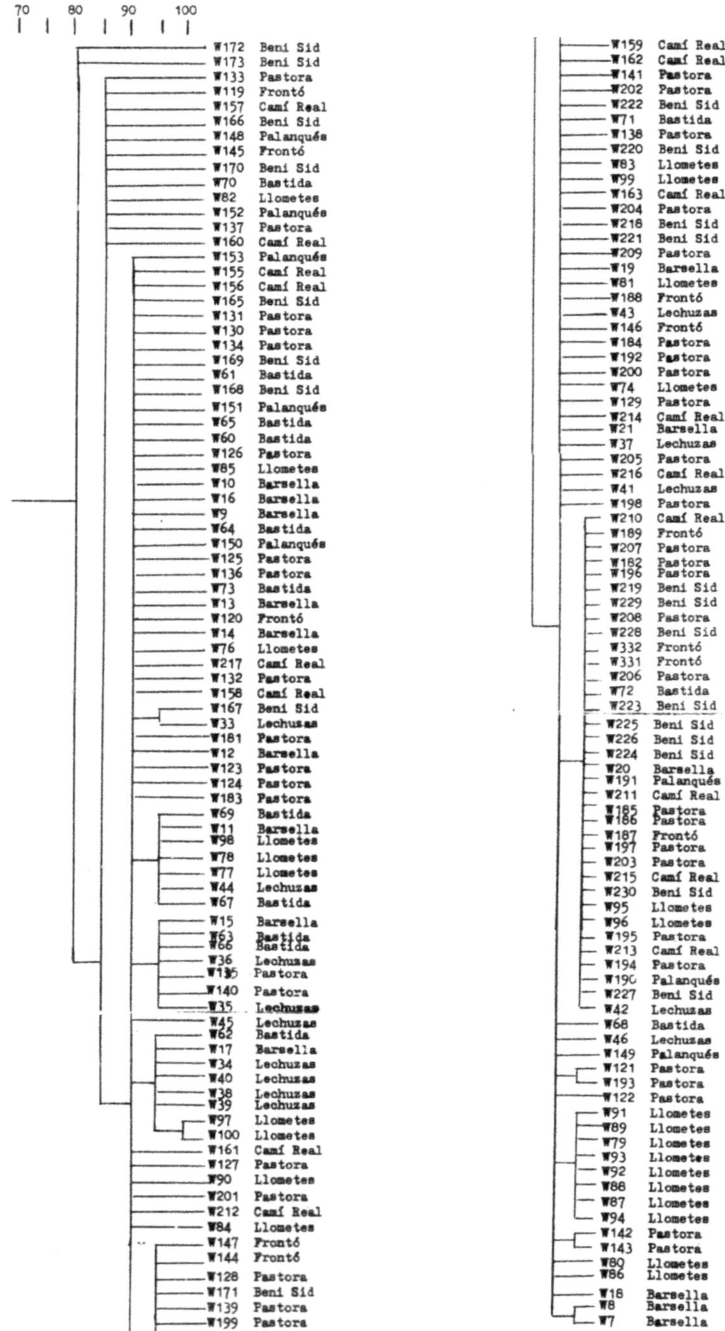

Prehistoric crania from nine southeastern Spanish assemblages (loose mandibles excluded) sorted for non-metrical data by GENSTAT single-linkage cluster analysis (loose mandibles excluded only).

Wn = data from Walker (1973)
[Jn = data from Jacques (1887)]

Dendrogram 8

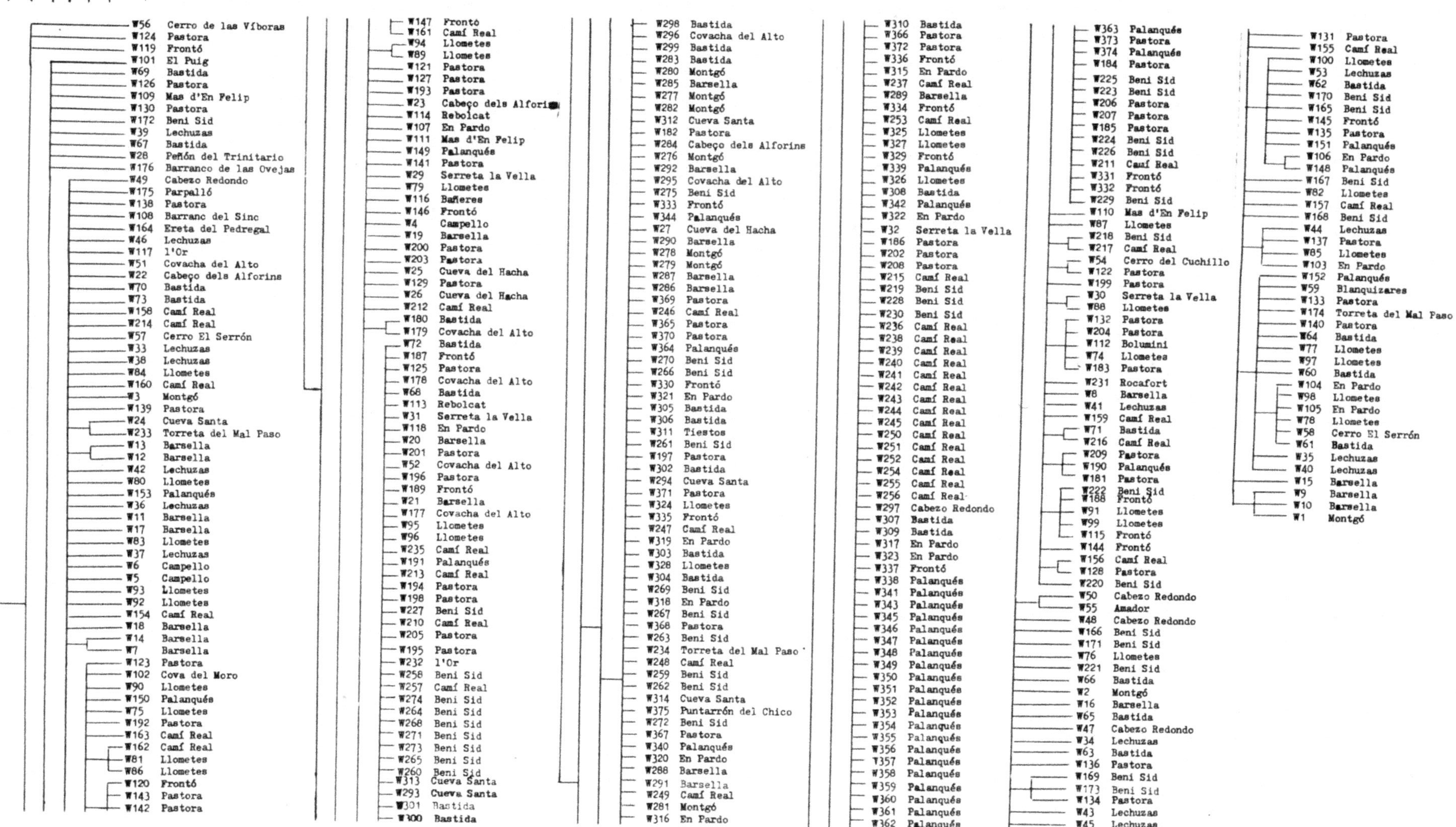

Prehistoric crania and mandibles from all southeastern Spanish sites except El Argar sorted for metrical data by GENSTAT single-linkage cluster analysis. Wn = data from Walker (1973).

Dendrogram 9

70 75 80 85 90 95 100

W119 Frontó
W124 Pastora
W69 Bastida
W130 Pastora
W126 Pastora
W172 Beni Sid
W39 Lechuzas
W67 Bastida
W46 Lechuzas
W138 Pastora
W139 Pastora
W131 Pastora
W158 Camí Real
W214 Camí Real
W70 Bastida
W73 Bastida
W220 Beni Sid
W13 Barsella
W12 Barsella
W33 Lechuzas
W84 Llometes
W80 Llometes
W42 Lechuzas
W38 Lechuzas
W153 Palanqués
W160 Camí Real
W11 Barsella
W17 Barsella
W83 Llometes
W36 Lechuzas
W37 Lechuzas
W171 Beni Sid
W66 Bastida
W16 Barsella
W65 Bastida
W34 Lechuzas
W63 Bastida
W136 Pastora
W169 Beni Sid
W173 Beni Sid
W134 Pastora
W221 Beni Sid
W76 Llometes
W166 Beni Sid
W45 Lechuzas
W43 Lechuzas
W15 Barsella
W9 Barsella
W10 Barsella
W167 Beni Sid
W157 Camí Real
W152 Palanqués
W133 Pastora
W140 Pastora
W64 Bastida
W77 Llometes
W98 Llometes
W78 Llometes
W97 Llometes
W60 Bastida
W61 Bastida
W40 Lechuzas
W35 Lechuzas
W100 Llometes
W62 Bastida
W170 Beni Sid
W151 Palanqués
W135 Pastora
W145 Frontó
W148 Palanqués
W165 Beni Sid
W155 Camí Real
W82 Llometes
W44 Lechuzas
W137 Pastora
W85 Llometes
W168 Beni Sid
W93 Llometes
W92 Llometes
W18 Barsella
J66 Argar
J27 Argar

J67 Argar
J55 Argar
W123 Pastora
J36 Argar
J45 Argar
J19 Argar
J37 Argar
J18 Argar
J3 Argar
J68 Argar
J8 Argar
J60 Argar
J17 Argar
J48 Argar
J69 Argar
J12 Argar
J26 Argar
J62 Argar
J47 Argar
J40 Argar
J44 Argar
J61 Argar
J14 Argar
J9 Argar
J4 Argar
J41 Argar
J46 Argar
J65 Argar
J29 Argar
J2 Argar
J1 Argar
J54 Argar
J6 Argar
J32 Argar
J50 Argar
J20 Argar
J28 Argar
J49 Argar
J31 Argar
J13 Argar
J15 Argar
J51 Argar
J38 Argar
J10 Argar
J57 Argar
J16 Argar
J11 Argar
J53 Argar
J56 Argar
J24 Argar
J21 Argar
J5 Argar
J7 Argar
J59 Argar
J39 Argar
J63 Argar
J35 Argar
J22 Argar
J30 Argar
J58 Argar
J64 Argar
J33 Argar
J52 Argar
J42 Argar
J25 Argar
W90 Llometes
W150 Palanqués
W127 Pastora
W121 Pastora
W192 Pastora
W163 Camí Real
W162 Camí Real
W81 Llometes
W86 Llometes
W120 Frontó
W143 Pastora
W142 Pastora
W147 Frontó
W161 Camí Real
W94 Llometes
W89 Llometes
W75 Llometes

J23 Argar
W193 Pastora
W79 Llometes
J43 Argar
W125 Pastora
W212 Camí Real
W87 Llometes
W128 Pastora
W156 Camí Real
W144 Frontó
W19 Barsella
W200 Pastora
W218 Beni Sid
W217 Camí Real
W122 Pastora
W199 Pastora
W88 Llometes
W132 Pastora
W204 Pastora
W74 Llometes
W183 Pastora
W8 Barsella
W41 Lechuzas
W159 Camí Real
W222 Beni Sid
W99 Llometes
W91 Llometes
W188 Frontó
W71 Bastida
W216 Camí Real
W190 Palanqués
W181 Pastora
W209 Pastora
W203 Pastora
J34 Argar
W180 Bastida
W129 Pastora
W72 Bastida
W187 Frontó
W68 Bastida
W20 Barsella
W201 Pastora
W224 Beni Sid
W226 Beni Sid
W211 Camí Real
W229 Beni Sid
W332 Frontó
W331 Frontó
W196 Pastora
W189 Frontó
W185 Pastora
W21 Barsella
W95 Llometes
W96 Llometes
W235 Camí Real
W207 Pastora
W206 Pastora
W182 Pastora
W197 Pastora
W184 Pastora
W223 Beni Sid
W225 Beni Sid
W186 Pastora
W202 Pastora
W208 Pastora
W215 Camí Real
W219 Beni Sid
W228 Beni Sid
W230 Beni Sid
W213 Camí Real
W194 Pastora
W227 Beni Sid
W210 Camí Real
W195 Pastora
W205 Pastora
W146 Frontó
W149 Palanqués
W141 Pastora
W14 Barsella
W7 Barsella

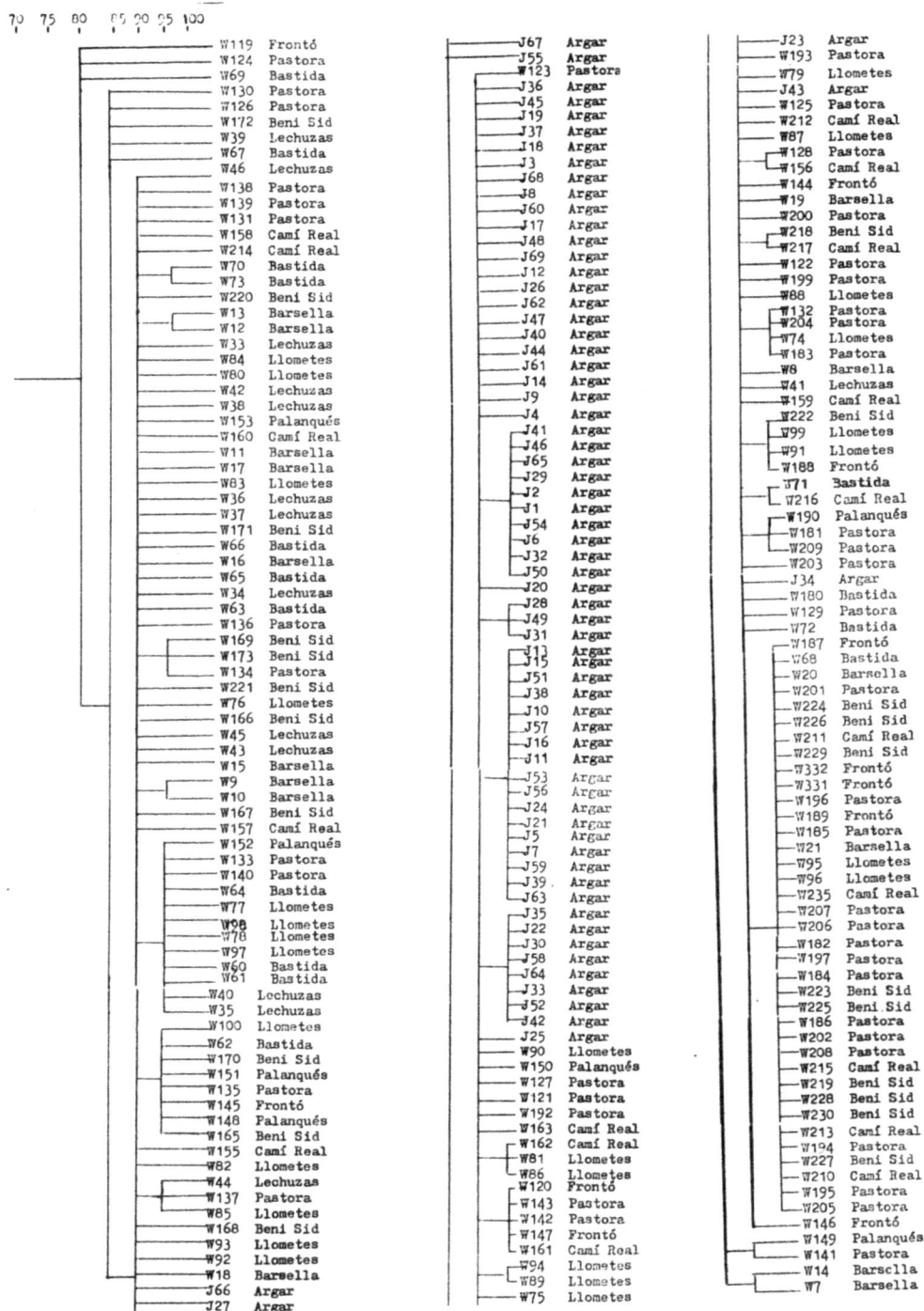

Prehistoric crania from ten southeastern Spanish assemblages sorted for metrical data by GENSTAT single-linkage cluster analysis. Loose mandibles were originally included but formed a long chain at the 100% level of similarity because of the abundance of missing entries (for other cranial measurements) and that has been excised from the dendrogram.

W<u>n</u> = cases measured by Walker (1973)
J<u>n</u> = cases measured by Jacques (1887)

www.ingramcontent.com/pod-product-compliance
Lightning Source LLC
Chambersburg PA
CBHW061000030426
42334CB00033B/3308
9780860543350